ART and DESIGN FUNDAMENTALS

Margaret R. Lazzari

University of Southern California

Clayton Lee

University of California, Los Angeles

 VAN NOSTRAND REINHOLD
New York

Copyright © 1990 by Van Nostrand Reinhold

Library of Congress Catalog Card Number 89-37294
ISBN 0-422-31943-6

Printed in the United States of America

Van Nostrand Reinhold
115 Fifth Avenue
New York, New York 10003

Van Nostrand Reinhold International Company Limited
11 New Fetter Lane
London EC4P 4EE, England

Van Nostrand Reinhold
480 La Trobe Street
Melbourne, Victoria 3000, Australia

Nelson Canada
1120 Birchmount Road
Scarborough, Ontario M1K 5G4, Canada

16 15 14 13 12 11 10 9 8 7 6 5 4 3 2 1

Library of Congress Cataloging-in-Publication Data

Lazzari, Margaret R.
    Art and design fundamentals : a text for cultural production /
Margaret R. Lazzari, Clayton Lee.
        p.   cm.
    Includes bibliographical references.
    ISBN 0-442-31943-6
    1. Visual perception.   2. Pattern perception.   3. Proportion (Art)
4. Communication in art.   5. Communication in design.   I. Lee,
Clayton.   II. Title.
N7430.5.L36   1990
701'.15—dc20   89-37294
                                                                    CIP

To our families and friends

Contents

Preface

This book began as a series of discussions during the spring and summer of 1987. We were both teaching art and design foundation courses but were dissatisfied with the nature of the material covered in these classes, a situation that is not unusual. Many art and design departments in colleges and universities offer foundation courses whose scopes are either poorly defined, too narrowly defined, or not defined at all. Many departments have no clear concept of what comprises foundation courses or, if that concept exists, no consensus among faculties on the importance of these areas to a student's progress. Given this situation, we were not surprised to find no texts that adequately covered art and design fundamentals.

We decided to develop a textbook that not only would be suitable for art and design fundamentals but also might suggest possible ways to restructure an entire visual curriculum. Rather than a limited text, we decided on an inclusive text that would contain these basic premises:

1. Foundation studies for art and design students should be the same, with no distinction in the fundamental training for either group of students.

2. Foundation studies should be a thorough introduction to the theory, history, and practice of art and design.

3. Foundation studies in art and design should introduce students to many media.

Thus began 18 months of work. We developed the concepts and structure of the book together, with Clayton Lee providing the bulk of the theoretical and historical material and Margaret Lazzari much of the studio and technical information. All first drafts of the text and appendix materials were written by Lazzari, with frequent joint revisions. The illustrations were compiled or executed by Lazzari, who also wrote the assignments and classroom-tested the projects and the concepts contained in the text. Reflected in the text are our own individual educational backgrounds, personal interests, and work experiences: Lazzari in painting, graphics, computers and advanced technologies, art history, and humanities; Lee in printmaking, graphic design, photography, advanced design technology, art history, architectural history, geography, communication theory, and urban design.

We hope this text defines an excellent foundation course for art and design students. The material and approach are innovative and appropriate to a number of varied contexts, from the small college art department to the most advanced design school. Journalism and mass communications instructors may also find this a useful introductory text. Because of the broad scope of our material and approach, we invite readers' comments and suggestions.

Acknowledgments

We wish to thank those who contributed to this textbook. Thanks to our editor, Lilly Kaufman, for her support, suggestions, and insights. The University of Southern California provided support for this project with grants through Project Socrates, Faculty Research and Innovation Funds, and Innovative Teaching. Dr. Richard Kaplan, USC Vice-Provost for Academic Computing, provided equipment support. The administration, faculty, staff, and students of USC School of Fine Arts have been most helpful with advice and with technical, clerical, academic, and moral support. Steve Stolz of the staff of USC's School of Fine Arts assisted in printing final drafts and illustrations for this book. We also acknowledge the 1987 and 1988 freshman art students at USC School of Fine Arts, our guinea pigs as Lazzari tested the assignments in the classroom. Dain Olsen helped during classroom testing, advised on the assignments, and good-naturedly assisted in projects that never made it to the final stage. David Heintz of California College of Arts and Crafts read the manuscript from the point of view of a professor interested in defining the nature of foundation courses. Thanks also to Maroun Harb at University of California, Los Angeles, for equipment support and working space, and to Joyce Herleth for advice.

Finally, our family and friends were assets beyond value. Many supported the project in small and large ways and have our gratitude.

Introduction

This book is intended for college students taking their first art class, which may be called Basic Design, Design Fundamentals, Art Foundation, or some similar title. Although texts for this course are plentiful, our book is unusual among them. We believe this text gives a better explanation of the information covered in existing texts and also addresses areas that have been lacking in all.

This book addresses both art and design as parts of the same discipline rather than as different activities. Art and design are not simply the making of objects but are cultural processes and activities. Therefore, we consider the way art and design objects are influenced by the audience that receives them and the values and meanings they communicate. Because designers and artists must understand these aspects of art and design, this text unites the practice of art and design with the theory of how artists, designers, and the objects they make are culture.

Because the English language has no common term for both art and design, we have invented one. *Visual production*, which is both the act of making art and design product and the final product itself, is the subject of this book. Visual production is also the audience's reception of the product. Therefore, visual production is the interaction of culture, objects, individuals, and institutions, in addition to the fabrication of objects. Visual production includes painting, sculpture, and graphic design and also conceptual art, video, film, architecture, landscape and urban design, industrial design, interior design, and all other areas in which visual elements are important means for communicating cultural information. The scope of this text is inclusive rather than limited.

As a student in this class, you will study visual production as an act of both expression and communication because visual products are both self-expressions and the communication of ideas to an audience. A competent visual producer needs to (1) understand how human vision works physiologically; (2) be competent in various media; and (3) understand meaning and value as they are communicated in a visual product. We outline a process that you can use in your own creative works and that will help you understand what factors communicate your ideas to others.

A visual producer has to be visually, verbally, and mathematically competent. Visual producers are not mystics, idiots savants, or people who can afford to limit themselves to narrow areas of interest or focus. The subject matters visual producers deal with encompass the whole range of humanity, and practitioners need a broad background, vision, and thorough education.

This book introduces you to various current visual ideologies. We also present the impact of advances in technology on your understanding and creation of visual products. We have attempted to identify and define more precisely certain art and design terms that have developed multiple meanings. We have also eliminated the arbitrary distinction between two-dimensional and three-dimensional art and design and have integrated various media into the projects. Overall, the text presents more challenging and contemporary concepts than other foundation texts. It is meant to be challenging for college students. Ideally, a student rereading this text after four years of study will still find its concepts provocative.

USE OF THIS TEXT

The book is divided into five chapters on perception, pattern, proportion, reproduction, and power. Within each chapter are five sections that reflect again the main topics of the book. The chapters contain theoretical and historical information on visual production. We have organized the book in this manner because these main topics are not isolated discussions unrelated to each other. What you perceive, how it becomes information, how your perceptions relate to you, how you reproduce your perceptions, and what those perceptions mean are interrelated in visual production. To put it another way, you organize your perception into meaningful patterns, which relate to you through proportion; subjective perceptions are reproduced as visual products; when you grasp the meaning of your role as a visual producer, you acquire power; and these actions are all related.

Chapter 1 discusses perception, what is visually perceived. The environment is known through information acquired with the senses. That information serves as the basis for all visual products. We begin the discussion of art and design production in the context of visual perception as studied by visual psychologists, especially James J. Gibson.

Chapter 2 is concerned with the organization of sensory perceptions into meaningful patterns of information that are essential to organizing elements in visual products. Those who see visual products also organize their perceptions into patterns of information and meaning.

In Chapter 3, proportion is discussed as the subjectivity of perceptions and how visual products relate to any individual. The perceiving subject sees the world from a unique point of view, as does every other individual.

Proportion refers to the relative point of view and subjective perceptions and preferences an individual exhibits; it also can be seen in a broader sense within the culture.

In the fourth chapter, we discuss the composition, context, and act of making visual products. Because of the many reproduction media in visual production, we have focused on the historical development of drawing technologies. Twentieth-century innovations in production and reproduction have changed the value and meaning of art and mass-produced objects. We discuss at length how this change affects perception of visual products.

The final chapter is about power, one's own competence and skill, the meaning, value, and practice of all visual production.

Each chapter is followed by assignments that link theory and practice and engage the student in the practice of making objects as a visual producer, relating the content of the text to the visual products made. The projects introduce a variety of media. The class discussions following the assignments examine the role of the audience as visual producers. The assignments are where students test both their visual literacy as producers of visual products and as the audience for the visual products of others.

The appendices contain technical information that supplements the text and provides background information for the assignments. Combined with the bibliographic listings, they serve as a basic resource of technical and theoretical information.

This book can be used for both one- and two-semester courses and for two-quarter or three-quarter sequences of courses. In order to present more advanced concepts and to present information in a unified theoretical context, we have made the text information build from one chapter to the next and one assignment build upon the previous one. We do not recommend approaching the material out of sequence. However, each instructor can tailor the information and assignments in the text to fit the time available.

PERCEPTION

CHAPTER

1

THE BASICS OF PERCEPTION

What do you think about or see when you wake up in the morning? Your alarm clock is broken, but you are awakened by the sunlight shining through your eyelids. Your vision is blurred, and you need to find your glasses. You need to see adequately before you can begin the day. You start to get out of bed.

The action *getting out of bed* is a series of simple and natural motions. Motion is one of the essential elements of human sight, and the light available in the room is another essential element (see Appendix A for a further discussion of visual perception). The light in the room brings information about the room to your eyes. Your own motion allows you to see your waking environment from different points of view. As you open your eyes, you squint to focus your vision. Along with motion and light, your eyes compose the third important element in visual perception.

In order to acquire information from your environment, you use your senses. This acquisition, called *perception,* is your awareness of elements in the environment through physiological sensations. However, perception is more than just sensations. Perception is connected to thinking and accumulating knowledge. This connection is called *cognition.* In visual perception, cognition integrates the physiological processes of retinal perception and brain functioning (see R. L. Gregory, 1979).

Vision is an important source of perceptual information because, of all your senses, vision has the greatest range. Usually you can perceive more distant things with your sight than with any other sense. Visual perception has been identified with thinking. Consider the many conceptual terms, such as *visionary*, that associate sight with understanding; you say, "I see" when you understand something.

Sighted persons depend on light to connect brain, eye, and the world. This connection occurs whether you watch television or create objects with your hand. As a visual producer, your initial creative instrument is not your hand but your vision organized by thought. A *visual producer* makes art and design products. To be a competent and successful visual producer, you must do more than make things. You must be visually literate. *Visual literacy* refers to your understanding of how you make, use, and value visual products. Your culture strongly influences how you make visual products, how others understand those products, and how you comprehend the visual products of others.

Have you overslept? The angle and strength of the light through the window tells you if you will be early or late for class. You know if the skies are cloudy or clear from the color and strength of the light and its reflections in your room. *Ambient light* is the total available light at any moment (Fig. 1-1). The angle, color, direction, and strength of the ambient light gives you specific information about the environment. (For basic perceptual terminology, see J. J. Gibson, 1966, 1979). This light can tell you where you are and ultimately how to evaluate your surroundings. You can translate the perceptual information about your environment into visual products. *Visual products* are the output of visual producers and include but are not limited to art objects, design objects, performance, architecture, film, video, urban design, and information systems. This perceptual information will be necessary for both the visual producer and the audience for the artwork.

Are you in your bedroom or has someone kidnapped you? How do you know where you are? You know you are in your bedroom because your perception of the objects and lights are familiar patterns. The dimensions of the room are in familiar proportions. Because everything is still as you remember it before you fell asleep, the image from your memory of last night is a reproduction of what you are seeing now. The scene before you is your familiar surroundings and the space over which you have control or power. As major themes, perception, pattern, proportion, reproduction, and power are covered in depth throughout this book. The appendices contain a more technical discussion of the perceptual concepts covered in this chapter.

But what do you see? You can see luminous and reflective objects in the room. Luminous objects are those that emit light—you can see them in the dark. Reflective objects are those that depend upon ambient light to be seen. The color of reflective objects changes with changes in the ambient light. While sitting on the bed, you notice you left the television on all night. The pizza is still on the floor in front of the set. It looks blue. Have you poisoned yourself? But when you switch on the lamp, the cheese is yellow again. The color of the pizza changes because the pizza reflects the glow from the television tube or the light of the incandescent bulb.

The amount of light affects your perception of objects. The luminous television screen also projects or emits a light whose appearance is altered by the room's painted walls. If you raise the window shade so that the sunlight shines on the television screen, the television image fades. Large amounts of ambient light diminish our perception of light-emitting objects.

The general ambient light in your environment is altered by the objects around you. As a light-emitting object, the television screen adds a blue glow to the ambient light in the room. As light-reflecting objects, the pizza and the furniture absorb some of the ambient light and reflect back some portion of it. Moreover, your perception of the ambient array may undergo a refractive change. If you happen to look at the pizza through a nearby fishbowl, the water bends the light and distorts the image of the pizza. Because luminous, reflective, and refractive objects change the ambient light in your environment, you know they exist and can be seen.

Figure 1-1. The ambient array is composed of all light rays in the immediate environment. This includes both the light rays that radiate directly from a light source and light rays that bounce off the various surrounding surfaces.

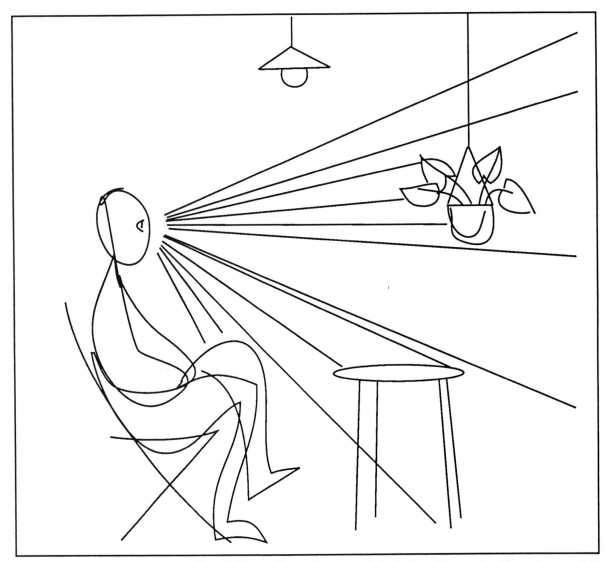

Figure 1-2. The optic array is composed of only those light rays from the environment that enter the eyes. It is in contrast to the ambient array (Fig. 1-1), which is composed of all light rays in the environment.

Although ambient light is all available light in your immediate environment, only a portion of those light rays enter your eyes to be perceived. The light rays entering your eyes are a specific sample of ambient light, called the *optic array* (Fig. 1-2). In contrast to ambient light rays bouncing in all directions, the light of the optic array is composed of rays specifically shining at your eyes. These include rays emitted directly toward you by a

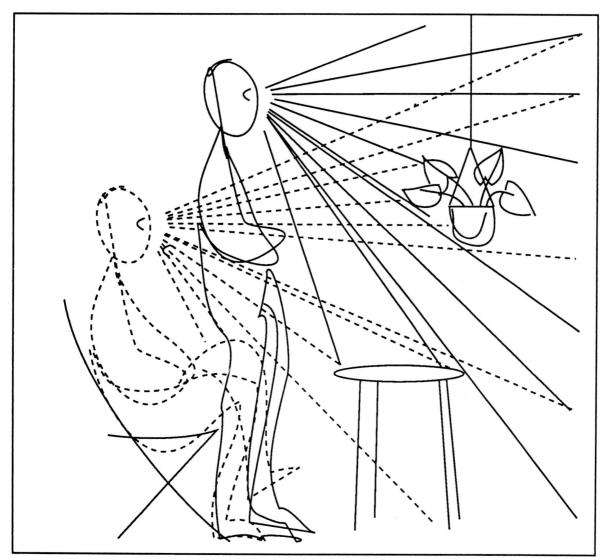

Figure 1-3. Every individual in every unique position sees a different optic array. Every movement changes the optic array, and the environment is seen differently.

light source or reflected directly toward you from some surface. The ambient array is unstructured light; the optic array is patterned and structured light. From any single point of view, at any instant, you see a unique optic array composed of light rays from objects to your eyes (Fig. 1-3). The optic array defines your position relative to the objects you see in space (Fig. 1-4). Read Appendix A for more information on your visual perception.

A

Figure 1-4. The optic array defines location relative to the environment. These three arrays define location as near the ceiling looking down (A), standing on the floor (B), and sitting on the floor looking up (C).

VISUAL PATTERNS

Where's the bathroom? In order to move toward the bathroom, you need to organize perceptual information into meaningful patterns so that you don't stub your toe or walk into a door. Getting off the bed and finding the bathroom requires both motion and previsualization, the ability to imagine a scene, image, or action before optically seeing it. Because you know where the bathroom is, your actions are guided by mental images, which are based on your behavior patterns. Previsualization maps your trip to the bathroom.

You see patterns by moving. In visual patterns you detect edges, edges in depth, slants, and corners. These pattern elements can be described by changes in colors, tones, and surface textures. We will define these new terms below and return to our attempt to get up and go to school later in this section. Remember that you are studying these terms in relation to perception. Later we will discuss how these perceptual sensations are translated into visual products.

B   C

Colors, Tones, and Surface Textures

Color is perceived as a person's visual system responds to differing qualities of light. Color is not the eye's response to different amounts of light
but to different kinds or wavelengths of light. The names of various colors,
such as *red, blue,* and *green,* are called *hues. Tone* is the eye's response
to different quantities of light, with more perceived light referred to as
bright and less perceived light referred to as *dark.* A synonym for *tone* is
value. Surface textures are the eye's perception of surface irregularities
such as lawns, gravel, or fur.

Edges, Edges in Depth, Slants, and Corners

As you move through space, you perceive changes in color, tone, and
surface texture that prevent you from running into the wall. When these
elements indicate differences in surfaces, edge—the transition from one

area or surface to another in the environment (Fig. 1-5)—is detected. The optic array is a pattern of light rays filled with edge distinctions. Edges are discontinuities in what is seen. Where the frame of the bedroom door is connected to the wall is an edge. You see edges-in-depth when you see the bathroom beyond that door frame. Edge and edge-in-depth may be indistinguishable from a single point of view (Fig. 1-6) but may become clearer as you walk, because you see the same things from different points

Figure 1-5. Examples of edges in the environment.

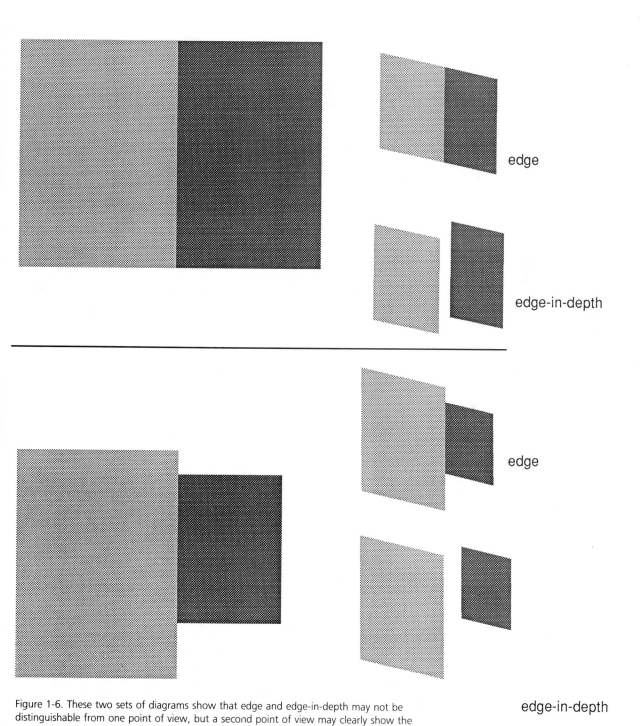

edge

edge-in-depth

edge

edge-in-depth

Figure 1-6. These two sets of diagrams show that edge and edge-in-depth may not be distinguishable from one point of view, but a second point of view may clearly show the spatial relationship of the two planes.

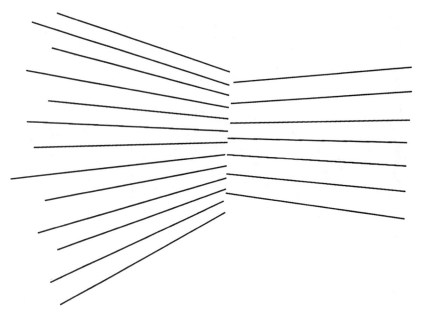

Figure 1-7. This diagram shows two slanted surfaces that meet at an edge, resulting in the perception of a corner.

of view. As you move through the door, the door frame appears to change shape and position and moves to the outside or periphery of your vision. The bathroom comes into greater focus because it provides a denser visual pattern than the bedroom.

A continuously modified surface can indicate slant. If a surface exhibits continuous change in tone, color, or surface texture, then the surface seems to slant away from or toward the viewer. Of the three, change in surface texture is the most specific indication of slant. A corner is the junction of two differently slanted surfaces (Fig. 1-7).

Other Complex Surface Patterns

Vision acquires pattern qualities when certain specific conditions are perceived in the environment. Light perceived to be reflected from many irregularly slanted surfaces enables vision to acquire pattern qualities. Areas facing the light receive more light and thus reflect more, and areas facing away from the light reflect less. This light pattern is called *surface texture* when it appears relatively small, for example, crumpled paper or a rough concrete wall. A mountain range and an architectural facade are examples of such light patterns increasing in size (Fig. 1-8).

A surface can also make visual perception appear to be a pattern if the surface has areas of dark and light grays or areas of apparently different colors (Fig. 1-9). Perception of a flat surface may have various tonal or color patterns if the surface is painted different colors.

A

B

Figure 1-8. Visual perception is patterned when complex irregular slanting surfaces are perceived. The road surface (A) is composed of rock fragments that have irregular slanting surfaces. In the optic array, these surfaces are patterns of light and dark tones. At a larger scale, these slanted surfaces may occur in the environment as footprints in the sand (B). Viewing mountains from the window of an airplane is this same visual phenomenon at a larger scale.

Shadows also cause patternlike visual perceptions. A surface can be distinguished if it has a shadow on it or if color changes or changes in slant are seen. The shadow has a penumbra and does not alter the texture of the surface upon which it is cast (Fig. 1-10). A *penumbra* is the partially illuminated fringe of a shadow.

Figure 1-9. Vision becomes patternlike when surfaces with color or tonal changes are viewed. In this photograph, indications of color and tone variations are apparent in the wood grain.

Figure 1-10. Vision becomes patternlike when shadows cast upon a surface are viewed.

PROPORTIONAL TRANSFORMATION OF YOUR PERCEPTIONS

Perception is proportional. It is not a complete, unchanging, or universal experience. The environment is perceived as the sum of information from all the senses. Although perception has often been considered to mean only vision, vision is a small portion of total perception. Perception combines all senses when acquiring information from the environment. Surface texture is an example of those combined perceptions because it is perceived as a visual experience of a surface, a tactile experience, or both. The tactile experience must exist, or the visual experience must strongly suggest the possibility of the tactile. Media such as photography or video enhance this illusion of tactile contact.

Adults in Western culture believe that sight, the optic experience, is the major source of information about the outside world. You can receive information or images without being in physical proximity or manual contact with what you see, yet young children examine almost every new experience with sight, touch, smell, hearing, and taste. Almost as soon as they see new toys, children pick them up and put them in their mouths. Even adults touch something they have not previously encountered, although convention and childhood memories generally restrain them from putting it in their mouths. Some perceptual psychologists propose that touch and motion are primary experiences over sight. Any visual producer's visual literacy requires more perceptual interaction with the world than sight alone.

Sight itself is a proportional, relative experience. Visual perceptions of the environment are modified by size, distance, motion, time, and previous knowledge. People make judgments about their surroundings based on how the surroundings appear in relation to them, their movement, and what they know. However, visual perceptions can be unreliable.

Having awakened, you are now in the kitchen. You look out the window and see the people below. They look like cockroaches. They are cockroaches! You were looking at the window ledge instead of the street below. Several factors contributed to your mistaken perception. First, you made a judgment based on size, but size is a relative concept. *Large* and *small* have no absolute meaning but gain significance in proportion to your experience. Your own body becomes the significant standard for evaluating the size of objects in your environment. You mistook the bug's dimensions for those of humans at a distance. The second factor in your mistake was your interpretation of apparent distance. Thinking the bugs were people means that you presumed they were very far away. You made a mistake because you misinterpreted the distance and therefore the relative scale of what you saw.

Scale is a dimensional relationship in which you use actual or apparent distance to compare the relative proportions of objects to yourself. It is

Figure 1-11. In order to understand spatial layout, looking at something from different points of view may be necessary. For example, whether a drawer is opened or closed may not be apparent from one angle only (A). Viewing the same object from a different location may clarify the actual spatial relationship (B).

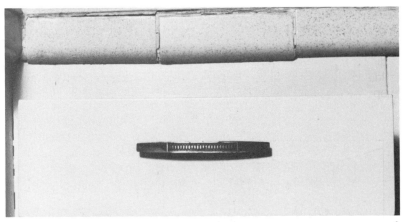

A

B

the relative size of things compared to you, the perceiving subject. People perceive objects in relation to themselves. Like the Lilliputians and Gulliver, you use sight primarily to judge the scale of things in the world, relate things or people to your own size, and compare them to what you know.

You get your insecticide and look elsewhere for more bugs. Knowing about the spatial layout of the environment is important. Your knowledge of your environment increases proportionally as you look from additional points of view. For example, a single stationary point of view may give ambiguous information about edge, corner, or depth. Once you move, however, the situation is clarified. If the edge is in fact an edge-in-depth, one surface progressively wipes out or reveals the other. By moving around objects or planes, you can determine the spatial configuration of the objects seen (Fig. 1-11).

An extreme example of how you learn about your environment in relation to your movement is the experiment in which visual psychologists have constructed highly eccentric, trapezoidal rooms that appear to be ordinary rectangular spaces from a specific point of view. The illusion holds only when the observer is still; once the observer moves, the true shape becomes apparent (Fig. 1-12).

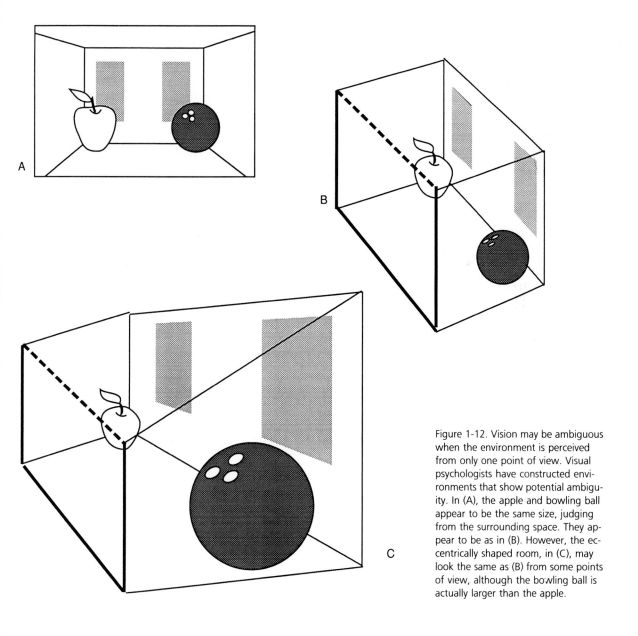

Figure 1-12. Vision may be ambiguous when the environment is perceived from only one point of view. Visual psychologists have constructed environments that show potential ambiguity. In (A), the apple and bowling ball appear to be the same size, judging from the surrounding space. They appear to be as in (B). However, the eccentrically shaped room, in (C), may look the same as (B) from some points of view, although the bowling ball is actually larger than the apple.

Figure 1-13. When only part of the optic array moves, the viewer is stationary and some object in the environment is moving. In these three images, note the movement of the woman relative to the center mark indicated by the triangle. The rest of the image does not shift.

Finally you leave your home, walk to the corner, and take the bus to school. You take the seat of a person who rises and moves to the rear door to get off the bus. A child near you drops a ball, and you watch it roll down the aisle. For all these experiences, you may ask, "What has moved?" Have you moved or has your environment moved around you? Was the ball rolling, or was it stationary as the bus moved beneath it? You receive motion information from your optic, haptic, kinesthetic, and aural senses. *Optic* refers to visual perceptions, *haptic* refers to touch perceptions, *kinesthetic* refers to perceptions from within the body such as balance, and *aural* refers to hearing perceptions. From the point of view of this book, vision linked with cognition is the most important sense for judging motion. You make judgments about motion in the environment all the time, based on your visual perception from your relative point of view. Your visual judgment is based on the constantly changing optic array you see.

If only part of the optic array moves, then you know that an object is moving (Fig. 1-13). If the total optic array moves uniformly, then you

Figure 1-14. When the total optic array moves, the viewer is moving. In these three images, note how the entire image shifts relative to the center mark indicated by the triangle.

know that your own body is moving, whether by your own power or some external means (Fig. 1-14). Vision is a primary information source about different types of viewer motion; for example, the changes in the optic array are much different if you are walking to the bus stop as opposed to riding in a bus. Sometimes you may be misled by sight. Looking from the window of the bus as it backs up slowly, you may think at first that the world is gliding forward.

When you move through space, you need to know where you can safely walk and whether you will collide with something. If you are approaching a surface, the optic array seems to expand outward and become less dense and proportionally quite large as you near impact (Fig. 1-15). However, if you are moving through space, the optic array expands

Figure 1-15. When a person is approaching impact with a surface, the optic array becomes progressively less dense at the center (marked by the triangle). The decreased density in the optic array is more apparent in the texture of the fence in each successive image, as impact with that surface becomes imminent.

toward the edges but always remains dense straight ahead, at the center of your vision (Fig. 1-16). A contracting array indicates that you are backing away. When you look out the back window of the bus as it moves forward, the world seems to contract toward the center of your vision (Fig. 1-17).

You judge the relative distance between objects and yourself while you move. Close objects move quickly across your optic array as you pass them. Distant objects move proportionally more slowly through the optic array than close objects (Fig. 1-18).

At last, you arrive at school.

Figure 1-16. With movement through space, the optic array continues to be densest at the center. Compare the constant center density in these three images to the decreasing center density shown in Figure 1-15.

Figure 1-17. Moving backward through space, the optic array contracts to the center. In these photographs, which reproduce what can be seen from the back window of a moving bus, objects seem to shrink and move toward the center of the array. Observe the location of objects relative to the center mark.

Figure 1-18 (facing page). With movement through space, the closeness of objects can be judges. In these photographs and corresponding diagrams, close objects, such as the single tree, move more rapidly across the optic array than distant objects, such as the distant group of trees.

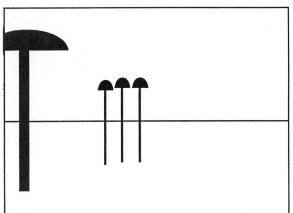

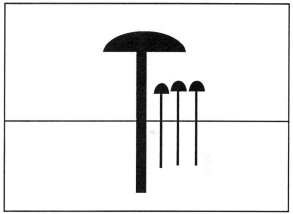

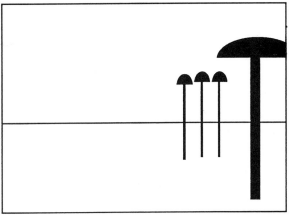

REPRODUCTION

As you head across campus, you pass a couple on a bench. One person appears quite hideous but may only have a bad haircut; the other seems also to have gone to the same barber and is really using too much hairspray. You have based your judgment on a sequence of views produced as you walked by them. Vision is not composed of just a single image. You reproduce a series of images that change slightly in sequence. Unlike a photograph, which isolates and frames a single scene, your vision is continuous and frameless, with sequences of scenes very much like the ones that preceded them.

Motion is important in vision because it reproduces a series of related but varying images on the retina. Binocular vision functions like movement because your two eyes are constantly seeing something from different points of view (Fig. 1-19). As you move, fixed or moving objects are reproduced in different locations on your retina. Their passage from center vision to periphery and their apparent movement relative to other objects enable you to determine their location, calculate their size, and understand their spatial layout. To decide whether the haircuts were really similar and/or hideous, you had to look at them from more than one view. Seeing those bad haircuts makes you go into the rest room and look in the mirror to check your own hair.

A mirror surface presents a unique perceptual condition. Unlike light-reflecting or light-emitting surfaces that are perceived in relation to your point of view, mirror surfaces reproduce the point of view of a hypothetical viewer. This viewer implied by the mirror scene would be as far behind the mirror as you are from the front (Fig. 1-20). Not all mirror surfaces give complete reflections. For example, perhaps you tried earlier to check your haircut in the reflection from a store window. At certain angles a piece of glass may be invisible or may show several scenes at the same time. While looking in a store window, you may see simultaneously the inside display, your reflection, and the street scene behind you. A similar example is the pool you passed before going to the rest room. A still body of water may show the surface beneath it. Rippling water may reveal at once the bottom surface, the surface of the water itself, and a scattered image of the sky and trees above.

Visual products reproduce your visual perceptions. As you cross campus, you pass many art and design products. They reproduce some aspect of what you see in the environment. Although they do not duplicate exactly your primary perceptions of the world, they translate those perceptions into visual conventions in the visual product. *Visual conventions* are the commonly accepted symbols, processes, and styles in any culture that are used in visual products. They are understood only within the context of a culture.

Following are some visual conventions that are ways to translate your

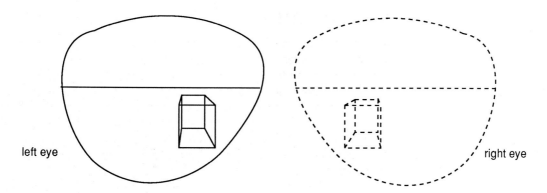

left eye   right eye

This diagram indicates the disparity between the optic arrays perceived with the left eye and with the right eye.

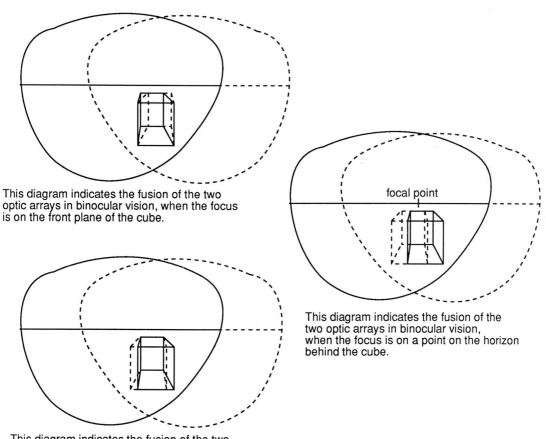

This diagram indicates the fusion of the two optic arrays in binocular vision, when the focus is on the front plane of the cube.

focal point

This diagram indicates the fusion of the two optic arrays in binocular vision, when the focus is on a point on the horizon behind the cube.

This diagram indicates the fusion of the two optic arrays in binocular vision, when the focus is on the back plane of the cube.

Figure 1-19. The fusion and disparity of binocular vision.

visual perceptions into art and design products. They are important for understanding the reproduction process.

1. Because the eye is a sphere, the straight lines are curved when the lens projects them onto the surface of the retina. Right angles may not seem true at a quick glance. Although people do not actually see straight edges, straight lines are visual conventions of art and design. The dimensions of the Parthenon' in Athens were designed to compensate for the apparent distortions in straight lines (Fig. 1-21). Read Appendix A for information about the structure of the human eye and visual perception.

2. Edge is the transition between two different surfaces. In pictures and diagrams, edge is often represented as a line. Drawing a line to represent an edge, eliminating the differing surfaces, and indicating their boundary with a continuous mark are visual conventions. If the line curves around and the ends meet, the result is an outlined shape. Shape and line exist only in pictures and diagrams, where they function as visual conventions representing edge. *Shape* is a closed area whose boundary is established by a continuous edge. A *line* is the continuous extension of points between any set of two points. Shape, line, and edge all imply discontinuous surfaces and reproduce spatial interruptions. The comprehensive term *edge* encompasses shape, line, and form (Fig. 1-22). *Form* refers to shape that is structured or systematized. (We avoid the term *form* in this book for several reasons. Form as applied to art and design education has become ambiguous because it has acquired too many meanings. In some cases,

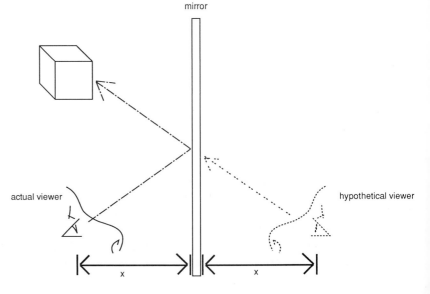

Figure 1-20. An object is seen in a mirror as a hypothetical viewer would see it if that hypothetical viewer were behind the mirror and as far away from the mirror as the viewer looking into the mirror is.

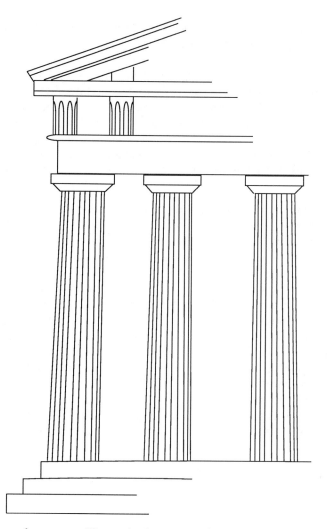

Figure 1-21. Although the various parts of the Parthenon in Athens (448–432 B. C.) appear regular and consistent, actually it has very few straight structural lines. The top step of the structure is convex. The columns tilt slightly toward the center of the building. The outer column is more closely spaced to its neighbor than inner columns and is slightly wider than the other columns.

form refers to specific aesthetic systems that dominate visual production, such as formalism. *Formalism* is the set of beliefs that the object exists autonomously in isolation from a cultural or physical context. Further discussion of formalism is found in Chapter 5.)

3. Color and tone can be reproduced with art and design media such as drawing, painting, photography, sculpture, and landscape design. Various light levels can be reproduced through white, black, and gray or by realigning surfaces to represent changing light quantities. Chroma or color differences are reproduced by many methods, including light reflection from pigments, dyes, or emission of certain light frequencies from a source such as a television. The two primary divisions for reproductive media are reflection and transmission. *Re-*

flection media rely on light reflected from surfaces, such as painting and photographic prints. *Transmission media* rely on projected or emitted light, such as television and computer display terminals.

4. Linear perspective drawings are diagrams that indicate the spatial relationships among objects and the observer. These diagrams reproduce a single monocular point of view and therefore are very different from actual human sight. In a linear perspective drawing, a small object next to a bigger one may indicate either actual size or depth differences. To make the ambiguities clear, linear perspective never presents a second point of view like the human binocular vision. Rather, it reproduces other spatial clues, including overlapping, shadows, continuous ground lines, and position relative to the horizon line, that clarify spatial layout (Fig. 1-23). Read Appendix D for more information.

Figure 1-22. Edges are the results of tone, color, or surface texture changes in the environment. A visual producer draws lines and shapes as the pictorial equivalents of edges.

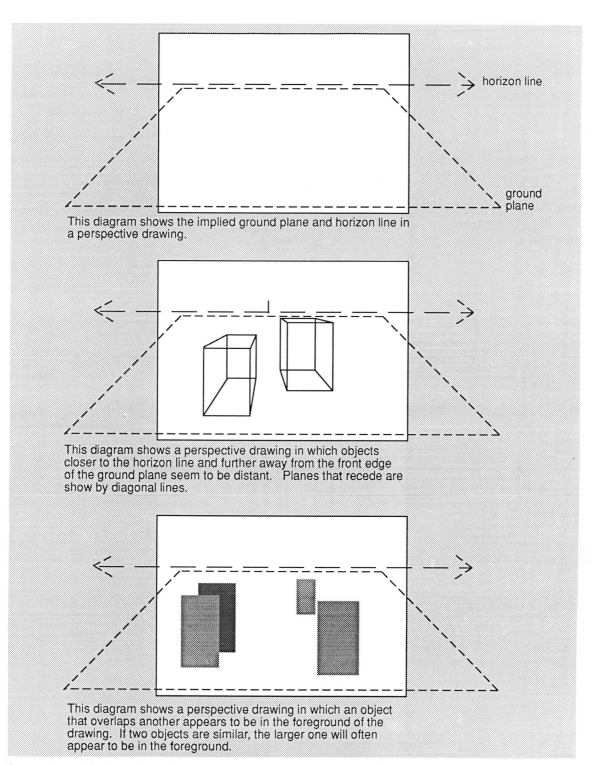

This diagram shows the implied ground plane and horizon line in a perspective drawing.

This diagram shows a perspective drawing in which objects closer to the horizon line and further away from the front edge of the ground plane seem to be distant. Planes that recede are show by diagonal lines.

This diagram shows a perspective drawing in which an object that overlaps another appears to be in the foreground of the drawing. If two objects are similar, the larger one will often appear to be in the foreground.

horizon line

ground plane

Figure 1-23. Spatial indicators in linear perspective drawings.

Figure 1-24. With movement through space, the architecture and landscape create specific views and vistas that are seen in succession.

5. When you walk through space or approach a surface, the optic array seems to expand outward and become less dense at the periphery. When you look from a moving vehicle, an expanding optic array indicates forward movement; a contracting array indicates that you are looking to the rear. In cinematic terms, these effects can be compared to zooming in and zooming out. The built environment—architecture, landscape design, and urban design—creates and reproduces specific views and vistas to be seen in succession while you move through the space (Fig. 1-24).

THE POWER OF PERCEPTUAL INFORMATION

All environmental information is derived through perception. A visual producer attains power by using perceptions as information in the creation of visual products. Exercising power in the realm of visual production requires two skills: (1) the ability to create images and objects that express personal ideas or the ideas of others and communicate these ideas to the audience; and (2) the ability to be an intelligent viewer, to understand not only the obvious message in any image or object but also the culture in which it operates and its associated messages. These skills are two aspects of the same activity. Both artist-designer and viewer are cultural producers, and both are participants in the process that uses and gives cultural meaning to visual products. Visual literacy is based on cultural competence and ability to produce visual products based on that competence.

Concrete and Abstract Perceptions

People tend to think that seeing a photograph is looking at reality. However, what is actually perceived is a combination of concrete and abstract perceptions. To be visually literate, understanding the difference between concrete and abstract perceptions is important.

Concrete refers to the immediate experience of actual things or events. A concrete experience is often the direct experience of the surrounding environment using all the senses. *Abstract* refers to the conceptual experience of things or events. Viewing a visual product that refers to an object is experiencing that object abstractly. The experience is abstract because the visual product is not identical to that object. For example, a photograph is a combination of concrete and abstract perceptions. People assume that the photographic print is actually how they concretely see with both eyes, but it is really the abstract visual product of a monocular or single lens. Concretely the photograph is a series of photochemically produced tones. When these tones are interpreted as an image of something, the photograph is perceived as simultaneously concrete and abstract because something is seen beyond what is concretely there. A photograph of a person is simultaneously a silver grain emulsion on paper, an actual image, and something that refers to someone not present.

The dichotomy of concrete and abstract is a simplification of the complex nature of perception. Vision simultaneously consists of both concrete and abstract perceptions of things that could be objects, events, or situations. Concrete perceptions are things seen as they are. Abstract perceptions occur when things refer to something else. People see a synthesis of concrete and abstract perceptions.

People perceptually comprehend their environment. Perception is also the basis for making visual products. In the next chapter, we consider how perceptions are organized into meaningful patterns and how this process affects visual products.

PERCEPTION ASSIGNMENT 1

Composition Exercise A

Your vision does not have distinct limits or edges, in contrast to a visual product, which has defined edges. In this exercise, you will organize visual elements within these edges. This perceived organization of a visual product's elements is called *composition.*

Materials

3 sheets heavyweight drawing paper, 18" x 24"

3 sheets black paper, 18" x 24"

Cutting knife, ruler, pencil

Glue: rubber cement or glue stick

Procedure

Select any five shapes from Figure 1-25. Enlarge them so that the largest one is approximately 18" x 24", the next is about half that size, the next is again half in size, and so on. Cut these shapes alternately from black and white paper.

Figure 1-25. Select any five shapes.

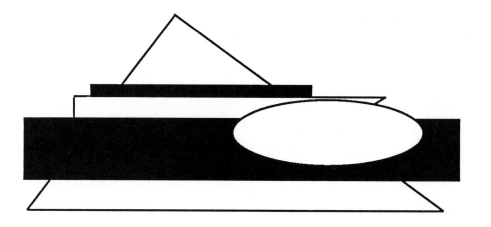

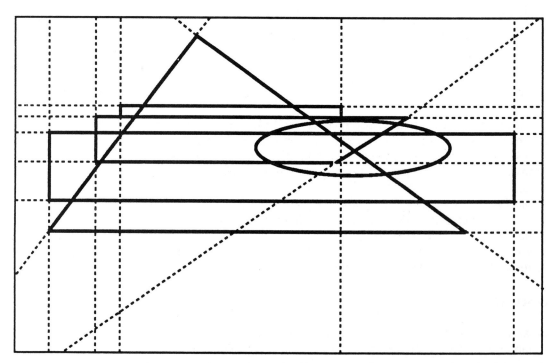

Figure 1-26. Select another student's assignment. Place it on paper, draw the shapes, and extend the lines until they reach the edges of the paper.

Within the largest shape, arrange these other black or white shapes to emphasize *one* of the following directions within the shape. Glue them in place.

1.   Emphasize the center of the shape.

2.   Emphasize the horizontal axis of the shape.

3.   Emphasize the vertical axis of the shape.

4.   Emphasize one of the diagonal axes of the shape.

5.   Emphasize one of the corners.

Composition Exercise B

In this exercise, you will organize visual elements by using a different medium, acrylic paint. By using another student's project as a starting point, your visual product will be the result of the creative labor of two people.

Materials

Heavyweight drawing paper or one-ply bristol paper, 18″ x 24″

Acrylic paint, painting supplies

Pencil, ruler

Procedure

Select another student's black-and-white project from the previous assignment. Draw the shapes of the previous project with ruler and pencil on 18″ x 24″ paper. Extend the lines you have drawn until they reach the edge of your paper. Your paper is now covered with shapes and lines (Fig. 1-26).

Mix five different tones of gray, excluding black. Paint the grays within the shapes to emphasize a direction within the rectangular paper: horizontal, vertical, diagonal, corner, or center.

When you are finished, compare the rectangular gray paintings to the corresponding black-and-white projects.

Discussion

What was the difference between organizing visual elements within a rectangular shape and organizing within a nonrectangular shape?

Composition Exercise C

Now you will learn about color mixing and about the effect of ambient light on color perception. See Appendix C for further discussion of color perception and paint mixing.

Materials

Acrylic paint, painting supplies

3 sheets heavyweight drawing paper or one-ply bristol paper, 3" x 4"

1 sheet heavyweight drawing paper or one-ply bristol paper, 12" x 16"

Cutting knife, ruler

Glue: rubber cement or glue stick

Procedure

Select one color sample from the color chips the instructor provides. Mix

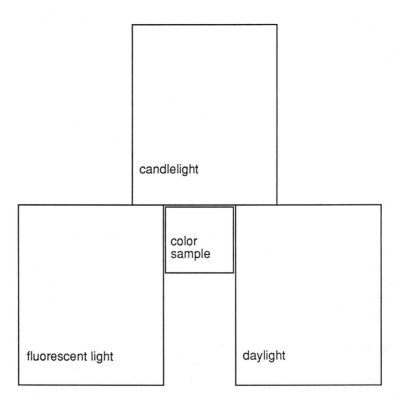

Figure 1-27. Arrange the mixed colors next to the original color, as shown above.

your acrylic paints to match the color of the paint chip you selected, under these different light situations:

1. Under candlelight, in an enclosed room

2. Under fluorescent light, in an enclosed room

3. In daylight, outdoors

Paint each mixture on one 3″ x 4″ piece of paper. Glue each mixture and the original color chip onto the large sheet of white paper, and arrange them so that each paint mixture touches an edge of the color chip (Fig. 1-27).

Discussion

How do you account for the differences and similarities in the paint mixtures?

Composition Exercise D

In this exercise, you will see how the addition of color affects a tonal composition.

Materials

Acrylic paints, paint supplies

Scraps of one-ply bristol paper

Glue

Cutting knife

Procedure

Return to the rectangular gray painting you did in Composition Exercise B. Paint some colors on scraps of bristol paper in colors similar to the ones you painted in Composition Exercise C. Cut the color samples into any desired shape and place the colors on your tonal composition from Exercise B, so that the addition of color reinforces the directions and locations you wish to emphasize. Glue them in place.

Discussion

Are the color areas focal points of all the compositions?

PERCEPTION ASSIGNMENT 2

Memory Exercise

You can arrange visual elements in groups or place them randomly in a composition. In this exercise, you will see how various arrangements of visual elements affect recall and see the perceptual differences between individuals.

Materials

10 sheets bond typing paper, 8½" x 11"

Wide-tipped black marker

Procedure

With the wide-tipped black marker, draw six to nine lines on one piece of paper. The lines may be curved or straight, and can be any length between 2 and 9 inches. Arrange them in one of the following ways:

1. All lines touching each other
2. All lines grouped very closely together
3. All lines pointing in the same direction
4. Lines arranged to suggest a simple geometric shape

On a second piece of paper, draw the same number and length of lines, but arrange them as randomly as possible.

Break up into groups of five students. Show your drawings, one at a time, to the other students in your group for approximately 1 second each. On separate pieces of paper, the other students should try to reproduce each original drawing, including the length, arrangement, and placement of lines.

When they are finished, you should gather all the drawings that reproduced your own.

Discussion

From the results of this project, did individuals show perceptual differences?

Were the random line drawings or the grouped line drawings more accurately reproduced?

PERCEPTION ASSIGNMENT 3

Sketch Exercise

Your perceptions from all your senses serve as a basis for your visual products. You must learn certain visual conventions to transform what you perceive in the environment into a visual product.

This exercise will help you learn some simple drawing techniques that will help you visualize spatial relationships in the environment.

Materials

2 sheets graph paper (scale: 8 or 10 squares per inch), 11" x 14"

Pencil, eraser, ruler

1 piece corrugated cardboard, 10" x 12"

Cutting knife

Procedure

You will make two different types of drawings that reproduce an interior space. Both drawings are based on your perceptions, but each records different kinds of information.

Drawing 1. Break up into groups of four. Group members should measure the floor dimensions of a room, hallway, and an adjoining room. Note the placement of doors, and measure where the walls of one room join along the walls of another room.

Using the collected information, each student should draw on graph paper a simple floorplan that reproduces the spaces and their relative locations. Indicate proportionately the actual room measurement. Show the location of the doors (Fig. 1-28A).

Drawing 2. Cut the center out of the piece of cardboard to leave a rectangular window 8" x 10". With a pencil, mark 1-inch increments on the cardboard on all four sides along the edge of the window.

On the second piece of graph paper, draw an 8" x 10" rectangle, and mark 1-inch increments on all four sides of the rectangle.

Holding the cardboard window at arm's length, look through it at the classroom. Reproduce the scene you see through the window on the graph paper. Notice the markings on the window where the edges of the ceilings, walls, and floor seem to meet the cardboard window edge. Find the corresponding markings on the graph paper, and reproduce the shapes in those locations (Fig. 1-28B).

A. Drawing based on abstract mathematical information.

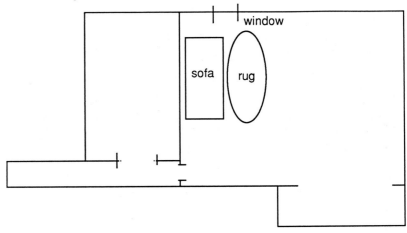

B. Drawing based on concrete visual perceptions.

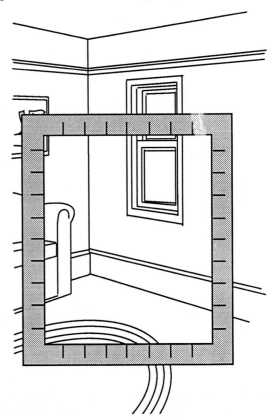

Figure 1-28. First draw a room and other adjoining spaces based on mathematical information. This drawing is a floorplan (A). Then draw a view of the room as seen through a cardboard rectangle. This drawing is based on concrete visual perceptions (B).

Discussion

Drawing 1 relates to your experience and your environment and is a reproduction of a space familiar to you. However, it is a more *abstract* image because you can never actually see at any one instant what this drawing depicts.

In Drawing 2, you are attempting to reproduce your more *concrete* visual perception of the room because you are depicting your visual perception of the room and its contents as you saw them from a fixed point. Because your drawing has distinct edges, no color, and few fine details and is composed mostly of lines, however, it is only a partial reproduction of your concrete perception.

Discuss how these drawings relate to your visual and nonvisual experience of the rooms. What information gathered from your other senses about the rooms do these drawings not reproduce at all? How does each drawing seem more or less complete than the other?

PERCEPTION ASSIGNMENT 4

Viewer Motion and Perception

Your perceptions give you information you need for everyday life and even for survival. For example, with your visual perceptions you can detect possible paths that enable you to move through space and avoid collisions. If you are approaching a surface, the optic array seems to expand outward and become less dense and proportionally quite large as you near impact. When you are moving through space, the optic array expands toward the edges but always remains dense straight ahead, at the center of your vision.

In this exercise you will learn more about how your vision is structured. In addition, you will make a visual product based on your visual perceptions.

Materials

Small map of the campus

Floorplan of art building

Colored markers

Procedure

Demonstration. The instructor or teaching assistant will use a portable video camera to record what you see as you walk through a series of rooms. When playing back the tape, you should be able to see the varying densities in your optic array as you move through space. For example, as you move through a doorway, the frame and surrounding wall areas become visually less dense and more peripheral, while denser arrays are emerging from behind the door's edges.

Exercise. Indicate on a small campus map the routes you have taken through the campus today. Visualize the route as completely as possible, until the point where you entered the building for this class. The following color code should be used in marking the map:

Black: paths taken while walking

Green: stop at any location (e.g., attending class)

Red: locations of emerging optic arrays, as when you move through a doorway or walk between two buildings. In the video demonstration, you saw how optic arrays emerge from behind edges, such as doorways or buildings.

The teacher will prepare a similar, large map of the campus. On the large map in the classroom, all students draw the paths they took that day to class, just as they drew on their individual maps.

Follow the same procedure on the floorplan of the building, show the paths taken until the time you entered the classroom and reproduce them on the large floorplan.

Discussion

Observe the patternlike result when all students trace their paths on the same large map. This pattern conveys information about the students' foot and traffic patterns. Compare how various students recall emerging arrays where two or more maps overlap.

PERCEPTION ASSIGNMENT 5

Motion and Cultural Distances

At school, you follow paths that are convenient for you. The physical distance you maintain from the strangers who surround you is called *personal space.* A well-designed campus and classroom building provide you with convenient paths and adequate space. You become aware of your surroundings if you are inconvenienced or if your personal space is invaded.

In this exercise, you will plan a visual product that will make viewers aware of their surroundings.

Materials

1 sheet 18″ x 24″ heavy bond paper or bristol paper

Pencil

Colored pencils

Ruler

Procedure

Study the map of the classroom building from Perception Assignment 5 to choose a location in the building with considerable foot traffic (e.g., doorways, rest rooms, vending machines, courtyard entrances).

Plan a way to alter or impede foot traffic around the building. You should change paths often taken or force a compression of personal space.

Communicate your ideas visually using drawings, plans, and diagrams. Also write descriptions of your ideas, the amount of time you need to execute the project, and what reaction you anticipate from the audience. This is called the *documentation* of your idea.

Discussion

Do Not Enter signs, velvet ropes, sawhorses, fences, and metal grates are some of the many kinds of barriers. Discuss barriers and your willingness to accept them in specific situations: at amusement parks, in a bank, police lines, freeway detours. Which define privileged spaces, which keep order, and which deny access?

Discuss how personal distance changes according to the culture and to the particular situation.

EXTRA CREDIT

Buildings are now being constructed so that some entrances are accessible to handicapped persons, but frequently these entrances are remote or inconvenient. Plan handicap accessibility for your classroom building, or critique existing handicap entrances. In the plan, you should enable handicapped and nonhandicapped people to use the same paths and all entrances; require a similar effort for both to enter the building.

PATTERN

CHAPTER 2

Because you decided not to eat the leftover pizza, you were still hungry when you arrived at school. You pass through the campus sculpture garden to go to the cafeteria for an early lunch. You accidentally walk into the wrong dining room and find that the faculty have a different room for their meals but are served the same food. Printed reproductions of famous paintings decorate the walls of the faculty dining room, in contrast to the bare walls of the student dining area. You recognize paintings you saw as slides in your art history class.

After finding the correct entrance, you join the crowd in the serving line to get your food. People in line are standing too close to each other. They touch and bump against you. You finally reach the salad bar. You spoon out what you think is blue cheese dressing onto your salad. The person behind you informs you that you have put lumpy tapioca pudding on your lettuce. You made this mistake because the desserts are next to the salad dressings and in similar containers.

The bag of french fries you chose was under the warming lamp too long, and oil has soaked into the bag. The ink used to print the clown face on the bag has turned from pink to green. You finally get past the cashier and attempt to find a seat. You trip because you misread the edges of the steps while ascending the stairs to the upper dining room. You lose your footing and an apple falls off your tray. No one notices.

ORGANIZING YOUR PERCEPTIONS

You see the world as many edges. Perception of these edges is necessary for performing the simplest task, such as walking up steps or going to the cafeteria for meals. The edges seen are distinguished from each other and organized into patterns.

The difference between seeing, looking, and perceiving is one of degree and attention. People see things without being aware of details they would notice once they really begin to look at them. Perception is the synthesis of these actions, in which raw data perceived become visual information.

Figure 2-1. Examples of foreground-background relationships.

Edge perception is one example of that raw data that become visual information. It is the apparent distinction between two contrasting areas of color, tone, and surface textures (see Fig. 1-5). Edge perception is simple and uncomplicated and one of the basic processes of vision. When any edge appears, differences among phenomena within the optic array are perceived, indicating distinctions among areas of color, tone, and surface texture. Many such differences at any one time produce patterns of edges. Some of these patterns combine to produce images. This process occurs constantly in visual perception. In this chapter we discuss how complex edges or systems of edges produce pattern. Visual literacy includes how a producer or an audience understands these patterns.

In any optic array, elements and groups of elements are often composed of many complex edges. *Foreground-background* refers to the perception of elements within optic arrays (Fig. 2-1). Foreground-background relationships occur when more attention is paid to the elements perceived and less to the background. In this *center-periphery* relationship, the element that has gained attention becomes the center of the optic array. The surrounding elements at that same moment fade to the periphery of vision. Foreground-background structures the optic array.

Foreground-background relationships often change in the optic array. Perception is a dynamic activity, a constant scanning and rescanning of the array as a person focuses on different elements. New foreground-background relations are available within the same array. With a change in focus, an apparent foreground becomes a background. For example, a certain shape may alternately be a hole or an element surrounded by white spaces (Fig. 2-2).

The term *figure-ground* occurs often in other texts and classes, but here we use *foreground-background* for a number of reasons. *Foreground* is a more appropriate term than *figure* to describe the subject of attention. For example, *figure* is an inadequate descriptive term when the focus is on an area without edges or on a group of objects instead of a single figure or object. *Figure* primarily is associated with the human figure. *Foreground* may refer to many kinds of visual elements including the human figure. Paying attention to something brings it to the foreground of awareness or to immediate perceptual attention. In the optic array the foreground corresponds to a spatial location in contrast to a background. Either close or distant objects in the optic array may be brought to the foreground. Foreground-background implies a continuum in which the

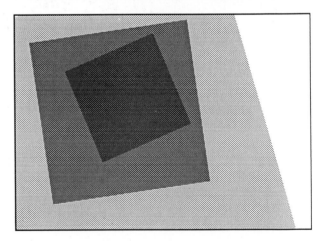

Figure 2-2. Foreground-background relationships are not constant. They shift as the viewer's focus changes. The various squares in each diagram may appear as holes that become background or as closed shapes that become foreground.

foreground is distinct from the background at the same time that it is part of the total optic array; figure-ground implies a simple dichotomy that inadequately describes a complex set of visual relationships.

Perception is more than colors and tones. Focusing attention interprets the colors and tones perceived; significant elements are selected over other elements from the environment. The salad dressing mistake is a good example of selecting and being misled by an ambiguous combination of foreground elements.

Perceiving is not passive but a creative act. Interpreting foreground or background does not depend strictly on the physical stimulation of the eye and its retina receptor cells. For example, when you look at printed text, you pay attention to the letters and words and ignore the surrounding surface. However, in your retina, both surface and letters stimulate photoreceptor cells. Your attention to the words is culturally conditioned. The page provides an environment for you to interpret the mutually interdependent foreground and background.

Why is this foreground-background relationship so important? Visual space is constructed by paying attention to foreground elements. The perceiving subject uses foreground-background to establish physical, optical, and conceptual relation to the artwork. That simple act of establishing location relative to what is perceived is valuable and powerful, especially when the visual producer can communicate that sensation to an audience by using visual products (Fig. 2-3).

Foreground-background gives meaning to spatial relationships and allows gauging of what is significant and insignificant. You pay more attention to those people who come closer to you. When you were crowded in line, you became aware of a cultural pattern concerned with how much personal space and distance you usually maintain between yourself and others. In a crowded urban environment, you use foreground-background relationships to identify paths, to detect signs for information, and to locate landmarks and familiar sites.

Visual producers manipulate the foreground-background relationships in their visual products in order to control or guide the viewers' gaze. This manipulation communicates both the order and meaning of the artwork and demonstrates in its practice the technical competence of the individual visual producer. In *Sunday Afternoon on the Island of La Grande Jatte* (see Color Plate 1 and Fig. 2-7A), Georges Seurat produced foreground-background relationships in the painting so that certain elements are more readily noticeable than others.

These foreground-background relationships are grouped to construct visual patterns, whether regular, irregular, organized, or random. These patterns give useful spatial information about corners, slant surfaces, edges-in-depth, scale, and spatial arrangement. Visual producers use patterns to communicate to their audience, and the audience acquires information from them.

Figure 2-3. People use foreground-background relationships to locate themselves relative to the environment. In these two photographs, relative distance from the objects can be judged, based partly on which objects are in the foreground and which are in the background.

PATTERN STRUCTURES THE VISUAL ENVIRONMENT

Pattern is structure. It is more than the idea of structure as a passive object, such as building or sculpture. Structure is both active and passive, and the viewer structures as much as the producer. You structure your visual environment into patterns as you perceive, and you structure visual patterns in products as you make them.

How are patterns structured? Like the patterns of English grammar, visual patterns are based on conventions such as grouping that change according to those who use them. Structural patterns evolve over time. English grammar is not the same now as it was 200 years ago. Like languages, visual patterns are related to social and cultural patterns. The pattern of arrangement of food in the cafeteria and the segregation of students from faculty is visual and cultural. The artwork in the faculty dining room suggests a higher status for faculty than for the students.

Pattern is composed of basic units that are organized structurally. For the moment, following a mathematical example, let us assign the abstract term *point* to such a basic unit. When you look at a group of points collectively, you may perceive them as pattern. For example, a line is the continuous extension of points between any set of two points. Complex pattern elements such as lines and planes are created by first connecting points in space. Points, lines, planes, and their combinations are parts of the essential structure of pattern (Fig. 2-4).

Pattern may be the foreground in a foreground-background relationship. You structure pattern elements in your optic array and in the visual products you make. A variety of concepts, including grouping, symmetry, and shape grammars, guide pattern perception and construction.

Grouping

When you group the elements of your visual environment into patterns, you structure random items and events into usable information. You perceive such grouping as foreground elements, with the rest of the array becoming the background, to make your perceptions meaningful to you.

Many of the grouping concepts listed below are similar to gestalt perceptual principles. (See Rudolf Arnheim, 1980, for further discussion of gestalt principles.) We do not use the terms and concepts from the gestalt psychology of art because gestalt theory has been challenged by subsequent research on the cultural and environmental bases of perception. (See Donis Dondis, 1973, for another perspective on the concepts of grouping.)

Comparison: grouping elements according to similar aspects. The degree to which parts of an array are comparable in some aspect is a

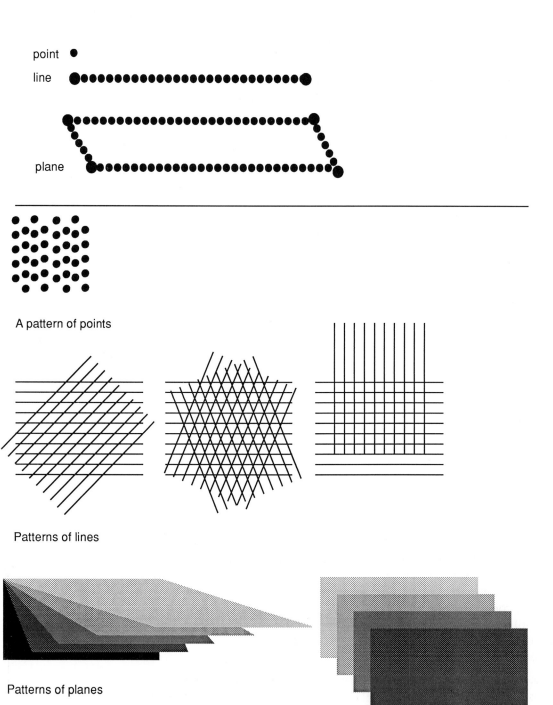

point

line

plane

A pattern of points

Patterns of lines

Patterns of planes

Figure 2-4. The point is the basic unit of pattern.

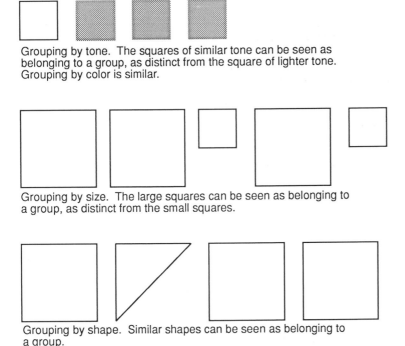

Grouping by tone. The squares of similar tone can be seen as belonging to a group, as distinct from the square of lighter tone. Grouping by color is similar.

Grouping by size. The large squares can be seen as belonging to a group, as distinct from the small squares.

Grouping by shape. Similar shapes can be seen as belonging to a group.

Figure 2-5. Grouping by comparable aspect. These diagrams show how figures can be grouped when they are compared on the basis of tone, color, size, and shape.

factor in their being grouped. These aspects include size, shape, color or tone, location, and direction or orientation (Fig. 2-5).

Contiguity: grouping elements that touch, which creates a foreground pattern (Fig. 2-6).

Proximity: grouping elements that are close, such as dots placed close together in a row to become a line. Elements that are closer to each other than to other elements in an array may be grouped (Fig. 2-6).

Simplicity: grouping elements to produce regular, simple, relatively symmetric, and closed relationships. Elements are grouped according to the fewest structural features possible. Unconnected parts are mentally connected when the connection results in a completed shape (Fig. 2-6). This concept is also called *closure,* which is a variation on simplicity. Grouping occurs with correspondence of parts across or along an axis. This concept is also called *symmetry.*

Motion: grouping moving elements. Movement in the same direction is a basis for grouping (Fig. 2-6). The different speeds of various moving elements may be a basis for grouping. These concepts may be found in visual products such as motion picture film, video, performance art, and kinetic sculpture.

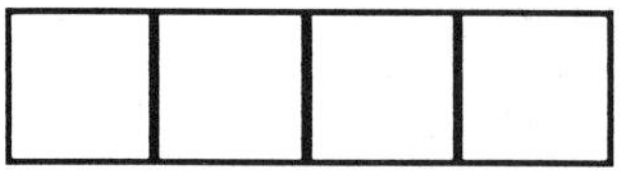

Grouping by contiguity, where shapes that touch each other are seen as part of a group.

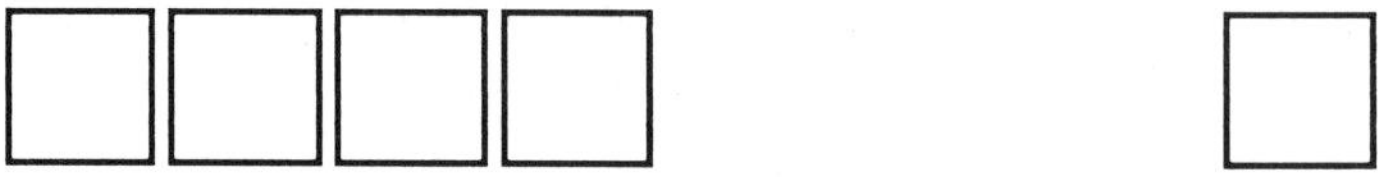

Grouping by proximity, where shapes close together are seen as part of a group that excludes the more distant shape.

Grouping by simplicity. In this case, the simplest process is to group each set of four lines and to consider them as squares. This may also be called closure.

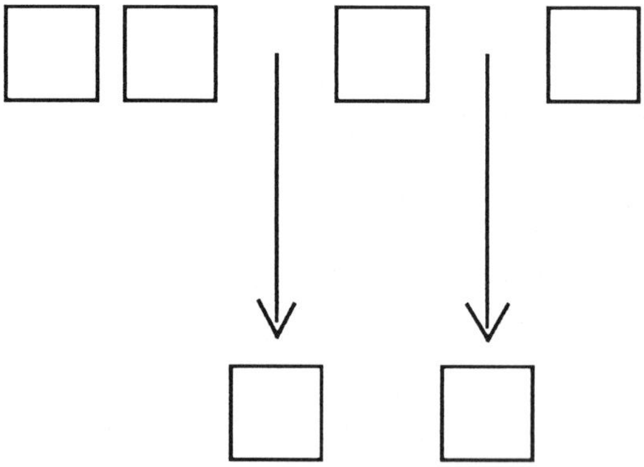

Grouping by motion. The shapes that appear to move are grouped, as distinct from those shapes that appear static. In addition, movement of the shapes in the same direction may be an added basis for grouping.

Figure 2-6. Grouping according to contiguity, proximity, simplicity, motion, and direction.

Convention: grouping elements according to habit, convention, or the accumulated experience of the visual producer. One example is the mistake with the pudding and salad dressing that you grouped by location and container. Also, the varied landscape colors are perceived as generalized blue tones at a distance and therefore distant objects may be grouped based on color. Another example in Western cultures is reading text left to right and top to bottom on a page. This process is habitual and the result of the accumulated experience of reading. The habit is carried over into looking at images; people look first to the center and then to the upper left of any page, canvas, or screen.

When an artist paints a painting or a designer develops a design, they use grouping concepts (Fig. 2-7). Grouping in perception is different from that of a visual product because perception has no distinct edges and a visual product has a definite size, shape, and boundary. This size, shape, and boundary affect how visual elements are grouped within a visual product (see Appendix B). For the graphic designer, that grouping is necessary for the audience to be able to extract the message from the entire area of an advertisement, screen, or billboard. The sculptor groups shapes and voids to convey cultural information. In urban and architectural design, building details and spaces are grouped to meet user demands.

Symmetry

Symmetry operates both as a grouping concept and as a structural concept. A structural concept organizes elements according to logical rules, in this case, symmetry rules. In symmetrical patterns, elements are divided and/or repeated systematically, mathematically, or geometrically. Elements within the symmetrical configuration become identified as foreground, with the rest becoming background. Following are some simple symmetrical transformations that regulate the placement of an element within a pattern:

Mirror: the reflection of an element or elements across an axis (Fig. 2-8). The configuration of the elements is repeated but reversed.

Glide: the repetition of an element along an axis (Fig. 2-8). In a one-directional glide, pattern elements are reproduced in a line. A two-directional glide results in a planar pattern. A three-directional glide yields a network, where elements are repeated in length, width, and depth, which may correspond to *x, y, z* graph coordinates (Fig. 2-9).

Rotation: repetition of elements around a center or axis (Fig. 2-8). Boat and airplane propellers are examples of rotational symmetry.

A

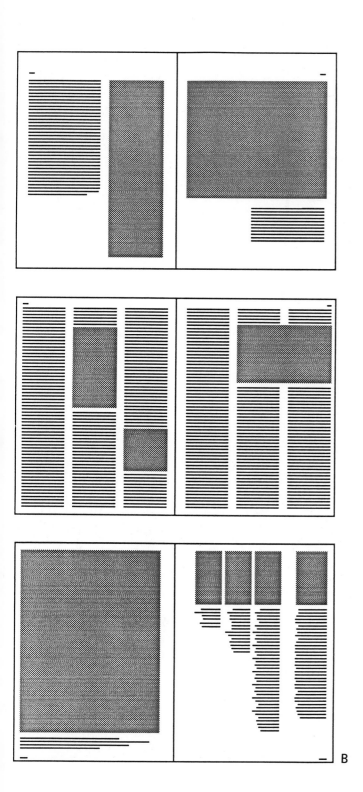

Figure 2-7. In Seurat's *Sunday Afternoon on the Island of La Grande Jatte* (see Color Plate 1), one possible grouping of shapes in the painting is according to tone, with the darker areas becoming the foreground (A). Example of page layout in which lines indicate text and the gray rectangles indicate images (B).

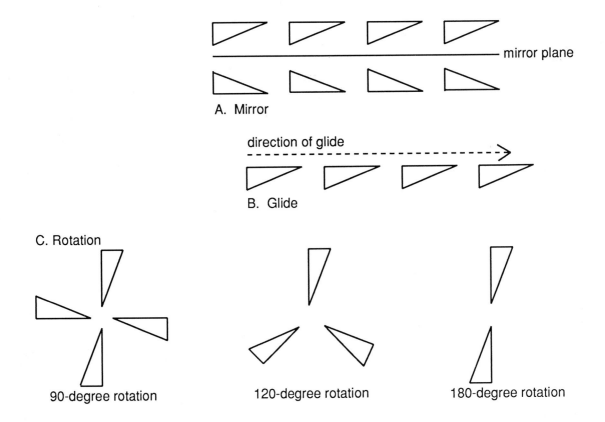

A. Mirror

direction of glide

B. Glide

C. Rotation

90-degree rotation   120-degree rotation   180-degree rotation

Figure 2-8. Symmetry transformations. Mirror, glide, and rotation are the three basic movements to any symmetry system.

These basic symmetrical transformations can be combined for more complex results. For example, the screw transformation is a combination of rotation and glide. An example of a screw transformation would be a spiral staircase, in which the steps are the elements that are repeated according to both rotation and glide. Layers occur when two symmetrical systems coincide, one atop the other (Fig. 2-10).

Symmetry applications are numerous. For example, symmetrical patterns are extremely common in decoration. Some cultures, such as Islam, are known for their decorative use of symmetry on tapestries, manuscripts, and buildings. Symmetry is frequently employed to structure large-scale or complex spatial designs, such as architecture and landscape planning, because the person using the space can understand the total layout and organization without having to experience it firsthand. Church architecture often uses simple, clearly visible symmetry. In industrial design, symmetry is used to design solar panels and heat deflectors and to solve ordinary packing problems. Symmetry can be used in systems design to develop complex processes such as corporate identity programs, urban transportation systems, and information networks.

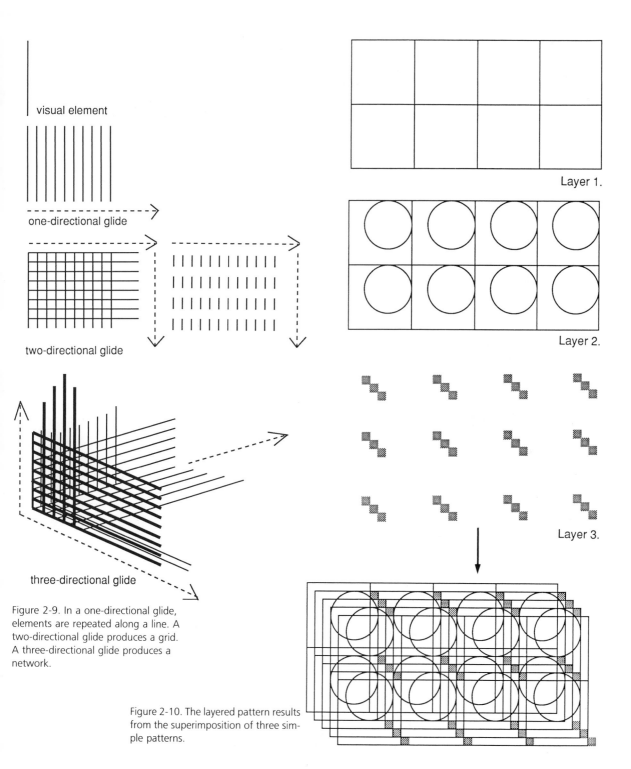

visual element

one-directional glide

two-directional glide

three-directional glide

Figure 2-9. In a one-directional glide, elements are repeated along a line. A two-directional glide produces a grid. A three-directional glide produces a network.

Layer 1.

Layer 2.

Layer 3.

Figure 2-10. The layered pattern results from the superimposition of three simple patterns.

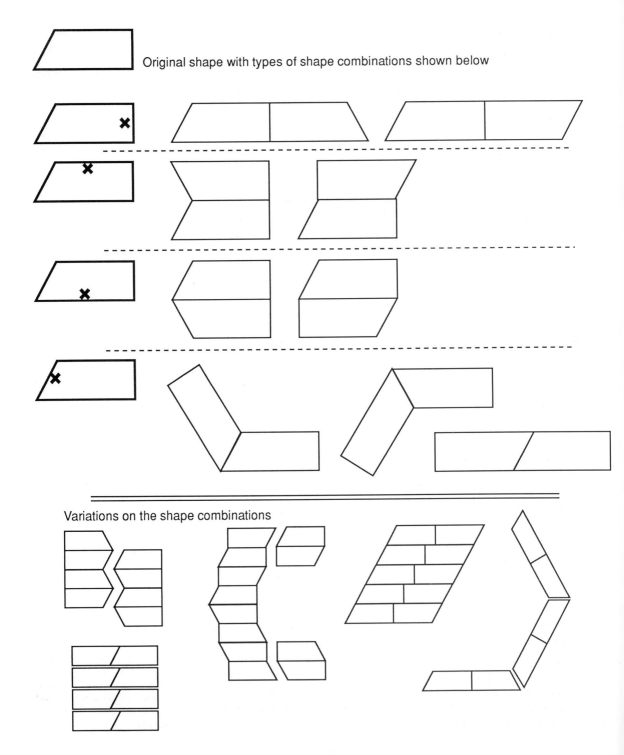

Original shape with types of shape combinations shown below

Variations on the shape combinations

Shape Grammars

In addition to symmetry and grouping, shape grammars are used for systematically organizing visual elements. Shape grammars attempt to structure pattern elements by determining how shapes are similar and may be transformed. Although shape grammar primarily involves geometric shapes, it has its sources in disciplines that study the evolution of complex biological structures, such as typology and morphology. *Typology* refers to the classification of shapes; *morphology* refers to the essential features and derivation of shapes. For example, ''Family resemblances'' are recognizable because the faces of members of one family are more similar than those of the larger human population. The biological methods of typology and morphology may be applied also to cultural objects. Shape grammar research applies biological analogies from typology and morphology to the fields of architecture and design by studying the similarity of plans and developing new systems for generating visual products (Fig. 2-11). It also is used as a creative tool in furniture design and drawing. (See William Mitchell, 1977; Philip Steadman, 1979, 1983; and George Stiny, 1975.)

Grouping, symmetry, and shape grammars are concepts used to organize and pay attention to the broad range of significant and important elements found in culture. These organizational and structural concepts pattern vision into meaningful information. The meanings and purposes associated with pattern configurations depend upon and change with cultural context. For example, different cultures may associate symmetry with diverse religious meanings and values.

PROPORTION OF ELEMENTS IN A FIELD

Scale

Previously, we have defined *scale* generally as the size of something relative to the observer. For certain visual products, however, scale is interpreted differently. In visual products such as painting, photography, and video, scale is the size of visual elements relative to the size of the frame that surrounds them. The size of a visual element is interpreted by comparing its actual size with the size of the painting, photographic print, film, or video screen.

These visual products have inherent boundaries: edge of the canvas, the dimensions of the photographic print, or the perimeter of the video or computer monitor. Human vision does not have these absolute boundaries. The relative boundaries defined by canvases, photographs, or screens are called *frames.* The frame may contain many fields. The *field* is a subdivision of the perceived optic array determined by point of view and the area upon which attention is centered from that perspective.

Figure 2-11 (facing page). Shape grammars investigate possible shape combinations. This diagram represents only a small proportion of the possible combinations based on the original simple quadrilateral.

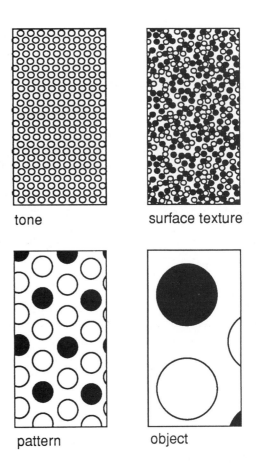

Figure 2-12. Tone, surface texture, pattern, and object can be perceived and reproduced by means of pattern at an increasing or decreasing scale.

Fields are established because the optic array is constantly changing and is bounded by blurred peripheral vision.

Perception of visual products is affected by the scale relationship between the frame and the visual elements it contains. A pattern changes in scale as it becomes larger or smaller in relation to the frame containing it. As pattern changes in scale, perceptions and interpretations of the patterns also change. Specifically, tone, surface texture, pattern, and object are perceived (Fig. 2-12).

Although framing a pattern affects perceptions of tone, surface texture, pattern, or object, a pattern may be perceived at more than one level. For example, in the same video frame, you can get close enough to perceive the combinations of dots on the screen and at the same time perceive tone, surface texture, pattern, or object in the dot patterns.

As scale diminishes, the individual elements within the surrounding frame are much smaller and frequently numerous. Conversely, at larger scales, individual elements are close in size to any surrounding frame. In a large-scale configuration, a visual element may approach the size of the frame that contains it. In that case, the frame defines the boundaries of a large foreground element within the larger optic array (Fig. 2-13).

This shift, where foreground becomes background in a visual product, or the reverse, also happens within the optic array. Imagine walking across a room with a distant door as the center of the optic array. The room is the foreground space. As you, the subject, move toward the door, the room shifts behind you. It becomes the background as it moves to the outer edges of the optic array. The door frame also moves to the periphery, and the scene through the door becomes the new center of the optic array (Fig. 2-14). Standing still, you can have a shifting foreground-background perception by focusing on different areas of the optic array.

Whether you travel through a landscape, view it from a fixed point, or attempt to construct a landscape, you are creating these shifting foreground-background relationships. Regardless of medium—videotape, photography, sculpture, architecture, or painting—you use these foreground-background relationships. The visual environment serves as patterns for the generation of new visual products. Being aware of the structural relationships of perception provides methods for organizing work. By the analogy of theme and variation in music, the theme establishes a pattern from which new variations in pattern may be generated or improvised. Your visual environment is the theme upon which you improvise while making new visual products.

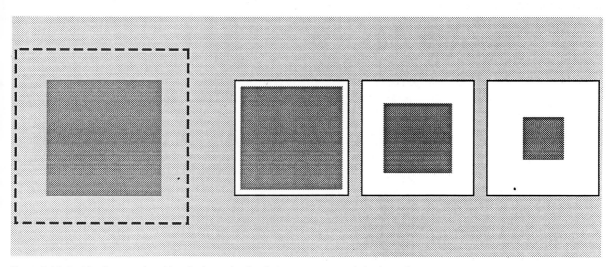

Figure 2-13. In this diagram, the object is shown by the dark gray square and the frame is indicated by the outlined square. An object can be increased in scale until it approaches the size of the frame. Once the size of the object is the same size as the frame, then the frame-object becomes the foreground within a larger implied background.

Figure 2-14. Foreground-background relationships can shift in the optic array, based on where attention is focused. In the large picture, the foreground-background relationship may be different than the foreground-background relationships in the smaller photographs.

PATTERNS THAT REPRODUCE TONE, SURFACE TEXTURE, PATTERN, AND OBJECT

In visual production, pattern is used at various scales to reproduce tone, surface texture, pattern, and object. Patterns based on points are essential for image production and reproduction. Pattern also operates in architectural, sculptural, urban, and landscape design.

Pattern that Reproduces Tone and Color Mixtures

Pattern is perceived as tone when the scale of the pattern is small and the elements are densely arranged within a frame. The perceived light levels of the environment can be translated into tonal equivalents in art and design media.

For example, a photographic print is composed of silver grains that are perceived as varying grays when viewed without instruments such as microscopes or grain magnifiers. The irregular pattern of silver grains against white paper creates the entire range of tones in a photograph. When this photograph is to be reproduced by industrial printing processes, as in this book, it is rephotographed through a screen to transform it into a halftone dot pattern (Fig. 2-15). The dot patterns are small in scale compared to the printed page and are perceived as tone. Due to the apparent fusion of dots, the dots collectively are perceived as gray tones similar to the tones of the original photograph.

A paint sample derives its color from the small pigment particles suspended in a clear, hardening liquid. White paint is white because the small pigment particles are white. Black paint is black because of black pigment. If you mix a gray from black and white, the perception of gray results from an irregular pattern of black and white pigment particles perceived as a unified tone (Fig. 2-16).

These grains, particles, points, and dots exist in many reproduction media: in the grain of the photograph, in the halftone printed image, and in paint pigment. The eye's individual photoreceptors respond to these halftone dots and pigment particles, and the brain groups them as tone. Large groupings of particles and dots collectively create images.

Like tone, color mixtures in art and design media are patterns on a very small scale. In color mixing, however, the visual elements that create perceived color mixtures are different from those that create the perception of tone. In color mixing, *primary colors* are those that combine to produce the largest number of new colors. Each art and design medium may have its own set of primaries. In paint, the primaries are red, yellow, and blue. When their pigment particles mix in a pattern on a microscopic level, they result in the perception of new colors. For example, the mixing of blue and yellow pigment particles results in the perception of green (see Color Plate 5).

Figure 2-15. The halftone dot pattern in the reproduction above has been enlarged below to show how tone can be reproduced by using pattern.

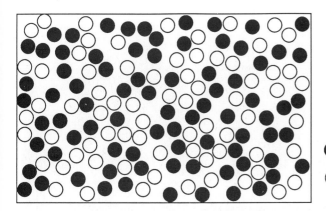

Figure 2-16. Gray is perceived in a mixture of black and white paint, which mingles black and white pigment particles.

● Black pigment particle

○ White pigment particle

In industrial printing, the primaries are cyan, yellow, magenta, and black. Cyan is a greenish blue color; magenta is a deep purplish red. Although cyan and magenta may appear similar to the blue and red of pigment primaries, they are actually very different, specific, and transparent colors. Layering separate, small-scale dot patterns of cyan, yellow, magenta, and black produces a wide range of printed colors. These printed color layers came off your french fry package (Color Plate 6). Both painting and industrial printing are reflection media, which means that they absorb some wavelengths of ambient light while reflecting other wavelengths that reach your eyes and result in your perception of color. In video, the primary colors are red, green, and blue. Color mixtures are created from the systematic arrangement of phosphor elements in small-scale triads of red, green, and blue repeated across a screen stimulated by an electron beam (see Fig. C-5). These red, green, and blue primaries combine to produce all other color video mixtures. Because video is a transmission medium, which means it emits light, the primaries and mixtures for video are the same as color mixing with light (see Color Plate 4). See Appendix C for a further discussion of color primaries and color mixing.

Pattern that Reproduces Surface Texture

When you perceive a pattern as tone, you perceive black and white particles or similarly sized points, uniformly dispersed, and small in scale. When these black and white points vary in size or are no longer evenly dispersed, however, a totally different perceptual experience occurs, in this case, visual or tactile surface texture. Surface texture may be either regularly or irregularly structured (Fig. 2-17). Examples include coarsely woven cloth, a thick paint stroke on an oil painting, the regular weave of a screen, and the printed woodgrain finish reproduced on plastic surfaces, such as kitchen countertops. Surface texture is sensed through either sight or touch.

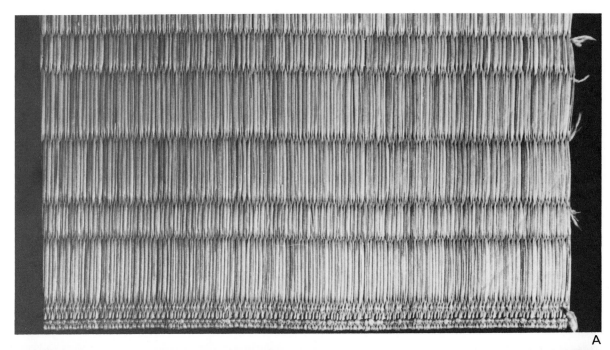

Figure 2-17. Examples of regular (A) and irregular (B) surface textures.

Surface texture can be visually reproduced in a variety of media. Halftone dot patterns can reproduce the illusion of tone or surface texture in photographic or industrially printed images. The perception of tone occurs when dots are uniformly sized, and surface texture appears when dot sizes vary. In painting, surface texture may be achieved by thick and uneven paint surfaces. Vincent van Gogh painted in a thick and textured manner. In addition, paint can provide the illusion of surface texture. You may have seen smooth-surfaced paintings where a rough wooden board looks convincingly tactile or other paintings in which the artist reproduced the visual texture of fur, fruit, cloth, or tile (Color Plate 7).

Surface texture is linked to materials. The visual product acquires meaning through the value associated with the materials used to make it. When you study a contemporary building finished with granite and marble, for instance, you perceive both the actual surface of the material and the implied monetary and class value symbolized by the material. Moreover, one material may be altered to resemble another. For example, vinyl shoes are often supposed to resemble and take on the associations of leather shoes. Although visually they appear similar, your other senses often tell you how differently these shoes function.

Pattern Itself

By increasing the scale of basic pattern units beyond surface texture or tone, you arrive at pattern itself. At a larger scale, the same halftone dots that produced the illusion of tone become a pattern (Fig. 2-18). At this scale, the structure governing the repetition of pattern elements can be perceived. Pattern elements are repeated within the frame according to natural processes or constructed formulae (Fig. 2-19). Natural sources of patterns include water waves, cloud formations, and erosion patterns. The structure underlying cloud and erosion configurations is discernible. Historically, organic objects such as foliage and their growth cycles have provided new pattern sources. Other structural patterns often require mathematics to explain the placement of elements. Recently developed mathematical processes such as fractal geometry can simulate natural patterns that model the growth and complexity of nature (Fig. 2-20). (For examples of fractal geometry and its application to visual production, see Benoit B. Mandelbrot, 1983.) Color is an important component in pattern structure and identification. Color placement within a pattern can make the underlying structure apparent (Color Plate 8).

Patterns can acquire symbolic significance within a culture. Specific patterns can be readily identifiable and serve as symbols for corporations, organizations, and locations. The five-circle pattern that symbolizes the Olympics is an example. In the 1984 Olympics held in Los Angeles, a complex system of patterns, with color coding, was developed and used at all

Figure 2-18. Pattern reproducing pattern. In this image, patterns of small black and white shapes create a larger overall gridlike pattern.

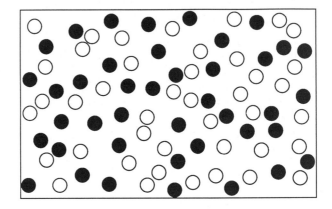

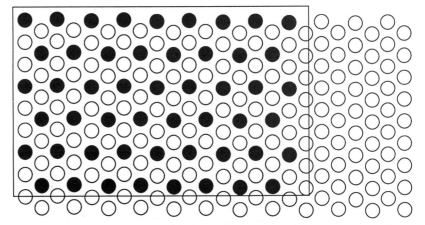

Figure 2-19. Regular and irregular pattern configurations.

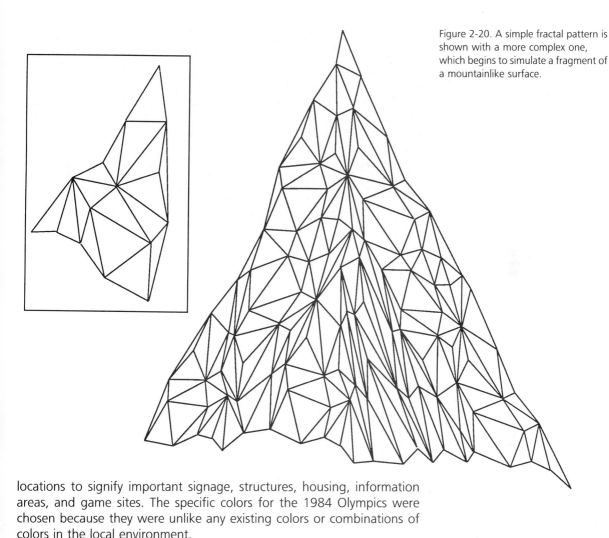

Figure 2-20. A simple fractal pattern is shown with a more complex one, which begins to simulate a fragment of a mountainlike surface.

locations to signify important signage, structures, housing, information areas, and game sites. The specific colors for the 1984 Olympics were chosen because they were unlike any existing colors or combinations of colors in the local environment.

Pattern that Reproduces Object

When only a few elements appear large within the field, they are perceived as objects. Rather than any object in particular, the word *object* names something physical or mental, of which the subject is consciously aware. The perception of object is an additional scalar increase from the perception of pattern. This scale relationship between elements and field makes important a specific individual element, as opposed to groups of elements. For example, a person standing with one other person encounters another unique human being; in the cafeteria serving line, however, one person becomes insignificant among the crowded pattern of bodies.

Tone, surface texture, pattern, and object are interrelated. What appears to be an object may be an isolated part of a larger pattern. The apparent absence of a pattern may be caused by too narrow a visual field. For example, a dot can be considered as a pattern. The dot is the foreground, surrounded by a background, which is a basic pattern configuration. Also, the dot is conceivably part of a large pattern of which only a segment is perceived (Fig. 2-21). No dot can be perceived in isolation. It requires a spatial and temporal context.

Frame boundaries in any visual product imply that only a part of a total scene is perceived. When a movie camera pans across a scene such as a landscape, that the hills and sky continue beyond the edge of the screen is assumed (Fig. 2-22). What is implied is that the framing cut off part of a large scene with an arbitrary boundary. In photography, framing operates both at the individual selection of a shot and in the sequence of photographs taken. For example, the photographic contact sheet represents pattern at many levels. The sum of the individual shots represents a framed set of patterns, and the roll of film records a sequential pattern

Figure 2-21. What is perceived as an object in a frame may be part of a larger implied pattern.

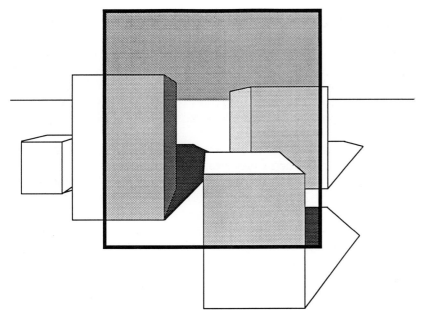

Figure 2-22. The implication is that a scene extends beyond the frame boundaries of a visual product.

of frames from the first to the last shot. Several photographs of an object may provide a pattern of framed points of view, where each represents a different subject-object relationship and a different moment in time.

Pattern that Reproduces Space

Spatial patterns are established by the presence or absence of objects. You become aware of spatial patterns as you move around objects in constantly changing environmental situations. The habitual path a person takes to work or school is a spatial pattern composed of encounters with objects and events. Spatial pattern is evident in any step taken through space or up and down stairs. Movement and awareness of edge establish spatial pattern. Objects and events establish spatial patterns that also are important for the visual producer.

When you look at an object, you do not simply focus on that object alone. You perceive virtual space, which consists simultaneously of the object's materials and the surrounding spatial environment. You visually complete that object by combining it with its particular site or situation, which includes its surroundings, the context in which you perceive the object, and the object itself. Moving around such objects, you experience many shifting foreground-background relationships. With these multiple views, you are able to understand the volumes of objects and the surrounding volumes that provide the context for objects (Fig. 2-23).

Figure 2-23. These photographs show Royce Hall on the campus of the University of California, Los Angeles, from two different points of view. The virtual space in each view is different because the virtual space is the perceptual combination of foreground and background.

Your perception of your own body is related to the concept of virtual space, based on the contrast between the internal space occupied by your own body and your body surrounded by external space. Immediate surroundings are important as personal space. Crowding in the cafeteria line compresses and diminishes virtual space. This sense of space changes in different cultures. Between two people arguing, for example, the mini-

mum comfortable distance between them is less in Mediterranean countries than in the United States.

You are aware of your body's interaction with spaces that are close to you in scale. However, spatial relationships become more complex at larger scales and beyond the immediate surroundings. Comprehending experience with expansive spaces such as landscapes composed of built

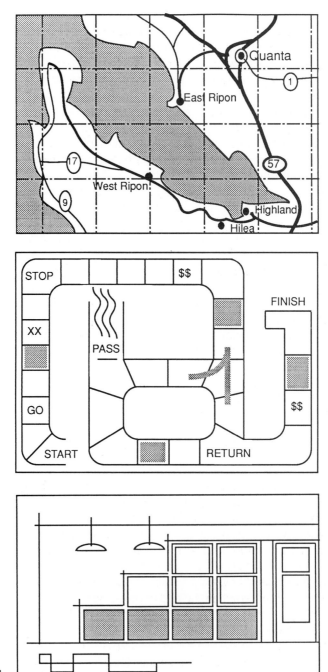

Figure 2-24. A map, game board, and wall plan are all examples of the segmentation of space into patterned units.

and natural elements is more difficult and requires other methods. At the most abstract levels of spatial comprehension, schematics such as maps, plans, or diagrams represent spatial pattern and experience. These maps, plans, or diagrams are abstract spatial patterns that structure space into measurable units. Such patterns appear in ground plans and the plan, elevation, and projective views of drawings of objects, for example, buildings or machines (Fig. 2-24). These patterned representations of space are the basis for the production of technological cultures. For example, the segmentation of space into measurable units is essential to planning land use, which further enables the production of cities, parks, and freeways.

Human behavior also establishes spatial pattern. Visual producers reproduce spatial patterns for individuals and groups when they design products for personal uses such as territory, privacy, socialization, and rituals. For example, the campus park provides a baseball diamond as territory, an occasional retreat for privacy, a meeting place for socialization, and a location for religious rituals such as weddings. The creation of campus parks structures contact with nature within the more artificial environment of a city.

We have discussed the patterns necessary to reproduce and plan various visual products. Deciding to create certain art and design products, such as city parks, connects pattern and power, particularly political power. We now analyze the relation between pattern and power.

PATTERNS OF POWER

Visual production is related to power. To understand that relationship, an understanding of the composition and context of a visual product is necessary.

The first aspect of a visual product's composition is the materials that constitute or are used to make the product. Examples of materials would be the clay and throwing wheels for ceramics or the actors for performance art. These materials are transformed through physical and mental human labor, making these raw materials into objects or events with meaningful symbols and visual information. Human labor is the second aspect of composition. The third aspect of composition is the actual use of the visual product. Remember that visual production does not end when a visual product is made but rather when the audience receives the product by experiencing it. Visual products have a wide range of social and personal uses such as a vessel to hold food and a painting to depict a historical event, both of which have cultural value or meaning. All three of these aspects—materials, labor, and use—are the composition of a visual product because they are the aspects of making a visual product that expresses meanings and values and communicates those concepts to the audience.

The first aspect of the context of a visual product is the economic network in which visual products are made and distributed, such as the prices for visual products and supplies used to make them. The price of a visual product may be different if the product is classified as art, design, or craft. A communicative network, such as journals and newspapers that review cultural events such as art exhibitions or fashion shows, provides meaning for visual products. This communicative network is the second aspect of context. The third aspect is the institutional framework that provides the location and the organizations for visual production. It includes schools, galleries, and design firms. These three aspects—economic network, communicative network, and institutional framework—compose the context of the visual product and influence the meanings and values attached to the visual product.

The composition and the context are the materials and meaning of visual products. They are not separate entities, even though we have discussed them separately and listed various aspects for each. Both composition and context are embodied in the same visual product. As an example, remember the previous discussion of a contemporary building finished with granite and marble that presents both the actual surface of the material and the implied monetary and class value symbolized by the material. The value of granite and marble as materials is both compositional and contextual.

The aspects of composition and context can be organized according to order, meaning, and practice, as compositional order, meaning, and practice and as contextual order, meaning, and practice (Fig. 2-25). *Order* refers to the structure of the elements within a visual product. *Meaning* refers to the symbolic qualities of the elements. *Practice* refers to the actual use of the elements. Thus, compositional order is the materials, and contextual order is the economic network. Compositional meaning is supplied by the physical and mental labor of the visual producer, just as the communicative network provides the contextual meaning. Finally, compositional practice is the audience's reception or use of the visual product. Contextual practice occurs within the institutions that support visual production, such as schools, galleries, and design firms.

The order, meaning, and practice of composition and context are similar to linguistic rules of syntax, semantics, and pragmatics. Just as composition and context make visual products intelligible to others, patterns of speech are governed by rules of language that make one person's utterances intelligible to others. In order to speak a language or make visual products, you should know their necessary patterns. Because of their cultural context, both language and visual products are vehicles for communication. As you become competent in visual production, you acquire the creative power to produce and interpret visual information. This competence in a visual "language" is *visual literacy*.

In the beginning of this section, we wrote that visual production is related to power. More accurately, we could say that visual production

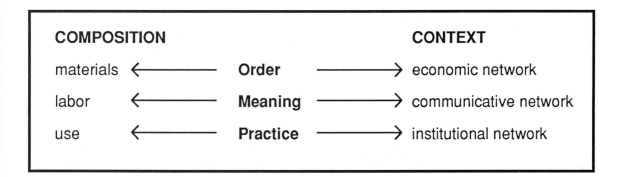

Figure 2-25. Compositional and contextual order, practice, and meaning.

and visual literacy are related to power; that is, power within society may define certain classes, groups, or individuals, and a person who is visually literate can better understand that power because patterns of power within a society are embodied in or represented by its visual products. The following are historic and modern examples of this relationship.

With the Renaissance revival of classical learning, new visual and literary languages promoted literacy across Western Europe. Renaissance artists rediscovered drawing methods for producing spatial patterns. By using linear perspective, those artists gained a power to reproduce images following geometric concepts. The practice of Renaissance artists visually represents a shift in a historically established pattern of relationships between people and God. They produced representations of the human figure and geometric space that suggested that knowledge was no longer divinely given but centered in human experience. In this same intellectual climate, geometry was used in astronomical research that challenged the Church's power to claim authority over scientific knowledge. Specifically, Copernicus and Galileo showed that the Church's position on the relationship of the earth and the sun was incorrect and suggested a shift in power to more secular authorities.

In modern art and design, power and pattern are interdependent. The use of the pattern to reproduce a tool, plan, or product has been a powerful technological element in the development of industrial cultures. Other patterns also reveal the underlying social structure of power. For example, the more abstract patterns of power in an office are apparent from the floorplans of the workplace. People with more power typically have offices at the corners of buildings or offices with windows. Floorplans show that people with less power have less privacy and fewer pattern elements, such as doors and windows, composing their work space.

In this section, we have presented a model of visual production comprised of compositional and contextual order, meaning, and practice to explain the broader concepts that govern and give meaning to visual production. In this model, we have expanded the meaning of pattern beyond the structure of visual patterns to include the patterns created by social and cultural rules and hierarchies. These two areas are related because the social and cultural patterns may be seen in visual patterns. Designers and artists often think they do not need to understand patterns of social and cultural power, but their activities comprise more than the objects they construct in their studios or workspaces. In addition to personal enterprise, visual production is part of a larger cultural system that obligates the individual practitioner to understand or to be exploited by it.

Famous historical examples of the exploitation of visual producers include the theft of cultural treasures by conquering armies or black market purchasing and the refusal to return them once their true origin had been revealed. For example, the Elgin Marbles in the British Museum will never return to their original site in Greece. In America, two contemporary examples of exploitation are the commercial exploitation of Robert Indiana's *Love* sculpture and Marlborough Gallery's manipulation of the estate of the painter Mark Rothko. (For further information on the Rothko estate, read Lee Seldes, 1974.)

In summary, visual production is empowered by knowledge of pattern. An awareness of pattern reveals underlying structural relationships in visual production and in society and culture. Composition and context are examples of these patterns that provide a means of making visual products and a method for understanding the visual products of others. In the next chapter, concepts of proportion are developed.

PATTERN ASSIGNMENT 1

Natural Pattern

Any pattern has two essential qualities: the repetition of elements and the structural arrangement of those elements. In natural patterns, these qualities are often the result of natural forces. For example, water rushing through soil may leave elaborate erosion patterns.

In this exercise, you will create a visual image based on a natural pattern.

Materials

Photograph of a natural pattern from a nature magazine

Blank 35 mm slide, black or with colors, but without image

Pins, needles, X-acto blades, small pieces of wire

Colored markers

Procedure

Look through a nature magazine for an image with a natural pattern. Examples may be plant or animal life, light and shadow patterns, geological formations, or landscape shapes.

Using these pattern images as a starting point, create a natural pattern on the blank 35 mm slide with pins, needles, X-acto blades, or any other sharp tool that can scratch the film's emulsion. Add color with transparent markers or make small cuts in the slide. However, use nothing that can damage the slide projector.

Project the slides in a dark room.

Discussion

When you project your image many times its original size, what effects do the medium and enlargement have on your work?

PATTERN ASSIGNMENT 2

Pattern and Scale

When you change the scale of an image, you also change the perception of tone, surface texture, pattern, and object.

Materials

20 sheets lightweight bond paper, such as typing paper

1 sheet one-ply bristol paper, 18″ × 24″

Photocopied images

Found images

Pencil

Glue

Procedure

Make a large number of rubbings, photocopies, drawings, or found images that contain surface textures and patterns. All images or rubbings should be black and white and approximately 4″ × 6″. From all your images, pick out those where similar visual elements are repeated on different scales. Arrange them so that the visual elements are gradually enlarged and are perceived as surface texture, then pattern, and finally object. Glue the images on bristol paper.

Discussion

Sometimes surface texture reappears inside the image that has been enlarged to be perceived as object. This surface texture may be pencil shading lines or photocopy grains. Do any of the students' projects have images that simultaneously show surface texture and object?

PATTERN ASSIGNMENT 3

Grouping Project A

In this assignment, you will group visual elements in many different ways.

Materials

1 sheet bond or typing paper, 8½″ × 11″

Black marker

Access to photocopy machine

Procedure

Draw three to six black points, half an inch in diameter, on the bond paper. Photocopy the image four times, resulting in five images that are the same. Exchange your five images with another student in the class. On each image you receive, connect the points together in different ways. Use as many lines as you wish and the front and back of the paper, if desired (Fig. 2-26). Number the drawings from 1 to 5 in the order in which you made them.

Discussion

When all students have finished, display the drawings on the wall in vertical columns, one column to each student. Start with drawing 1 at the top and drawing 5 at the bottom.

Is any relationship apparent between simplicity and complexity in connecting the points and the order of the solutions developed? Do any of the students' projects suggest sequence or development in their images? Which images exhibit closure?

Draw five dots on a page and make four photocopies.

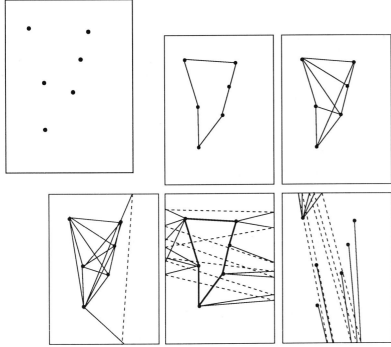

Connect the points in five different ways and number the order in which you completed the drawings.

Figure 2-26. Sample execution of Pattern Assignment 3.

PATTERN ASSIGNMENT 4

Grouping Project B

In this exercise, you will study the perceptual relationships that group shapes together. Because you will be working with other students' projects, the final results will show a division of creative labor.

Materials

4 sheets bond or typing paper

Black marker

Colored markers (optional)

Procedure

Select two of the geometric shapes from Figure 2-27 and draw each of them three or four times on the bond paper. You may draw them different sizes or make them different tones. Do not use color. Arrange the shapes so that you perceptually group them according to one of the grouping principles: comparable shape, size, or tonality or symmetry, closure, or proximity.

Label your image with your name and the grouping principle involved. Photocopy it and give the copy to another student, keeping the original. In turn, you should receive a photocopy from another student.

Cut apart, rearrange, draw on, add to, or alter the photocopy to change the grouping of the visual elements. A new grouping principle should then govern the arrangement of the visual elements (Fig. 2-27). Add your name and the new grouping principle to the bottom of the work.

If time allows, photocopy your original image two more times, exchange the copies with other students, and rearrange those groupings also. Make one grouping using color. In another, change the shape of your composition from rectangular to some other shape.

Discussion

All altered designs should be displayed by the original drawing for the class discussion. Arrange the projects in columns, with the original drawing at the top and the transformed projects vertically beneath it. Discuss how grouping operates among all the projects or within columns of projects.

Choose any two of the following shapes:

Random arrangement:

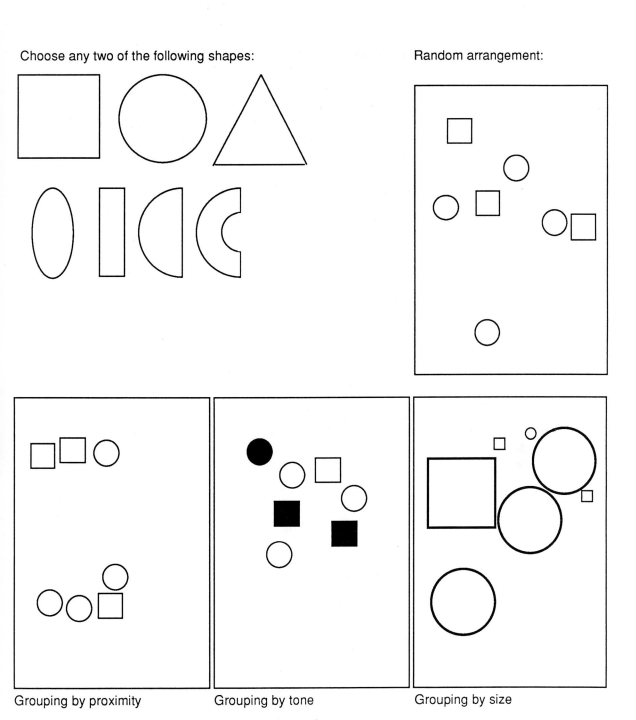

Grouping by proximity   Grouping by tone   Grouping by size

Figure 2-27. Sample execution of Pattern Assignment 4.

PATTERN ASSIGNMENT 5

Foreground and Background

When you look at your environment or at a picture, you can pay attention to different areas, which then become the foreground. The rest of the picture becomes the background. The foreground-background relationship is constantly shifting, depending on your focus. In this exercise, you will change the foreground-background relationships in an image.

In this assignment, we make a loose analogy between a photographic camera and the human eye to help you understand how foreground-background relationships can shift. Specifically, we discuss the autofocus camera, which is designed to determine which elements in the viewfinder should be in focus and what need not be considered in focusing. The focusing mechanism is designed to respond most to what is in the center of the viewfinder and then average that with the depth of the rest of the field.

Materials

Large newspaper or magazine photos

Acrylic paint, painting supplies

2 sheets bristol paper, 18″ x 24″

Glue: rubber cement or glue stick

Procedure

Part 1. Take a newspaper or magazine photo and photocopy it three times. On each of the three photocopies, indicate the foreground area by painting it a single, even color. Determine the foreground area as if you were using an autofocus camera that could focus on these different foreground areas (Fig. 2-28):

1. The foreground is whatever shape occupies the center of the image.

2. The foreground is the area of greatest visual activity (for example, the area with the greatest detail or surface texture).

3. The foreground is the largest shape in the whole image.

Glue the original photograph and all painted copies onto bristol paper.

Part 2. Take the results of Part 1 and photocopy each twice. On the first photocopy of each, paint the background area a saturated color and

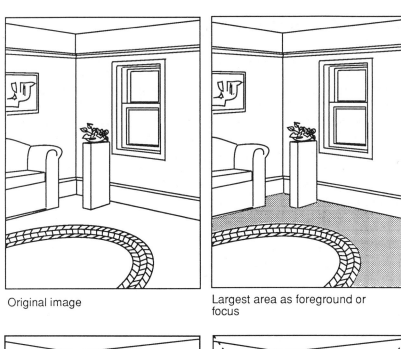

Original image

Largest area as foreground or focus

Area of greatest visual activity as foreground or focus

Center of image as foreground or focus

Figure 2-28. Determining the foreground of an image, based on its largest area, area of greatest visual activity, and area located at the center of the image.

the foreground area a desaturated color. On the second photocopy of each, paint the foreground area a saturated color and the background area an unsaturated color.

Glue all the painted photocopies onto the bristol paper.

Part 3. Select a magazine photo and photocopy it. On the photocopy, paint all areas that are middle gray or darker as one even, unvaried color. Then paint another even, unvaried color over all areas lighter than middle gray. Do not keep one shape distinct from another. Let them run together. Make no effort to keep the imagery readable in the picture. Glue the original photograph and the painted photocopy together on bristol paper.

Discussion

Compare the original and the painted photocopies, and discuss what happened to the foreground-background relationship.

Compare the color combinations on different students' projects. How do different color combinations affect foreground-background relationship?

PATTERN ASSIGNMENT 6

Exercises in Color Mixing Using Reflective Media

These exercises will help you learn about color mixing in reflective media. Reflective media, such as painting or industrial printing, absorb part of the ambient light and reflect the rest. You perceive the reflected light as the apparent color of the visual product.

In these exercises, you will compare color mixing in wet and dry media. You will make and arrange color mixtures to show the relationship between color tonality and color saturation. You will learn color mixing possibilities with an opaque or a semitransparent paint film. You will also see that your color perception results both from the media you use and from the color of the underlying surface.

Color Mixing Exercise A

In this exercise, you will study color qualities such as tone and saturation and color mixing in wet and dry media.

Materials

Acrylic paint, painting supplies

1 sheet one-ply bristol paper, 7" x 10"

1 sheet one-ply bristol paper, 18" x 24"

Colored pencils, professional quality

Pencil

Ruler

Cutting knife

Glue: rubber cement or glue stick

Procedure

Half the students should do this exercise with colored pencils; the other half should use acrylic paints. The procedure for the exercise is written for students using paint. Those using colored pencils should follow the same procedure but with the different medium.

Mix a wide range of tones between black and white. On the 18" x 24" sheet of bristol paper, draw several rectangles 1" x 2" each, and paint each tone over one of the drawn rectangles. Make sure that the paint is heavy and thick enough to be opaque and that you cannot see the paper through the paint film. (For colored pencils, put down a heavy application of color.) Be sure you have sufficient amounts of paint left over to use again later in this exercise.

When the paint is dry, cut out the small rectangles and select five grays that make an even tone scale. Also make a black 1" x 2" and a white 1" x 2". These five gray, plus black and white, show the range of tones possible with acrylic paint.

Select one of the following colors: red, yellow, green, blue, orange, and violet. Other students in your class should choose the other colors. Paint the color you selected on a 1" x 2" piece of bristol paper at full saturation, without mixing. Your perception of that color should be as intense and colorful.

Now, mix your saturated color with each of the five gray tones by using the paint you have remaining from the beginning of this exercise. In doing so, you will be creating less saturated mixtures of your color, in different tonalities. Paint these five mixtures onto small pieces of bristol paper.

Assemble all your small color and tone samples as shown in Figure 2-29. Each horizontal row should exhibit the same tonality. To achieve tonal matches, repainting some color samples may be necessary. The vertical rows indicate ranges in color saturation, with the single saturated color as the most saturated and the gray-plus-color mixtures showing less saturation. The white, gray, and black tones are the least saturated.

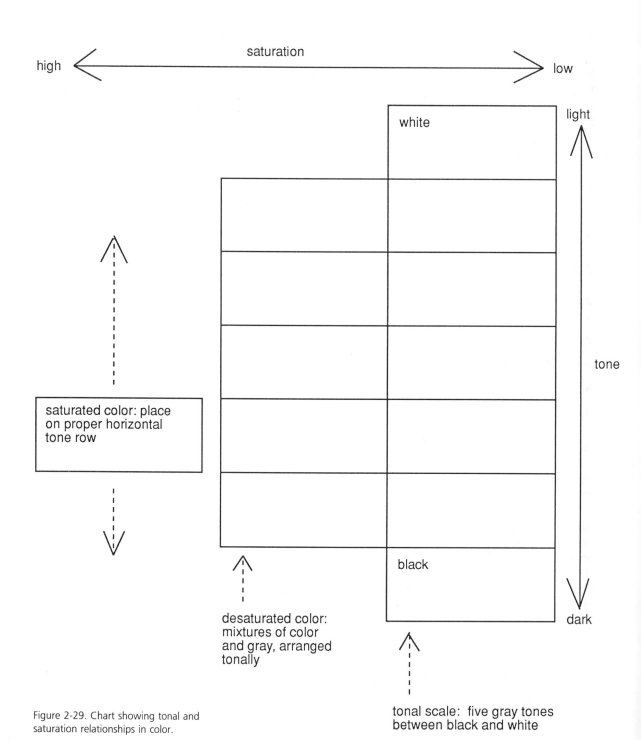

saturation

high ← → low

white

light

tone

saturated color: place on proper horizontal tone row

black

desaturated color: mixtures of color and gray, arranged tonally

dark

tonal scale: five gray tones between black and white

Figure 2-29. Chart showing tonal and saturation relationships in color.

Discussion

Compare the results of using paint and using colored pencils.

Arrange the students' projects like planes in a Munsell color solid (see Appendix C). Notice how the saturated colors are in different tonal ranges, with saturated yellow the lightest, and blue and violet the darkest.

Color Mixing Exercise B

In this exercise, you will apply semitransparent color layers onto colored paper. The colors you perceive in the finished visual product will be the result both of the medium you use and of the color of the underlying surface.

Materials

3 sheets heavyweight inexpensive colored paper, in saturated colors, 6" x 6"

Acrylic paints, painting supplies

Colored pencils, professional quality

Ruler

Pencil

Procedure

For this exercise, those who used acrylic paints previously should use colored pencils; those who used colored pencils should now use acrylic paints.

Figure 2-30 contains some simple drawings of geometric objects. Choose one of them, or invent a similar image. With a lead pencil, redraw the same drawing on three pieces of paper of different colors, so that you have three drawings that look alike except for different-colored backgrounds. One sheet of colored paper may be black, but none of the paper should be white. Select one of the following sets of colors and make mixtures from them.

1. Yellow, orange, and blue

2. Orange, red, and green

3. Red, violet, and yellow

4. Violet, blue, and orange

5. Blue, green, and red

6. Green, yellow, and violet

Thin the paint with water, so that you can see the background paper color through the paint as you apply it. (For colored pencils, put down a light application of color.) Paint all three paintings at once. Paint the same color mixtures in the same locations for all three paintings. Paint all parts of the geometric drawing and the background.

When finished, you should perceive different colors in the different paintings, even though you painted the same colors three times. This difference occurs because you perceive both the paint color and the background paper color at the same time.

Discussion

Compare the results obtained with colored pencils to those made with paint. How does the color of the paper affect the apparent colors in thin and opaque paint? How does it affect colored pencils lightly or heavily applied?

Figure 2-30. Two sample sets of images with geometric shapes.

PATTERN ASSIGNMENT 7

Symmetry Exercises

In the first symmetry exercise, you will organize visual elements according to symmetry by using mirror, glide, and rotation transformations. By layering visual elements, you will create new symmetry configurations.

In the second exercise, you will work with other students to enlarge and expand a symmetry pattern. It will change from being a drawing on paper into a large sculpture or installation in the space of the classroom. You will learn how to work with others to develop creative ideas and to complete visual products on a larger scale and in less time than you could working alone.

Symmetry Exercise A

Materials

2 sheets bristol paper, 18″ x 24″

2 sheets tracing paper, 18″ x 24″

Acrylic paint, painting supplies

Scissors, X-acto knife, glue

Pencil

Ruler

Procedure

Think of each sheets of bristol as two planes, one on the front and one on the back. Two sheets have four planes.

On one plane, draw a fairly complex series of shapes that will be your *motif,* the recurring thematic element in your project. Reproduce that motif, or parts or multiples of it, on all four planes, according to any combination of symmetry concepts you wish to employ. When repeating elements in this project, symmetry can be satisfied by duplicating the original element, creating a mirror image of the original, changing the color of the original, or negating the original (Fig. 2-31). Paint these four planes so that your symmetry system has color.

Now, choose any two completed planes, place them side by side, and lay the tracing paper over them. Using pencil only, draw a new symmetrical system on the tracing paper based on the symmetry project underneath. The shapes on tracing paper should be different from those be-

fronts: two sheets of bristol paper
Original drawing   Glide and mirror transformations

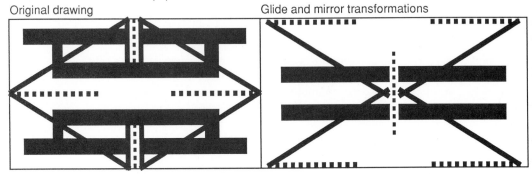

backs of same sheets of bristol paper
Original reduced, glide transformations   Original reduced; glide and rotation

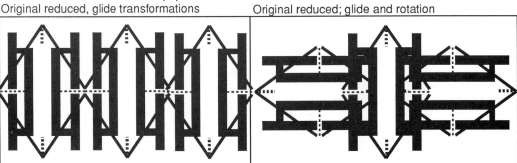

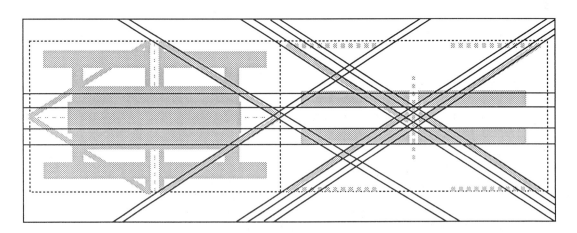

acetate or tracing paper overlay
The first two drawings were used as a basis for a new symmetry
drawing on the overlay.

Figure 2-31. Sample execution of Pattern Assignment 7.

neath, but the two systems ought to intersect in an organized, structured way.

The result will be a layering of two symmetrical systems that together yield a third (Fig. 2-31).

Symmetry Exercise B

Materials

Large supply of bristol paper, large sheets of colored paper, or cardboard

Acrylic paints, painting supplies

Cutting knife, scissors

Glue, masking tape, pushpins

Ruler

Pencil

Procedure

As a group, the class should select one project from the first symmetry exercise as a starting point for this exercise. Pick a project that the group as a whole wishes to enlarge and expand into the space of the classroom.

The class divides into three groups, each of which will adapt the original project in different ways. The groups should plan their projects simultaneously, with each group consulting the others about their plans and organizing all three parts to make a single work.

Group 1. Adapt the original project to make a large symmetry system that covers the wall. This part should be completed with paint on paper only. It serves as a basic symmetry pattern layer for the class project. Cover a 6' x 12' wall section or larger, if possible.

Group 2. Create geometric solids by cutting and assembling pieces of bristol paper, colored paper, or cardboard. The shape of these solids should be based on the original project and correspond with Group 1's work. With pushpins or glue, affix these shapes onto Group 1's underlying pattern. As much as possible, the walls of the solids should be cut away to allow much of the underlying symmetrical pattern to remain visible.

Group 3. Expand the symmetrical patterns into the space of the room. Elements of the symmetrical pattern may be arranged on the floor, suspended from the ceiling, or placed on temporary supports away from the wall.

Discussion

How was the creative and manual labor for the project divided among group members? How important is it for a single individual to execute all steps of a creative process and control the results? Can a group control the creative process? Can you think of aspects of traditional painting and sculpture that are actually social in nature?

EXTRA CREDIT

Three-dimensional planar patterns have many applications, such as solar panels, heat and sound deflectors, and traffic barriers. Buckminster Fuller designed large-scale complex geodesic domes. Research solar panels to find out essential information about size and arrangement, and adapt your symmetric planar design to fit those specifications.

Color Plate 1. This painter used the technique called *pointillism,* in which color mixing is achieved through a patterned application of paint. Georges Seurat, *Sunday Afternoon on the Island of La Grande Jatte,* 1884–86, 207.6 x 308.0 cm, oil on canvas, *Helen Birch Memorial Collection,* 1926.224. © 1987 The Art Institute of Chicago. All Rights Reserved.

Color Plate 2. Detail of Color Plate 1, *Sunday Afternoon on the Island of La Grande Jatte,* which shows more clearly the pointillist method of color mixing.

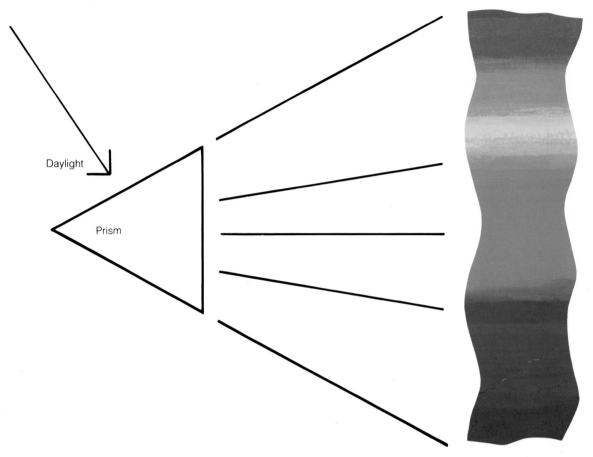

Color Plate 3. A prism refracts light to reveal how different wavelengths of visible light produce the sensation of color. White is perceived when a mixture of all wavelengths of visible light is seen.

Color Plate 4. In color mixing in light, the primary colors are red, blue, and green. The mixture of all primaries results in the perception of white. The mixture of two pairs of primaries results in cyan, magenta, and yellow. An object's shadow appears to be the opposite color to the light that is shining on the object.

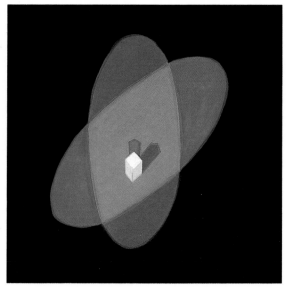

Red and blue

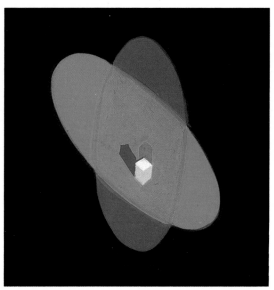

Green and blue

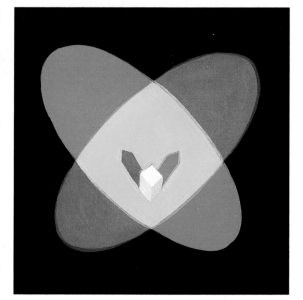

Green and red

Green, blue, and red

Color Plate 5. In color mixing in paint, the primary colors are yellow, red, and blue. The mixture of all primaries results in the perception of a dark, neutral color. Color mixing has a proportional quality. If yellow and blue are mixed to make green, the resulting green will appear more yellow or more blue, depending upon the proportions of the primary colors mixed.

Yellow plate   Magenta plate   Cyan plate   Black plate

Yellow and magenta   Yellow, magenta, and cyan   Yellow, magenta, cyan, and black

Color Plate 6. In color mixing in industrial printing, such as the printing used in the production of this book, the primary colors are cyan, yellow, magenta, and black. These colors are printed as dot patterns one over the other to result in the perception of a wide range of colors.

Color Plate 7. In Davidsz de Heem's painting *Still Life With Oysters,* surface textures are only visual but imply that a tactile sensation is possible.

Color Plate 8. Color may structure and organize perception of pattern.

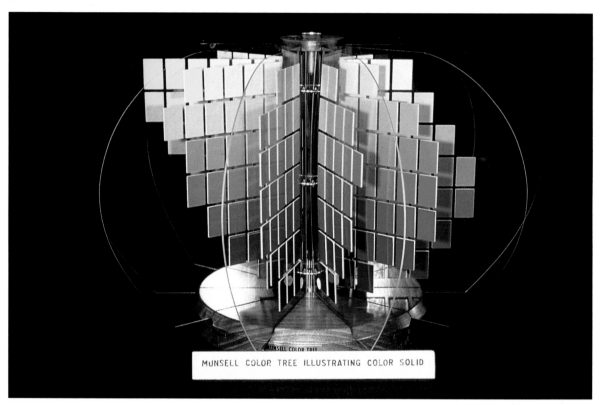

MUNSELL COLOR TREE

MUNSELL COLOR TREE ILLUSTRATING COLOR SOLID

Color Plate 9. The Munsell Color Tree organizes color according to tone, saturation, and chroma.

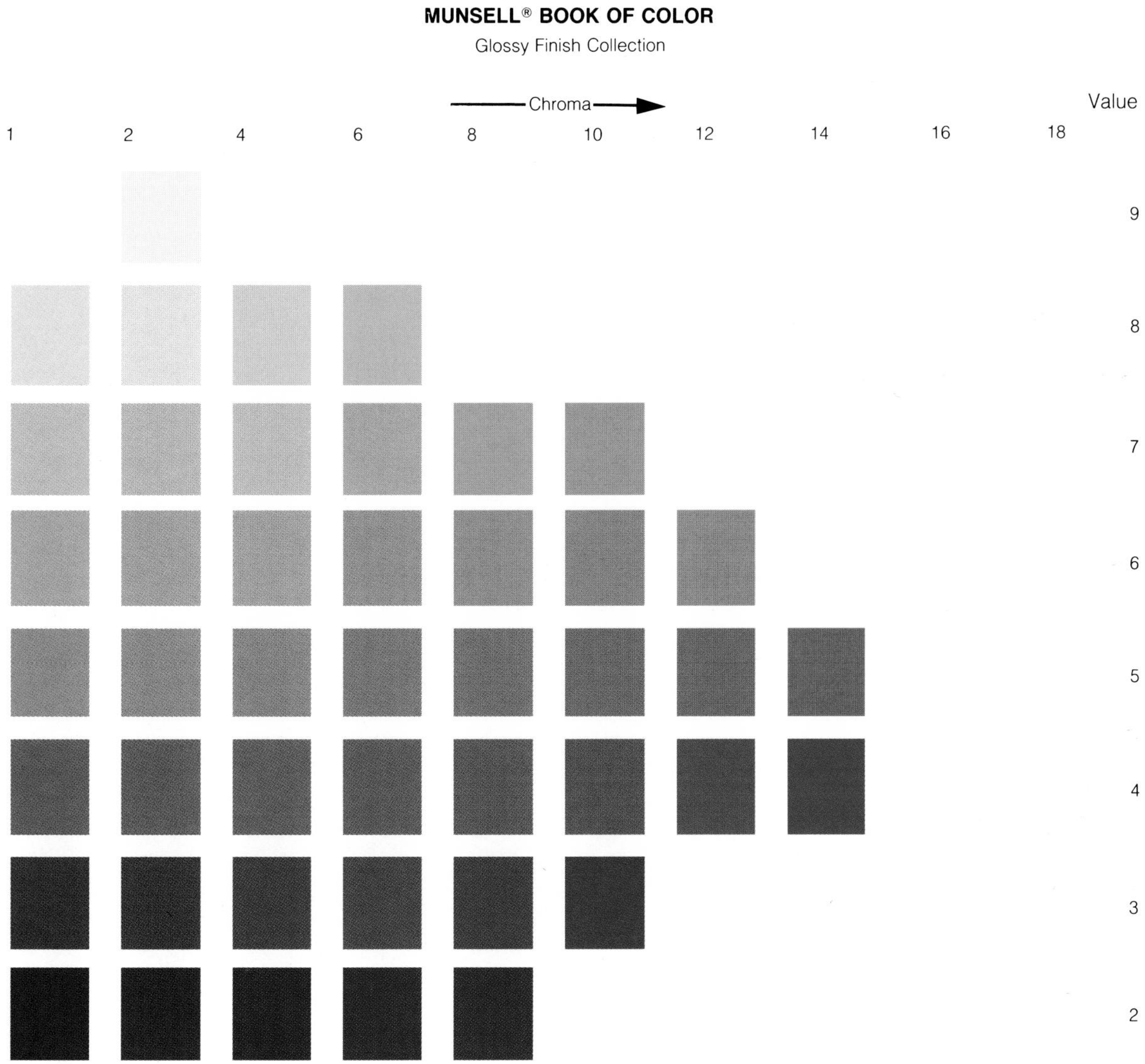
MUNSELL® BOOK OF COLOR
Glossy Finish Collection
Chroma
Value
1
2
4
6
8
10
12
14
16
18
9
8
7
6
5
4
3
2

Color Plate 10. This chart represents one page of the Munsell Color Tree. Darker tones are at the bottom of the page, and lighter tones are at the top. Reds of higher color saturation are on the right of the page, and reds of low saturation are on the left.

Color Plate 11. Color perception is relative. One factor that affects color perception is fatigue in the cones in the retina. Stare at the black dot at the center of the star for 30 seconds, and then look at a white wall. A temporary color shift should appear.

Color Plate 12. Color perception is relative. Besides fatigue, another factor that affects the perception of a particular color is the interaction with the surrounding color. In this diagram, the two center colors do not appear to be the same, but they are.

Color Plate 13. This computer graphic image shows decontextualized objects. The image of the Eiffel Tower has been altered so that the context in which the tower actually exists has been changed.

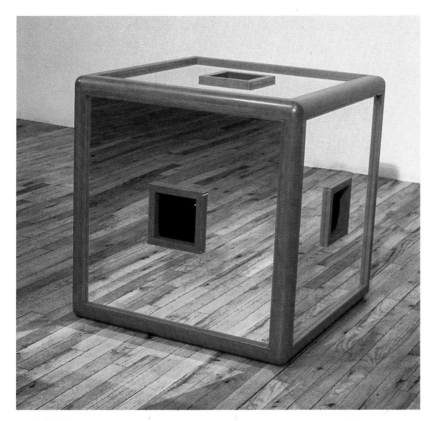

Color Plate 14. Jackie Winsor, *Interior Sphere Piece,* 31" x 31" x 31", mirrored glass, paint, 1985. This work is classified as minimalist art. Although the work seems to be composed of few elements, it refers to the relationship between craft and art and the use of industrial materials in art.

Color Plate 15. Hans Haacke, *Metromobiltan,* 140" x 240" x 60", fiberglass, three banners, photomurals, 1985. The artist is showing the relationship between large corporations, governments, and funding of art.

Color Plate 16. Jenny Holzer uses mass communication and industrial design media in her work. Holzer, *Under a Rock*, installation, granite benches and LED signs, 1986, and detail of same installation, *Untitled with Selection from UNDER A ROCK*, misty granite, 17.25" x 48" x 21"

Color Plate 17. Barbara Kruger, *Untitled (Your gaze hits the side of my face)*, 55″ x 41″, photograph, 1981. Kruger's work synthesizes art and design media and expression and communication.

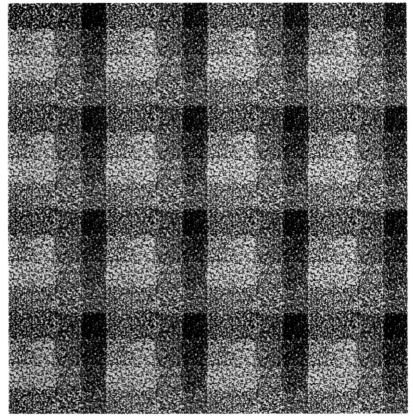

Color Plate 18. Ng Po Choy, *Untitled*, computer-generated image, 8" x 8", 1988. This image is output from numeric data. By combining and altering the computations made by the computer, variations of this image can be produced.

PROPORTION

CHAPTER
3

You are walking across the campus again, past the bell tower that serves as the campus's central landmark, and you decide to go inside and up the elevator to the top observation deck. You are worried about having registered for too many courses this term and need to think. You take a bite of the apple you have brought with you to eat. The sky is clear, and you see a spectacular view of the surrounding area. The bird's-eye view is wide and unobstructed. The comprehensive perspective and height of the building give you a sense of power, like a feudal lord surveying the land. The tower is named for the benefactors who gave the money for its construction, and what you see must have been the view they wanted. The view of the city's pattern, its urban design, tells you how the city has grown. You look for a trash receptacle for your apple core, but none is available.

You decide to use an available coin-operated telescope. Through this you see several scenes of street activity: leisure, commerce, crime. A police officer is pursuing a robber down a street. Your view of the whole land-scape lets you see around the corner, where the robber cannot see and where more police wait. As you track the path of the robber, you note that both robber and police officer are running as fast as possible. You shift the telescope but miss them because your own movements have to be slight as compared to the actual distance covered by the robber. You almost see the robber evade the police officer, but time runs out on the telescope's timer. You then decide to go back down to the plaza below. You throw the apple core away. The guard in the lobby yells at you be-cause you have thrown the core into a vase that you thought was a wastecan.

You proceed to the administration building across from the tower. You have to drop a class. The room has no tables, ledges, or counters for you to fill out the required forms. You sit on an uncomfortable steel chair under glaring fluorescent lights as you try to squeeze the necessary information into the form's tiny spaces. After waiting in a long line, you finally reach the window at the front and discover that you must talk to a higher-ranked administrator than the people at the windows. They tell you that you should go to the building with the classical columns next door. Unfortunately, of the two buildings next door, one has plain, heavy Doric columns and the other has tall, thin Ionic columns. Which one is classical? You pick the closest one. Running down the corridor, you get lost because the room numbers on the building directory do not match the floorplan mounted next to it. You finally arrive at the correct office, but after more bureaucratic delays, you find that you are still unable to drop the course. You get angry and wish you could get even.

This occasionally too true story provides examples of proportion. *Proportion* has several interrelated definitions. The most prevalent is the relation of one part to another or to the whole. In visual production, proportion is the relation of compositional parts to a whole visual product. When you see a visual product, such as a sculpture, you are aware of its internal proportions, which are the relationships between the parts of the sculpture.

Further, when you look at a sculpture, you are aware of its size compared to yours, which is another aspect of proportion. Proportion is the sense of scale, which depends upon distance and point of view. Proportion is the scalar, relational, and dimensional aspect of perception and visual production. The basis of proportion is in human proportions, which contextually relate humans to the visual products they use.

Although these statements define *proportion* in general terms, proportion is a human experience and therefore relative to the human who experiences it. An artist or designer shares the individual experience of proportion with other humans through visual products.

PERCEPTION AS A PROPORTIONAL EXPERIENCE

Perceptions are not some absolute or ideal set of sensations, nor are the meanings associated with them universal. Perception means your perception, or my perception, or someone else's. Perception changes depending upon point of view, distance and location, and perception of scale. Perception is not absolute; it is scalar or proportional to the individual. Scale is the relative size of things compared to the individual's own size. A visual producer must be aware of the proportional nature of perception. Any image produced has a proportional or scalar relation to other objects.

When you walked across campus, the view in most directions was limited by buildings. On the ground, you saw nearby buildings in large scale. You also saw building details clearly and judged the building's size in relation to yourself. At the top of the tower, your view was much more extended, and nearly limitless from side to side and upward. From above, you missed details and the buildings seemed small compared to your own size. You saw the relations of distance and location—often the result of city planning and urban design—that you could not envision while standing among the buildings.

Perceptions are a combination of direct and indirect experiences. For example, you have both direct and indirect experiences of distance. You directly experience the more immediate environment with your own senses: you see with your eyes to the limits of your vision, hear what is within audible range, smell what is near your nose, touch what is nearby, and taste what you can put in your mouth. The senses define the limits of direct experience of distance.

Indirect experience of distance is dependent upon technology, which alters your perception of actual distance relationships. The telescope on the campus tower brought the city below much closer and allowed you to perceive once again the same detail you see directly when you are near the buildings. With only a slight movement of the telescope, you were able to cover more distance than the cops and robbers could by running. Art and design media are other examples of technologies that alter distance relationships. Television broadcasts, movies, paintings, photography, and other visual media give you an indirect and altered experience of distance because you immediately can perceive things and events that may be occurring continents or even planets away. However, perceiving events by means of technology is limited in many ways in comparison to direct sensory perceptions.

A *medium* is a material or technical means that transmits visual information. Therefore, it is also the material or technical means of visual expression. Through use of a medium, ideas are made external as visual products. *Media,* the plural of medium, are used because most visual products are communicated not through one single medium but through a combination of them. All media alter, distort, expand, or reduce direct experience. These transformations of experience are called *mediation.* Experience of distance through the telescope is *mediated* because vision is altered through the use of some instrument or medium. A mediated experience is an indirect experience that is transmitted to the individual by some intervening mechanisms or instruments. Mediated perceptions, although incorporating direct perception, are different than direct perceptions. In contrast to direct visual perception, the view through the telescope is round, has distinct edges, reduces the amount of light available to the eyes, and alters distance relationships. A photograph of this same view through the telescope can be printed in an urban planning magazine as an illustration. This printed image would be an even more mediated or indirect experience of the original site and would require additional contextual information, such as captions, to explain it. All these qualities of mediated perception differ from direct, immediate visual experience.

PATTERNS THAT STRUCTURE PERCEPTIONS

Your own perception is scalar and proportional. So are the perceptions of others. You can only experience the perception of others through mediation. Because humans are social, they need to communicate their personal and varying perceptions to one another. This communication of perceptions and experience through media is only a partial, proportional representation of what was the actual, direct experience. Societies develop patterns of communication so that individuals have the means to convey some portion of their unique experiences to others. In a visual product, these patterns help to organize knowledge and structure visual elements in order to communicate ideas. You can use verbal and nonverbal descriptions to communicate and receive indirect, mediated perception. These descriptions may be represented with mathematics, writing, or visual production. Measuring systems are examples of proportional pattern, which is apparent from different descriptions of measurement. For example, the foot as a measurement was originally the actual foot of someone measuring something and was therefore a direct experience. A yard was the length between a person's outstretched arm and nose. A cubit in the Christian Bible was any of various units of length derived from the distance from the elbow to the middle finger. Sometimes a cubit was 18 inches, but it could be as long as 21. *Concrete* or direct measuring systems are those in which a person compares an arm or foot directly to some surface to determine size. To experience something concretely, that person must be in close proximity to the object, and the perceptions must be unmediated.

Concrete measurements must be standardized to be used collectively. If you used your own foot to measure and you know that everyone has different sized feet, then you would find no agreement on what length a "foot" represents. *Abstract* measuring systems are those with standardized proportional patterns. Eventually, the foot measurement was set to a standard size and became a socially accepted pattern for description. Once a foot became 12 inches and a yard became 3 feet, then the concrete act of measuring became more abstract and dissociated from any specific concrete instance. Other measuring systems, such as the metric system, are even more abstract because their basic units did not evolve from any concrete measurement.

The world can be indirectly experienced through scalar representations such as models, maps, and diagrams that rely on measuring systems. Measuring something requires holding up a scale that is a proportional representation of an object. A building can be measured directly by dropping a string from the top of the building or indirectly by parallax methods that require use of a telescopic surveyor's transit from the ground. If the tower on campus is said to be 180 feet tall, one aspect of it is defined, but no information about the structure, color, decorations, or materials of the building is provided. A scaled version of the building drawn on grid paper results in an even more mediated and proportional experience of the building. Although the scale drawing contains much information, a sense of the building's actual scale as it would be experienced concretely is lost.

Most architects include a scale rendering of humans in drawings of proposed buildings. The human is still the measure against which scale is judged, even in such a proportional, abstract, and mediated representation of the building (Fig. 3-1). The building as a composition is compared to the context of a human viewer. When you experience an actual building, you judge the scale of the building by relating its size to your size.

We now will discuss another aspect of proportion in visual products. When designing a whole building or when drawing, sculpting, or planning, you have to operate within parameters limiting size, time, cost, and materials. Within these constraints, however, many choices about the exact composition of the visual product are possible. The proportional aspect of these choices occurs when the visual producer makes decisions

Figure 3-1. Scale implies human scale. In architectural drawings, a human is often included to indicate the scale of a building.

about the internal proportions of visual products. If these individual proportional choices are repeated often, they may be standardized into socially pervasive patterns. The result of such cultural developments is style. *Style* is the similarity of composition or origin among any grouping of objects. When you were looking for a classical-facade building, you were looking for a specific pattern for its front. When confronted with two similar facades, you had to evaluate the two on the basis of their styles.

Figure 3-2. The ancient Greeks developed the Doric and Ionic orders, with columns of different proportions.

Doric Order   Ionic Order

Although both contain similar elements such as columns and pediments, the Doric and the Ionic are proportionally different (Fig. 3-2). Additionally, one was more appropriate for your purposes, which was to get your form signed.

Measurement and style systems are culturally based. Measuring systems and stylistic systems are proportional information that must be interpreted compositionally and contextually. A specific example of contextual and compositional analysis is the wastecan that was really a vase in the tower lobby. Compositionally, wastecans and vases are identical; both vessels have the same proportions and are made of similar materials. Stylistic systems can be used to evaluate the similarity of surface pattern used as decoration. Contextually, the location and cultural values such as price make such objects different. Compositional relations are contingent on contextual relations, and vice versa.

VISUAL PRODUCTION BASED ON HUMAN DIMENSION

Visual production covers a broad range of human activity and endeavor, from urban planning to broadcast systems to vase making. In Figure 3-3, visual production is described in four categories of increased scale starting with the human, personal scale. The visual products to the left in the figure are closer to human proportions. The scale of visual products increases at the right of the figure.

Of the things surrounding you, what do you most need? Food, clothing, and shelter are the most immediate necessities. The size of these objects is relative to human size. People's experience with these objects is immediate because they are in everyone's living and working situation. Moving from individual to social situations, structures are more complex and larger than immediate and familiar surroundings. Surroundings occupy a continuum from a relatively small and simple personal residence

Figure 3-3. All visual production is related along a continuum, with the individual person at the center, increasing in scale to either side.

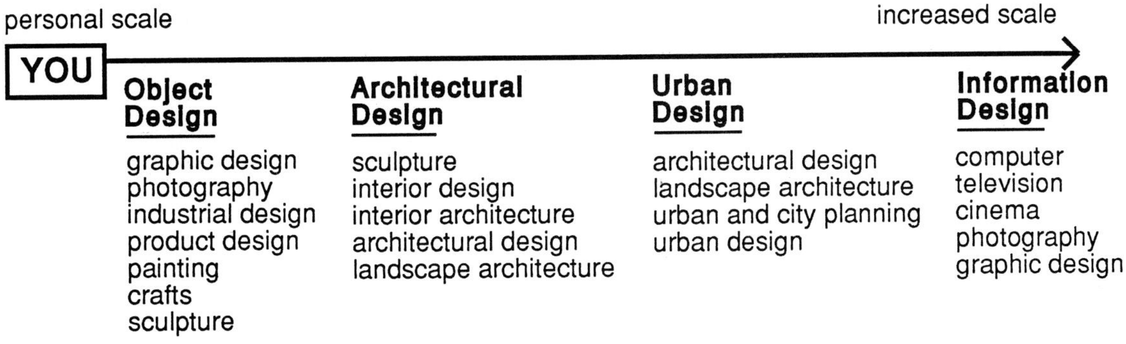

personal scale   increased scale

YOU	Object Design	Architectural Design	Urban Design	Information Design
	graphic design	sculpture	architectural design	computer
	photography	interior design	landscape architecture	television
	industrial design	interior architecture	urban and city planning	cinema
	product design	architectural design	urban design	photography
	painting	landscape architecture		graphic design
	crafts			
	sculpture			

to an increasingly large and complex surrounding urban environment. For example, the university is a more complex structure than a home. The development of the university required urban planning and landscape planning in addition to architectural design.

Personal objects in the immediate surroundings are proportional to human size. Experiences in using social objects become more complex. The continuum ranges from relatively small and simple personal objects to increasingly large and complex systems and networks that provide people with goods and information. This relationship between simple and complex visual production is itself complicated. The person who is alone, looking at an individual television set, is actually part of a community of isolated millions of viewers.

This model of visual production, based on human scale, integrates the diverse fields of visual production. It shows the structural similarities among apparently isolated fields. Your creative work is part of an entire system of interactions rather than the product of an isolated artist and designer (see Janet Wolff, 1984).

THE PROPORTIONAL NATURE OF REPRODUCTION

The reproduction of visual products has four proportional aspects. One involves how a visual product may be a proportional representation of an original. The second aspect involves the dimensional organization of color. A third concern is proportional changes in reproduction. The fourth involves the proportion of iteration or scale of production.

Proportional Representation

Plans, instructions, and diagrams that tell how to make or build something are common. The dimensions of these patterns may be expanded to reproduce some object, such as sculpture, buildings, or computer simulations for videogames. Other scalar representations of information are concrete physical models such as the scale model of a landform's terrain. More indirect, abstract models include maps. These models relate to actual experience. To use a map, for example, first you must determine your direction, which you can perceive directly from the location of the sun at certain times of the day or indirectly by using a compass, or comparing landmarks with the symbols on the map.

Some models or diagrams refer to more abstract concepts. For example, a chart showing the relative amount of light wavelength and saturation explains color perception (see Appendix C). In computer programming, complex computations are translated into binary instructions, which perform large numbers of individual computing operations to complete the computation. Because of the speed of the computer, the proportionately large numbers of computations are executed in proportionately short amounts of time. The products of these programs are numeric data that can be transformed into graphic representations (see Color Plate 18).

Any visual product proportionally represents an experience or an idea. When you were on top of the campus tower, you had an unobstructed view of the university, city, and surrounding countryside. A drawing or photograph of that view is a reduced scalar projection of that space. The drawing page or the photograph is a flat surface that acts like a proportional window or mirror, through which you see or which reflects an image toward you. Unlike perceptions, the drawing or photograph usually is rectangular, has distinct edges, and is more like a window or mirror.

The linear perspective drawing you make or the photograph you take is a model of the scene you see before you. Despite spatial differences, the edges, a scalar transformation, and a color shift, the picture refers to the original scene. The changes from the original scene to the image are transformations resulting from the medium, materials, and processes used to make the image. These transformations are produced at the discretion of the visual producer, who also acts as a medium for conveying some idea. The act of transformation is another instance of mediation.

Because the visual product is a model or representation of some original idea, scene, or object, it is a documentation of that original. Any model, diagram, map, or image refers back to and thus is a documentation of some original. In many disciplines, documentation for an idea must be produced before that idea can be realized. Architects, urban designers, landscape designers, and information systems designers generate substantial materials to support a project's proposal. In some cases, documentation is necessary before and after a work is executed. For example, many contemporary artists produce large earthwork projects, murals, or performance works for which proposals must be written and documentation must exist once the project is complete. These projects usually require large expenditures of money, time, and labor to realize the work. The proposals' diagrams and models, with any added mathematical or verbal information, are related or proportional to the final product. Neither models, diagrams, mathematics, nor verbal descriptions totally specify the final outcome. All are mediated versions of what finally is produced (Fig. 3-4).

These plans, diagrams, and documentation may seem to be "two-dimensional" representations of "three-dimensional" reality. Often the term *two-dimensional* refers to flat images and the term *three-dimensional* refers to solid volumes. However, all art and design products have natural and concrete dimensions. Every physical thing is three dimensional. Any purely two-dimensional experience represents a mathematical abstraction. Some cultures refer to two-dimensional objects such as paintings or book pages, but these objects have three-dimensional characteristics such as weight, mass, and surface texture.

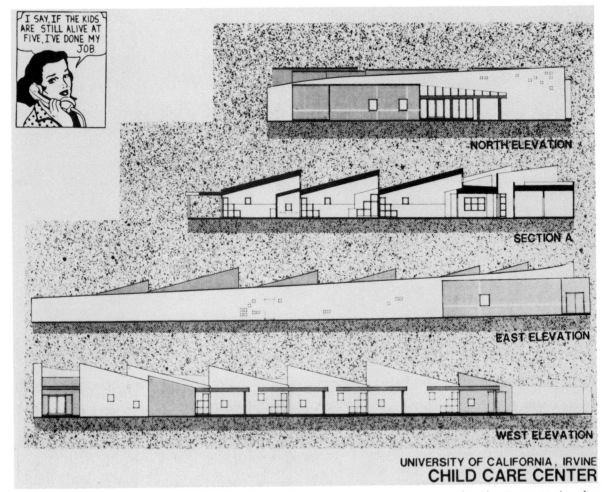

Figure 3-4. Documentation is a proportional reproduction of an idea. Documentation often includes written material, diagrams, and drawings. These are architectural drawings with which the architect is able to document the ideas for a building.

Dimensional Organization of Color

Color mapping, color systems, and color mixing have proportional and dimensional qualities. Color perception results from the stimulation of red, blue, and green cones. The combinations and relative amounts of cone stimulation produce a perception of a wide range of colors.

Colors can be fit into a spatial configuration to reveal specific color relationships in various ways. The eighteenth-century German philosopher and poet Johann Wolfgang von Goethe arranged colors into a triangle,

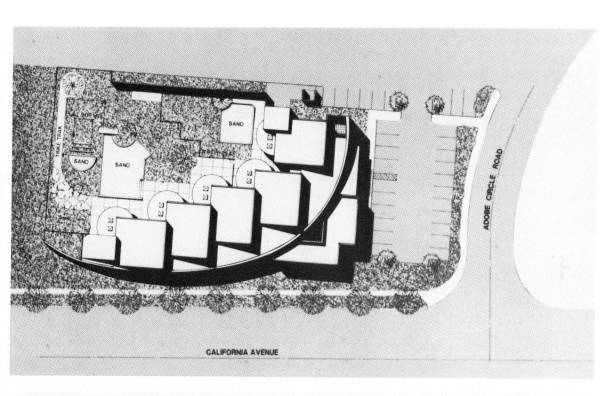

with red, blue, and yellow at the points and the mixtures resulting from each pair in between, to illustrate the relationship of certain colors in color mixing. We have already mentioned the Munsell color solid (see Color Plates 9 and 10 and Figs. C-1, C-2, and C-3), which relates color saturation and color tonality. Each of these illustrates proportionally some limited aspect of color relationships.

Color mixing is proportional. With pigment, mixing yellow and blue produces green. If the resulting mixture is too blue, proportionally more yellow can be added to the mixture (Color Plate 5). In industrial printing processes, a more yellow green is created when the halftone dots on the yellow plate are larger and closer together and the cyan dots are smaller. A bluer green is the result of larger dots on the cyan plate (Color Plate 6; see Appendix C for further discussion of color mixing and color theory).

Proportional Changes in Reproduction

To reproduce something means to make it again. Reproducing is an *iterative* operation, which means that in the repetitive making and remaking of something, it may be adjusted and refined to suit better the needs of its users. In the act of making an object again and again, its proportions may change. The evolution of the Cadillac tail fin is one example of iteration and proportional reproduction (Fig. 3-5).

Figure 3-5. Ant Farm, *Cadillac Farm,* located off Interstate 40 between Soncy and Hope Roads, Amarillo, Texas, 1974. Stanley Marsh III owned the Cadillacs, which were partially buried in the ground. The cars dated from 1949 to 1963. Ant Farm was the name of a group of artists based in San Francisco.

No one could say how many millions of times the concept of a house has been reproduced over the centuries. In repetitive reproduction, constant, often imperceptible proportional adjustments are made in the house design. These proportional changes often involve adjusting the size of one part relative to another within the house structure. In addition to being visual, these changes also may make the house more agreeable to its users, more efficient shelter in a certain climate, or less costly to build. Style development is a function of these gradual iterative changes. The Doric and Ionic columns are examples of iteration that resulted in two distinct styles of column. Proportion is the relation of parts to whole, and in iteration these relationships are worked out.

The development of style also can be seen in artistic output. An artist's style is often evaluated over a lifetime of production rather than by one object. Artists themselves are consumers of other artists' production and can become the audience for their own artwork. Artists' styles may develop as they repeat and reproduce similar compositions over their lifetimes, making gradual proportional adjustments.

The relationship of artists to their output is more than personal consumption. The style of their work also reproduces the general relationship between artists and their particular audience. For example, a royal portrait exemplifies an artist who produces for a specific class of patrons.

The Scale of Production

The vase in the tower lobby may have been made by an individual or by an industry producing many standardized products of that type. The individual craftsperson makes objects on a small scale of production. When mass-produced by a large industry, such vases are made at a large scale of production. *Scale of production* refers to the quantity of objects produced and the division of human labor allocated to the process. At smaller scales of production, the visual products generated are more distinctive and less standardized, in part because individual craftspersons are responsible for most aspects of making these visual products. At larger scales of production, the visual products are mass-produced and more uniform, because the individual craftspersons are absorbed into an industry of which they are only parts. Because many people contribute to the production of each object, standardizing all aspects of production is necessary to coordinate the efforts of all. Because no one makes an entire object, all producers in mass production are responsible for only a proportion of the total effort.

This segmentation of productive tasks is called a *division of labor*. When various individuals do only part of the work involved in creating a product, the scale of production can be greatly increased. When such a scale of production begins to produce more objects, the organization and division of human labor appear to produce things more efficiently. In addition, you may think that under modern technology, fewer hours of human labor are necessary in production. This is not the case.

Required human labor has been transformed or made abstract by the division of labor and the substitution of technology for human labor. For example, the computer is a product of advanced technology and perhaps was made by machines rather than people. In fact, quite a bit of human labor is necessary to make a computer. The scale of human labor necessary to build a computer seems to imply that its labor requires complex skills, but the type of unskilled labor involved in making a computer is actually not very different from that involved in making paintbrushes. You may think that the labor necessary to make tools is separate from the labor of a person who uses the tools to make visual products. A visual producer can use computers or paintbrushes as tools to make paintings. The use of computer technology may allow more visual products to be produced than could have been made by hand, but the total amount of labor necessary to make a visual product includes the labor required to produce its tools.

More value can be produced and accumulated at increasing levels of scale of production. For example, many people can share the same tool or can use those tools while others rest. At another level, the promise of technology is that machines can replace manual labor. However, every technological innovation or improvement is based on additional divisions of human labor, because human labor is used in making the machines of technology. The most radical and perhaps most dehumanizing version of this process is the mass-production assembly line that has made many modern products. Assembly lines are less dominant in the United States now than they were before World War II, but the American economy depends on products produced in variations on the original model of assembly-line production. Although initially productive, the assembly line eventually results in the accumulation and diversion of value that is not redistributed to the lowest levels of labor, because those people doing the producing tend not to divide among themselves the full amount of value accumulated. For example, the difference in wages between labor and management is often very great and does not represent an equitable distribution of profits.

Assembly-line production and its newer variants have resulted in a wider variety and greater quantity of goods available to at least part of the world's population. In some cases, attempts have been made to address the problems of quality control and dehumanization in production. For example, some assembly line workers are involved in their own quality control, and some groups of workers study the production system and suggest improvements. In some instances, this greater involvement has improved product quality and worker morale. However, it has not addressed the issue of the redistribution of the wealth produced by such production processes.

You may feel that, as an artist, this discussion does not apply to your production. However, your involvement in art production does not end with making an object. Your artwork may be bought and sold many times for amounts much greater than what you receive. In addition, the reproduction of that artwork, as posters or postcards, for example, many generate more value than the original work. Additional labor, including printers and designers, becomes part of the increasing scale of the production process. Despite being the original producer of the work, however, you might receive no compensation for the increased value generated by the poster sales. We discuss art production as a totality that includes production, distribution, and consumption in further chapters.

POWER

When you were at the top of the campus tower, the telescope could indirectly extend the limits of your direct vision only if you had the money to pay for the rental time. When you were trying to drop your class, you were frustrated by poorly designed forms, by waiting areas without writing surfaces, and by indistinguishable campus buildings with inaccurate campus maps.

These examples show how, in certain situations, you may derive a sense of power or powerlessness that depends upon your sense of proportion. The power you felt on the tower was the result of your commanding view in relation to the landscape. By substituting yourself for the benefactors you assumed their view on top of their building. Your sense of powerlessness in trying to drop your class was due to the complex bureaucracy and your perception that its huge proportions were beyond the scope of anything you could effectively handle. You were at a disadvantage because of the poor design of university forms, maps, rooms, and information systems. These examples of power were manifested in visual products.

The social dimensions of power and technological dimensions of power proportionally increase the power of an individual. Art and design products and instruments are examples of the technological dimension of power. These products and instruments enhance, alter, and mediate perceptions and have cultural and social value. Your use of the telescope is a combination of direct and indirect values created by using distance relationships. When you touch or look at the telescope, you experience it concretely as an object, but you want to look through it in order to see something else. Your amplified view, rather than the concrete object, has value. You put the money in the timer to see something specific, which is a direct exchange of one value for another. The indirect cultural value occurs when you see specific detail unavailable to your eye. This value is based on proportion; as an artist or designer, you value products and instruments that extend the capacity of your senses.

The indirect values are more mediated in that they place greater emphasis on meaning and value as opposed to the material objects themselves. They require a different king of perceiving to understand what you see with instruments. A historical example is that of Galileo and his use of the telescope to reveal new planet-to-sun relationships. Although Galileo's findings were concerned directly with astronomy, indirectly they had a religious impact, because they were seen as heresy by religious authorities. Visual producers, such as Eadweard Muybridge, used the photographic camera not only to produce visual products but also as a means of attaining knowledge. Muybridges's photographs investigated movement in humans and animals. For example, his work revealed the actual leg positions of galloping horses (Fig. 3-6). Before, galloping horses were painted with all legs extended.

Proportional differences help to establish a social dimension of power. For example, the scale of human bodies can be seen as one example of power. People are dimensionally more powerful and less powerful on the basis of physical size. The comparative size of one human to another, such as the big bullies who beat up smaller kids in the schoolyard, represents the direct power of proportion. Indirect power is based on direct power but is granted to individuals by larger social groups. Examples of more indirect power are teachers whose power is established by rules and police officers whose power is the law, which is directly enforced by guns and imprisonment. Such social power must be shown visually. For example, experiments in the 1970s changed police uniforms to blazers and squad car colors to pastels, but police perceived a loss of power in these experiments.

The dimensions of bodies, whether of males who play football or females who enter beauty pageants, use proportion as a type of power. Football players achieve superhuman proportions with shoulder pads, bodybuilding, and occasionally the illegal use of steroids; beauty pageant contestants alter their bodies cosmetically. These examples are direct because they involve physical bodies, but, because they are glamourized in print media or are broadcast over television, they also produce powerful indirect messages. The audience they influence and their impact through media is proportionally greater than their importance as individuals. The images of the football player and beauty contestant become caricatures whose physical dimensions and actions are largely choreographed or stylized. Their proportions gain power because the mediation of technology makes them proportionally gain more social and economic status (Fig. 3-7).

Power is connected to the historical rise of technology and law. The acquisition of power is tied to the use of proportional systems or technologies. An associated representation and reproduction of power also emerged. Renaissance artists used perspective systems or the classical orders to demonstrate artistic power. They used proportion to design and

Figure 3-6. Eadweard Muybridge's photographs show the positions of horses' legs as they are galloping. Muybridge, *Horse and Rider at a Gallop,* from *The Attitudes of Animals in Locomotion,* 1878–79.

Figure 3-7. The Lovely Elizabeth, Randy ''Macho Man'' Savage, and Hulk Hogan. Certain proportions, especially when combined with mass media exposure, are the basis for power.

Figure 3-8. Royce Hall, University of California, Los Angeles, imitates the proportions and details of the church Sant'Ambrogio in Milan, Italy, constructed during the eleventh and twelfth centuries. Frequently, university structures imitate the proportions of ecclesiastic structures to take on the heritage of Scholasticism.

reproduce larger-scale structures or murals than had been done before. These same structures proportionally and symbolically reproduced the power of the Church as a spiritual, educational, and political institution that governed a significant portion of the human population. The power of the Church became synonymous with its architecture and its accompanying artwork. Primary campus buildings in many twentieth-century universities resemble church architecture, thus borrowing the association of the church with scholastic power (Fig. 3-8).

Empowerment refers to the claiming or reclaiming of power by those who have been systematically or institutionally denied power. The role of power as empowerment is an important but largely ignored part of art and design. You felt powerless confronting the university's bureaucracy, forms, maps, furniture, and buildings when they were not designed to enhance your capacity for action. Had these objects been better designed for your use, you would have been to some extent empowered. As a user of visual products, your sense of power, or your ability to be empowered, is important.

In architectural, urban, and object design, many branches of science and areas of research study how humans can use products and work within their environment. Ergonomics is concerned with the application of biology and engineering data to problems relating people and machines. Human engineering and body metrics study the personal and cultural spatial needs of humans as they interact with surrounding space. Anthropometry compares and studies human body measurements and uses knowledge of human size, reach, and strength to produce better architectural spaces, urban design, and product design (Fig. 3-9). For the physically disabled or handicapped, these disciplines allow the user to be enabled and empowered.

A designer or artist who produces any kind of visual product—a building, a painting, a map, a hand tool, or whatever—gives the audience or user a sense of power if the product is designed well for human use.

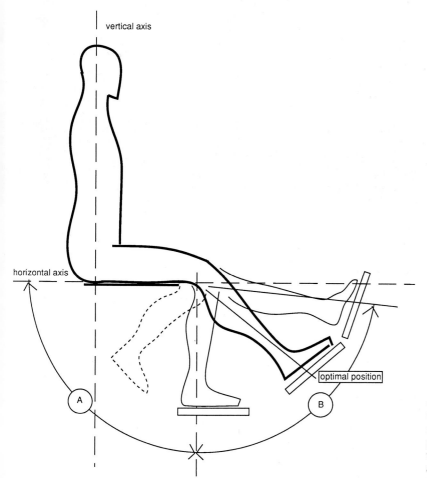

Figure 3-9. This anthropometric diagram shows leg positions for exerting light pressure against a pedal. The optimal position is shown, as are possible positions along the angle B. Although the leg can be placed in positions along angle A, exertion of pressure in those positions is not possible.

PROPORTION ASSIGNMENT 1

Proportion and Scale

Visual producers constantly make choices when they create visual products. Some choices are based on the limitations of the medium they use. Some are based on the needs of the audience who will use the visual product. Other choices are based on the visual producers' own sense of how parts of the visual product relate best to each other and to the whole. These last choices are called *proportional* choices.

The ancient Greeks believed that proportion was the key to beauty both in sculpture and in architecture. Polykleitos, in the fifth century B.C., devised a canon of proportions for the human form with the middle finger serving as the basic unit: two fingers equaled the length of the whole hand; three fingers equalled the length of the forearm, and so on. An example of the application of his canon of proportions is *Doryphorus* (450–440 B.C.).

The golden section is an ancient proportional guide, expressed as a:b = b:(a+b) in algebra or as the irrational number 1.61803398. The golden rectangle is based on the golden mean: the long side of the rectangle is drawn first and then is divided according to the golden section with the longer of the two resulting line segments becoming the short side of the rectangle. These proportional relationships were believed to link mathematics and beauty. The Fibonacci progression, in which each number is the sum of the two preceding numbers (1 + 2 = 3; 2 + 3 = 5; 3 + 5 = 8; 5 + 8 = 13; and so on), is related to these.

Materials

1 sheet 18" x 24" graph paper (scale: 8 or 10 squares per inch)

Pencil

Ruler

Photographs of architectural details

Procedure

Each student should select a photograph or reproduction of some architectural detail. Trace the major forms in one corner of the graph paper. Choose some part of the architectural detail as a starting point and redraw it in the middle of the graph paper. Now, redraw the other parts and enlarge each according to some mathematical progression.

You can use any of several mathematic progressions:

1. Fibonacci progression (1, 1, 2, 3, 5, 8, 13, 21, 34, 55 . . .)

2. Prime number sequence (1, 2, 3, 5, 7, 11, 13, 17, 19, 23, 29, 31, 37, 41, 43, 47 . . .)

3. Linear progression (1, 2, 3, 4, 5, 6, 7, 8, 9, 10, 11, 12, 13, 14, 15 . . .)

4. Geometric progression (2, 4, 8, 16, 32, 64, 128, 256, 512 . . .)

The results should be a proportional variation on the original image (Fig. 3-10).

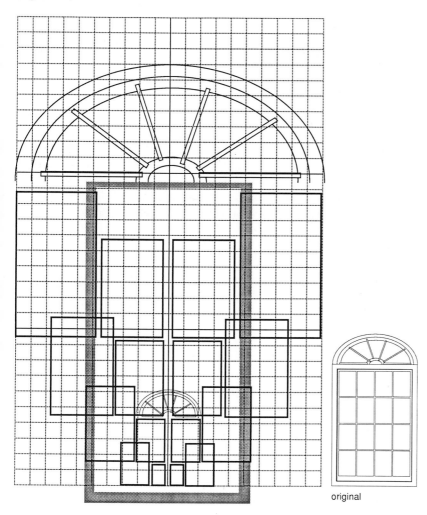

original

Figure 3-10. Change the proportions of the parts of an original drawing to create a new image.

PROPORTION ASSIGNMENT 2

Linear Perspective Exercise

Linear perspective drawings are proportional representations of space. The drawings consist of lines and shapes arranged on a flat surface according to culturally accepted rules to stand for spatial configurations. Your ability to understand linear perspective drawings as spatial representations is based on your cultural background. The Necker cube can be interpreted in a number of spatial and nonspatial ways (Fig. 3-11).

In this exercise, you will see how you can interpret line drawings in nonspatial ways. Read Appendix D for further information on ways to draw linear perspective drawings and Chapter 2 for discussion of pattern.

Materials

3 sheets 8½" x 11" bond paper

Pencil

Eraser

Ruler

Colored pencils or fine-tip colored markers

Procedure

The sample line drawings (Fig. 3-12) can be interpreted as patterns or as partially drawn perspective images. Choose one and redraw it large enough to fill one piece of paper. Complete the partial line drawing as a linear perspective drawing by drawing the horizon line and the construction lines to the vanishing point and then constructing the volume. Photocopy that completed linear perspective drawing.

Change the original drawing to stress a spatial reading by emphasizing volume outlines and shading the volume. On the copy, add tones or colors to the shapes created by the various lines, so that the drawing becomes patternlike. The final result should be one drawing with a strong spatial illusion and with an apparent object in the foreground of the drawing surrounded by background. The other drawing should diminish the illusion of space in depth, with shifting foreground-background areas (Fig. 3-13).

Follow the same procedure for two other sample drawings.

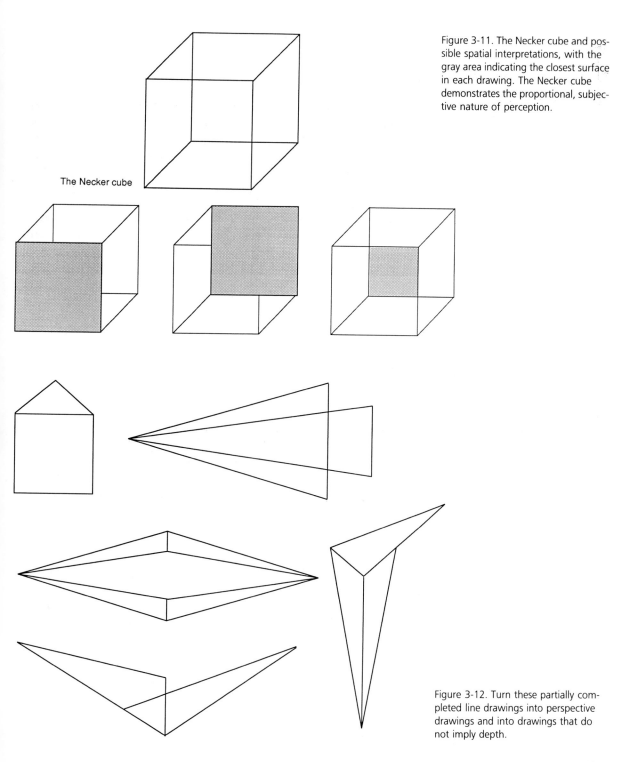

The Necker cube

Figure 3-11. The Necker cube and possible spatial interpretations, with the gray area indicating the closest surface in each drawing. The Necker cube demonstrates the proportional, subjective nature of perception.

Figure 3-12. Turn these partially completed line drawings into perspective drawings and into drawings that do not imply depth.

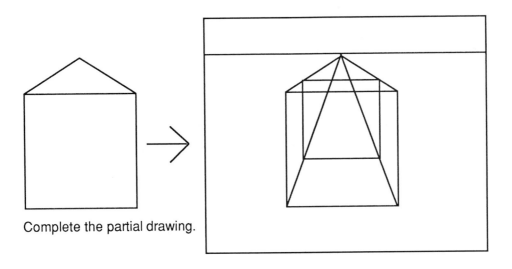

Complete the partial drawing.

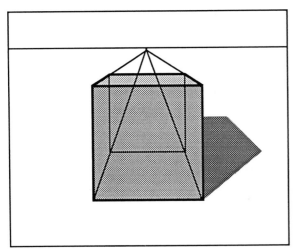

Modify drawing to increase the illusion of depth.

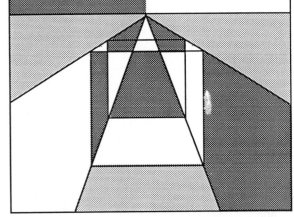

Modify the drawing to emphasize pattern and deemphasize the illusion of depth.

Figure 3-13. Sample execution of Proportion Assignment 2.

PROPORTION ASSIGNMENT 3

Linear Perspective Exercise 2

Drawing is a proportional representation of visual perception. The drawing page is a window that is proportional to your entire visual array. The drawing itself is a partial and proportional representation of what you see. Your position in relation to what you are drawing is your point of view.

You can transform visual perceptions into drawings, or you can transform numeric data into computer drawings.

Materials

Rope, heavy string, or tape

1 sheet 18" x 24" sketch paper

Pencil

Ruler

Procedure

Suspend rope or heavy string so that two taut, parallel, horizontal lines 18 inches apart are created across the room, about 5 feet off the floor. Then tie two taut, parallel lines 24 inches apart, perpendicular to the first two line. This process creates a rectangle suspended in the air.

The class should be divided into two groups facing each other across the suspended rectangle. Each student takes an appointed position in the room. Some students should be close to the wires, some distant; some should be seated on the floor, and others should sit or stand on elevated areas. Now, all students draw the room on paper as they see it through the suspended rectangle. The paper's edges correspond to the suspended rectangle. Carefully note where shapes in the room appear to intersect the rope edges, and place those shapes in the corresponding position on the paper (Fig. 3-14).

Demonstration

Take measurements of the room and use them as input to draw a ground plan and elevation of the classroom on a computer-aided design (CAD) system on a computer graphic workstation. The numeric data is converted to XYZ coordinates. The computer line drawing developed from the floor measurements and elevation can be rotated to simulate different points of view. You can see how this computer drawing, derived from numerical input, often resembles the results the students achieved by drawing.

Discussion

Place the finished drawings on the wall according to the position of the students as they were drawing. The suspended rectangle acted as a lens in determining what each student saw. Those seated low saw the ceiling of the room. Those up high saw the floor. Each student's drawing is like the visual perception of a single individual who moves in order to perceive a spatial layout from several points of view. Discuss how all the drawings together resemble a fragmented rendering of the space.

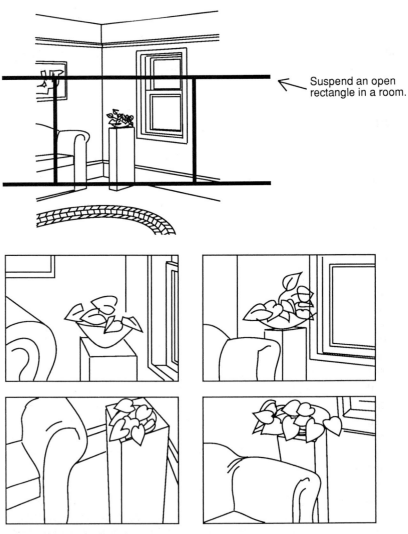

Suspend an open rectangle in a room.

Figure 3-14. Sample execution of Proportion Assignment 3.

Drawings made from different points of view through the open rectangle.

PROPORTION ASSIGNMENT 4

Mapping Kinetic Sculpture

In this exercise, you will learn how to map a object in space onto XYZ graph paper to partially reproduce spatial layout. In addition, you will make two other drawings that will show other positions of the object as it moves through space. The images you draw are related to the process of animation.

Your drawings are proportional reproductions of the original sculptures. When you make a scale version of an object, you reproduce it proportionately larger or smaller. In addition, this exercise allows you to study the internal proportions of the sculptures because in visual products proportion is also the relationship of one part to another or of one part to the whole

Materials

1 sheet 11" x 17" XYZ coordinate graph paper

Pencil

Ruler

Red pen

Procedure

Go to the library and find an illustration of a kinetic sculpture. Works by George Rickey or Alexander Calder are good examples of kinetic sculpture. If one is available where you live find an example of kinetic sculpture. Study the construction of the sculptures to find the pivotal points and determine what movement is possible.

Plot the position of the sculptural forms on XYZ graph paper. Photocopy this image. Redraw the movable parts of the sculpture in a second possible position superimposed on the photocopied drawing. Use red ink to distinguish this second position from the first drawing beneath it. This second position should be an extrapolation or extension of the movement implied in the first drawing. To *extrapolate* means to project, extend, or expand known data or experience to predict future development or movement.

Now photocopy the second drawing. On this photocopy, draw the sculpture in another possible position, this one an extrapolation of both the first and the second positions. Again, do not redraw the static parts, and draw the new position in red ink directly on the copied drawing.

Your final drawing should resemble a multiple-exposure photograph or sequence of animated images.

Extra Credit

Write and execute a program in BASIC or Pascal that will generate simple geometric shapes and show the kinetic sculpture in three possible configurations. Use the XYZ coordinates from this assignment as your input data. Make a printout of the image.

Many drawing, drafting, and design programs created for microcomputers allow you to draw or plot complex or simple volumes and then shift or rotate them. As an extra-credit project, complete this same assignment using a microcomputer with such a program.

Discussion

Discuss extrapolation and interpolation as a means of showing several locations of a moving item in space. What is their relation to animation and computer animation?

PROPORTION ASSIGNMENT 5

Load-Bearing Structures

In the first part of this assignment, you will have to resolve the problem of limited resources and visual considerations in the design of a chair or stool. The final proportions of your visual product may be influenced by the available resources.

Then you will redesign a chair or stool, based on the proportions and capabilities of the people who will use it.

Exercise A

Materials

1 sheet 8 1/2" x 11" construction paper

1 brick

Scissors, X-acto knife

3 sheets 4' x 8' corrugated cardboard

Binders: glue, contact cement wire, paper tape, staples

Procedure

Part 1. Build a shape from construction paper that will support the weight of one brick. Use the entire sheet of construction paper with none left over. Do not use glue, but you may cut or fold the paper. A prize will be given to the student who reaches the goal with the fewest number of cuts and folds in the sheet of paper.

Part 2. Break up into groups of four students. Design a stool or chair that will support the weight of one person by using corrugated cardboard and one kind of adhesive. Each group must use only the assigned binder:

Group A: white glue

Group B: contact cement

Group C: wire

Group D: paper tape

Group E: staples

Group F: no binder

Exercise B

Materials

1 sheet 18" x 24" graph paper (scale: 8 or 10 squares per inch)

Ruler

Pencil

Procedure

On half of the sheet of graph paper, draw one of the chairs or stools the class produced. This drawing is a scalar reproduction of its proportions. Redesign it so that it is appropriate for the human proportions of one of the following groups:

1. 2-year-old children

2. Adults weighing more than 300 pounds

3. Frail elderly persons

Draw your redesigned chair or stool on the other half of the graph paper and show the new proportions.

REPRODUCTION

CHAPTER

4

You have returned home after dropping your class and turn on the television. The program that comes on is a home-improvement show that tells you how to make a table from raw materials. On this program, the artisan begins with a tree stump and, using seventeenth-century tools, splits, carves, and turns the wood into a table you think is very beautiful. You turn the channel to a game show displaying a similar table called a "Scandinavian designer table." What amazes you is the table's high price, revealed when the contestant correctly guesses the price. At the close of the program, you see a promotional-consideration announcement and a 15-second commercial for the same table with a telephone number to order it with your credit card. You remember that you saw the same table in a catalog for $100 less.

As your mother's birthday is near, you would like to purchase the table as a gift. However, you notice in a following newscast that the Scandinavian table you would have purchased was made in Southeast Asia. You decide that you might be able to design a table like the one on television and maybe even start your own company. You begin to plan your production. You make preliminary sketches, assemble a list of tools, and start to draw the table in plan and elevation. You wonder whether you could hire others to make components for your table.

PERCEIVING A VISUAL PRODUCT

The story relates many examples of visual production and reproduction. We will start with the most basic example of visual reproduction, vision.

Perception is an act of visual reproduction. On a direct level, when you look at an object, you immediately perceive something; on an indirect level, you compare your original perception with your experience of other, similar objects or events. As you compare, you also reproduce, through the use of memory. Your perception also reproduces yours and someone else's ideas and experiences.

You express and communicate through a visual product. Making a visual product is producing an actual object. Simultaneously, you are reproducing your ideas in order to express them. Your self-expression is also communication because you always express these ideas to someone else, an audience. Each individual in the audience responds to the work both as internal responses and external responses to others. In their responses they express the cultural knowledge they have already accumulated from other sources.

A visual product represents and reproduces you and other individuals. For example, prehistoric humans painted on cave walls to reproduce their perceptions. These paintings represented imaginary projections of self and others engaging in hunting or ritual. These representations were self-expression and communications that became a kind of knowledge. Once self-expression becomes externalized as artwork, it can be interpreted in various ways by both the artist and the audience. A contemporary example of this same process is how advertising uses broadcast television to represent and reproduce projections of self to sell products to a mass audience (Fig. 4-1).

The medium used to reproduce the visual product changes perception because it changes how the product is experienced. You could experience something by looking at a photograph of it or by reading the description of it written by someone else. Although both experiences reproduce that original object, they are obviously different from each other and different from the original object. The transformation of the visual product and its effects are called *mediation.*

Expression is also transformed by different media of reproduction. In music, the individual self-expression of the performer is transformed by the distribution system that communicates that performance to an audience. Before a live audience, a musician performs differently than in a recording session. The audiences attending a live music concert, hearing that concert as a recording, watching that same concert on television perceive those products differently.

The scale or size of the audience may range from an individual to a global mass audience. The scale of the audience affects the direct and indirect perception of the visual product. Communication of that product to a mass-market audience becomes increasingly indirect due to the technology used to transmit or mediate it. An individual may visit the Vietnam Veterans Memorial in Washington, D.C. (Fig. 4-2) or be part of a mass audience that experiences the memorial through a television program. In that case, perception is more mediated because the experience is transmitted audio and visual perception without the more complete sensory information acquired by actually being there. For example, the television viewer is unable to touch the monument, which so many visitors are moved to do. Your visual perception is framed both by the camera and by your television screen as well as by the narrative that structures the program. Although it combines a broad range of expression and communication, your experience lasts only an hour.

Figure 4-1. Advertisements reproduce images of self and others. Advertisement: Southwestern Bell Telephone.

Figure 4-2. The Vietnam Veterans Memorial, Washington D.C., Maya Ying Lin, designer, completed 1982.

Expression and communication are a continuum based on human perception and expanded by mediation. Visual products are mediated expression and communication. The excitement of being able to externalize and express ideas and emotions is one of the great attractions of creating visual products. Although most visual producers understand their work as self-expression, too few understand how visual products communicate ideas or the mediated nature of their work. The ability to mediate the experience of others through visual products gives the visual producer power and challenges them to structure the knowledge and emotional responses of others.

PATTERNS OF REPRODUCTION

A visual producer, must not only understand how to produce a single object but also grasp the total pattern of reproduction. The pattern of reproduction is composed of three distinct sectors: production, distribution, and consumption (Fig. 4-3). *Production* is the making of visual products; *distribution* is the circulation of those visual products, and *consumption* is the using of the same visual products. The basic pattern of visual production and reproduction is a dynamic process that develops historically.

As a visual producer, you are part of each sector: When you make a visual product, you obviously engage in production; when you present or display a visual product,you are distributing or circulating it in order to communicate your experiences and ideas to an audience; you perceive your own visual product as an audience member and you also receive the responses of your audience; in this way, you also act as a consumer.

As an audience member, you participate in visual production, distribution, and consumption. When you go to a museum, you are engaged in the process of reception. You are a member of an audience involved in cultural activity that includes visual production. Reception is perceptual reproduction. In the distribution of a visual product, you experience what others also have experienced, which is primarily the ideas reproduced and externalized by the artist. Your reception is also an act of consumption because your use of visual products is connected to needs and desires.

The pattern of reproduction for visual products is manifested in direct, concrete ways and in indirect, abstract ways. A visual producer directly produces for self-expression; the visual product is a self-production or production of self. Direct distribution is producing objects or performing services to sell or barter in order to survive. Direct consumption is when visual products are used for self-satisfaction and for the satisfaction of those who use the object.

In an indirect way, abstract patterns of value and meaning are applied to this system of reproduction. They are abstract because values such as monetary prices are associated with but not identical to the visual products themselves. A *monetary system* is a set of indirect patterns that abstractly represent the value of products. In some cases, the same object may have many different values given to it, which shows again that monetary values are abstract systems applied to objects and not the objects themselves. An example of this is the varying prices for the Scandinavian table.

The use of visual products is acquiring status. Owning a particular painting or driving a certain style of car can be signs of belonging to an elite class. Status can be established through acquired or inherited wealth or professional education, such as law or medicine. *Status* is an abstract value of relative prestige or position, which is represented in a hierarchy

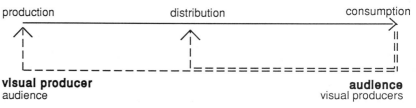

Figure 4-3. In visual production, the relationship between the producer and the audience is complex. Both groups express and communicate, that is, both groups produce and consume. The visual producer makes objects to communicate to the audience. The audience produces cultural responses for the artist or designer. The visual products and the cultural responses are consumed by both producers and audience.

by higher social standing, participation in elite cultural activities, and the consumption of privileged objects. This abstract value is produced, distributed, and consumed. For example, in production, indirect pattern of status includes the hierarchy of business management, that is, the decision-making structure as opposed to labor. In distribution, status is supported by marketing that uses advertising, sales, and shipping to circulate values such as health, wealth, and desire that are associated with products. In consumption, status is derived through the use of some object and the price of that purchase.

The status associated with owning a particular object may depend on the object's country of origin. In an effort to increase the status associated with an object, an advertiser may obscure the actual manufacturing location of that object. For example, much of the authentic Scandinavian furniture available in the United States is actually made in Southeast Asia, Eastern Europe, or Latin America. The craft knowledge and designs necessary to make the table are reproducible patterns that in this case come from Scandinavia and are transmitted to native craftspersons in Southeast Asia. You might pay more for an object advertised as Scandinavian rather than as Southeast Asian, although two such objects might be the same. You might also gain more status with the purchase and display of such an object. The greater value for one table over the other, based on where it was made, is supported by publicity and fashion.

Why should you, as a visual producer, know about status and about production, distribution, and consumption? You need to know how your visual products function in society and what expectations your audience has of your work, based on the medium you use. A visual producer should be aware that the objects made may be desirable because of the status that may be associated with them. This function of status is especially apparent if you seek to have your art or design work identified with elite art objects. You may choose to produce objects without aspiring to appeal to an elite who usually collects such work. Even so your visual products may be desirable because the person who purchases them sees them as a way to increase status.

PROPORTIONAL REPRODUCTION

The eighteenth-century British economist Adam Smith used a pin factory as an example of specialization and the division of labor. Instead of an individual craftsperson making a complete pin, the tasks could be divided among many assembly line workers, each performing one part of the process of production, such as sharpening the points and putting on the heads. This is an example of proportional reproduction because the entire task of making an object was divided among many individuals.

In the example of the Scandinavian table from Southeast Asia, the labor needed to produce the table is divided proportionally between the table designers and the craftspersons who actually fabricate them. This division of labor is between designers and craftspersons. Who is the actual creator in this process? The Scandanavian designer could be said to be the real creator. In addition, the craft tradition originally was developed in Scandinavia and reproduced in Southeast Asia, which has a different craft tradition. However, despite the training given to the craftspersons and the accuracy of Scandinavian designers' plans and instructions, the Southeast Asian artisan actually made the table. The creative process occurs over the total scope of reproduction, including designing and fabricating.

All visual products, including these tables, are the products of social and technical division of labor. *Social division of labor* refers to the human participation in the production of visual products. It may be physical or mental labor. Mental labor, which is perception and cognition, can be called *creative labor* and is often misidentified as intuition. *Technical* refers to all other resources, whether natural or technological. It may be the most elementary of tools, such as a rock used as a hammer, or it may be a space shuttle used as a carrier pigeon for the satellites that transmit electronic imagery.

Artists working in their studios may appear to be self-sufficient and independent producers who work alone, but artists rely on technical and social division of labor. They depend on paint manufacturers and canvas suppliers for materials. In many cases they rely on families or spouses to support their artistic production. Artists need museum curators, gallery owners, and art critics to reproduce and distribute the meaning and image of their work. Labor such as museum personnel and the printing trades are also part of this division of labor. The consumers of artists' works are collectors, other artists, visitors to galleries and museums, or purchasers of reproductions like postcards or posters. (For further explanation of technical and social division of labor in art, see Janet Wolff, 1984.)

All artists are small business operators in an art market, despite the stereotypic image of the autonomous artist struggling in the studio. The working artist is an example of the division of labor in object design. The graphic designer's dependence upon suppliers and vendors of photographic, photomechanical, and printing services is a similar example of that division of labor. Divisions of labor exist in each overlapping area of object design, architectural design, urban design, and information design.

In architectural design, the division of labor appears in the roles of architects, developers, contractors, suppliers, and construction workers. The architect is alternately the master and the slave of the real estate developer and sometimes functions in both roles. Individual architects often believe that they are the sole creator when the actual designing is done by the building contractors or individual workers during the construction of buildings. Sometimes a sculpture may be added to an architectural space, which is another division of labor, with the sculptor being separated from the architect's creative process. The architect James Wines said that sculpture placed within architecture only as an afterthought becomes a "turd in a plaza" (comment made at the International Sculpture Conference, Toronto, 1978). Cooperation among all divisions of creative labor is necessary for all art and design products.

In urban design the construction of the larger urban environment obviously requires complex divisions of labor. However, it also reveals another aspect of the proportional differences among types of labor. Using extensive divisions of labor, some autocrats have reproduced historical images of power manifested as cities that were developed or transformed according to their vision. An example of this is the development of cities by such politicians with their designers as Napoleon III with Baron Haussmann and Adolf Hitler with Albert Speer. The relocation or proposed relocation of capital cities by governments such as Brazil, India, and Australia suggests that urban design reproduces a larger image of state power beyond human proportions.

Information design—the production, distribution, and consumption of messages, usually visible and audible, using modern technology—also has complex divisions of labor. The television industry, for example, has producers, directors, camera operators, engineers, makeup artists, grips, advertising sales, writers, secretaries, managers, accountants, talent, and many more, including assistants for these people. The industry also has vast quantities of tools, machines, and other necessary resources. This division of labor applies to information design's production sector only. This sector is often referred to as an "industry," even though that word is usually associated with the industrial factory and its assembly line. Some people such as receptionists and chauffeurs work in proportionally noncreative tasks in this industry, often primarily to be associated with its creative products.

Why must the visual producer understand the division of labor in all visual production? Although most designers, architects, and urban planners understand the necessity of using the labor of others to realize their projects, many artists operate under the mistaken notion that they produce art objects by themselves. In fact, what artists produce are only potential art objects. The work of critics, collectors, educators, and museum and gallery personnel are required to transform the artists' works into art objects. Artists must operate within the social context for art production, which often is called an *artworld* (see Howard Becker, 1982; and George Dickie and Richard Sclafani, 1977). Those who "go off and do their own work" lack the complete process of cultural production. In addition, understanding the social dimension to visual production is important because too often successful artists, designers, or architects are falsely accorded the qualities of solitary geniuses for their work. This attribution represents a misunderstanding of how culture is produced and ignores the roles of many others who are essential in cultural production.

PRODUCTION AND REPRODUCTION

We will now examine various methods of drawing as specific examples of production and reproduction. The visual producer has to represent ideas visually, beginning with a mental visualization that must be made physical in some way. The many different methods of drawing are reproduction technologies that allow the externalization and reproduction of the idea. This section concerns expression of ideas through various media, how these media are related and have developed historically, and how innovations in technology affect reproduction.

Copying

You have an mental idea for the table you want to make. When you begin to design the table, you need to make drawings to determine the dimensions, methods, and materials for your visual product. You may choose from many types of reproduction. At the most manual level of drawing as reproduction, you can imitate or directly copy from an existing pattern or original. Transfer rubbing or tracing follows the exact contour of the original. In this method, each gesture produces a mark that corresponds to a related mark on the original. This simple method is similar that used by Renaissance artists who transferred a preliminary drawing to the surface of the fresco they were about to paint. They put many pin holes along the lines of their drawings, attached the drawings to the fresco surface, and dusted a fine powder over the drawings that would filter through the holes and deposit on the surface beneath.

Projection Geometries

At the next level are more abstract and geometric or mathematical reproduction methods, metric and projection geometries that include perspective drawing and other types of diagrams and schematics. These drawing methods require geometric drawing tools like rulers and compasses. Their purpose is to depict geometric spatial relationships on a flat surface.

For a *metric* drawing, the simplest geometric drawing, the spatial relationships from a single plane of an object or structure are reproduced. Verticals indicate vertical space; horizontals indicate horizontal space. Diagonals indicate diagonal direction on the plane and do not indicate depth. Space is reduced to a planar pattern. Examples of metric drawings can be found in Egyptian wall paintings and in some types of technical drawing (Fig. 4-4).

Although a metric drawing geometrically represents a restricted spatial relationship, *projection geometries* depict more complex spatial relationships. With projection geometry, diagonals often indicate depth or planes that appear to move away from the viewer. Vertical and horizontal edges usually indicate planes that are parallel to and face the viewer. Objects in front frequently overlap other objects. A ground plane is often implied that connects the bottom edge of the page with the horizon line, which is the schematic representation of the sky "meeting" the ground. Objects whose bases are on the ground plane near the horizon line are further back than objects whose bases are close to the bottom of the paper (Fig. 4-5).

Projection geometries include paraline and projective drawings. In *paraline* drawings, frontal planes are shown with vertical and horizontal

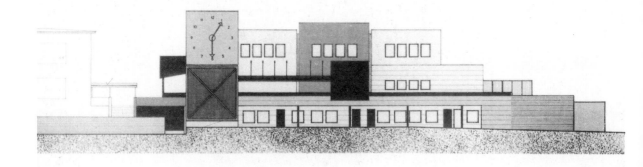

East Elevation

Figure 4-4. Both the metric diagram (above) and Egyptian painting (facing page) reproduce space horizontally and vertically. The architect's drawing of the elevation of the building is a metric diagram. In *Pool in the Garden,* a fragment of a wall painting from a unloaded Theban tomb, elements of wildlife and vegetation rarely overlap, but occupy space in horizontal and vertical relation to each other.

lines. Receding planes are shown as diagonals parallel to each other. Paraline drawings are also called *axonometric* or *axiometric*. Paraline methods of depicting spatial relationships are more often used in a variety of technical drawings, such as architectural plans. However, some traditional Japanese paintings also use this device to convey space (Fig. 4-6).

Paraline drawings include oblique, dimetric, and isometric types, as shown in Figure 4-7. (For further information on paraline drawings, technical drawings, and other architectural and mechanical renderings, see books on drafting and technical drawing such as John R. Hoke, Jr., 1988.)

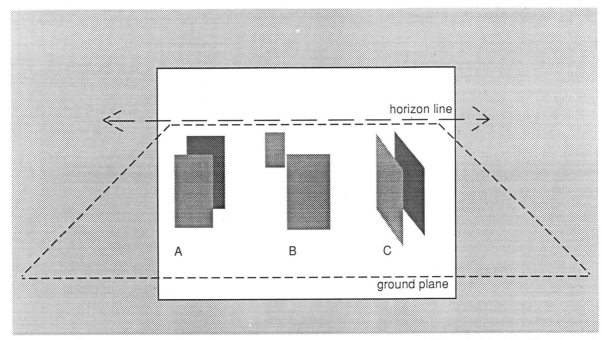

Figure 4-5. In linear perspective drawings, you can indicate spatial relationships using overlapping (A), size and placement relative to the ground plane (B), and receding planes (C).

Figure 4-6. Some Asian paintings reproduce space like a paraline drawing. *Scroll with Depictions of the Night Attack on the Sanjo Palace,* from the Heigi monogatari emaki, thirteenth century, Japan.

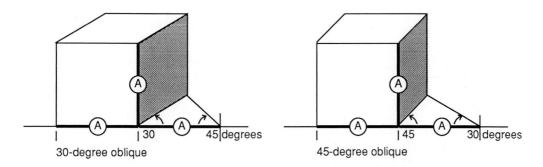

30-degree oblique

45-degree oblique

Oblique paraline drawings: frontal planes are drawn with horizontal and vertical lines. All receding planes are drawn parallel to each other and at a constant angle. All lines marked A are the same length.

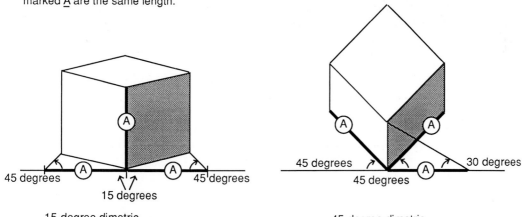

15-degree dimetric

45-degree dimetric

Dimetric paraline drawings: all planes are rotated so that a vertical edge is closest to you. All lines marked A are the same length.

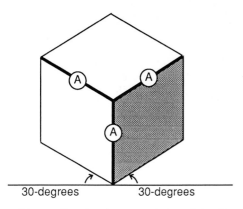

Figure 4-7. Paraline drawing variations: oblique, dimetric, and isometric.

Isometric paraline drawing: a variation of the dimetric, in which linear measurements are maintained.

Figure 4-8. Space reproduced in a linear perspective drawing. In Pieter-Jans Sanredam's drawing, the artist used linear perspective methods to draw the floor of the church. Sanredam, *The Choir and North Ambulatory of S. Bavo in Haarlem, November 1634*, pen and brown ink and watercolor, 39.1 x 37.6 cm.

In an *oblique* drawing, frontal planes are shown with horizontal and vertical lines. Receding planes are drawn at a 30-degree or 45-degree angle from the bottom edge of the frontal planes. The length of receding lines is determined as shown in Figure 4-7. In an oblique drawing, the shapes and spatial relationships within the frontal plane remain undistorted, and the side planes are shown with some distortion, more in the 30-degree and less in the 45-degree oblique drawing. *Dimetric* drawings are similar to the oblique, except that the drawn object is rotated so that an edge appears to be closest to the viewer. Receding planes are shown at either a 15-degree angle or a 45-degree angle. The lengths of the receding planes are determined as shown in Figure 4-7. Dimetric drawings eliminate the frontal planes and distort side planes equally. The 15-degree dimetric allows the viewer to see more of the side planes and less of the top; the 45-degree dimetric drawing makes more of the top visible. In an *isometric* drawing, all axes of the object, except the vertical, are rotated and kept at the same angle of projection, usually 30 degrees from horizontal. All dimensions are equally distorted, and therefore receding lines or frontal lines all maintain their original proportions. Isometric drawings are commonly used in architectural renderings.

Linear perspective drawings that artists frequently use are *projective* projection geometry. *Perspective* is the geometric depiction of spatial relationships on a flat surface. In projective renderings, vertical, horizontal, and diagonal edges have the same spatial meanings as in paraline drawings. However, the diagonal lines do not remain parallel to each other, but converge on one or more vanishing points. Space can be conceptually divided into a distinct checkerboard pattern, in which objects are placed. Some Renaissance paintings and drawings follow modified versions of projective linear perspective (Fig. 4-8). See Appendix D for further information on various projective geometries used in linear perspective drawings.

Metric or projection geometries are abstractions of visual perception in that edge distinctions are reproduced as lines. Also, they frequently reproduce no color or surface texture, and they are not atmospheric. Atmospheric depictions of spatial relationships attempt to reproduce the blurring, loss of detail, and bluish cast perceived when you look at different, distant objects.

Optic, Mechanical, and Electronic Reproduction

Ideas can be reproduced without projection geometries. The next development in reproduction beyond the use of geometric drawing methods involves optics or the use of lenses and other technological instruments. The *camera lucida* and *camera obscura* are early examples of optic reproduction, in which an optic array from the environment is projected and focused as an image onto a flat surface. With the development of the photographic camera, the technology of the camera obscura and camera lucida is extended. The image from the optic array is projected and recorded onto a surface such as photographic film or paper coated with light-sensitive chemical emulsions (Fig. 4-9).

People today are accustomed to being surrounded with images, but 150 years ago the reproduction of images was less common. Industrial printing and later twentieth-century innovations have raised the level of

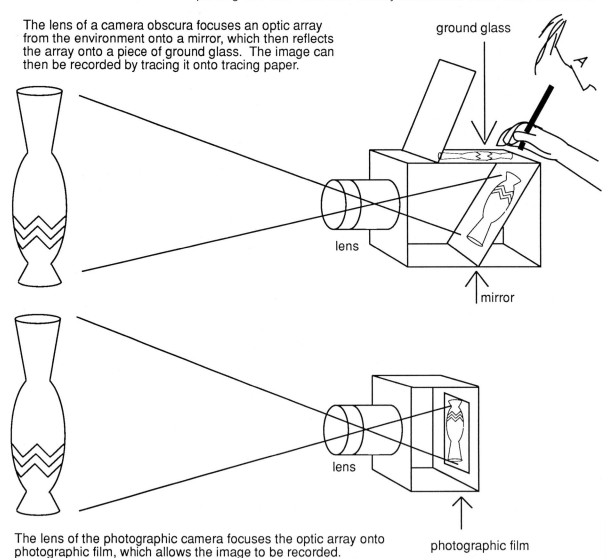

The lens of a camera obscura focuses an optic array from the environment onto a mirror, which then reflects the array onto a piece of ground glass. The image can then be recorded by tracing it onto tracing paper.

ground glass

lens

mirror

The lens of the photographic camera focuses the optic array onto photographic film, which allows the image to be recorded.

lens

photographic film

Figure 4-9. The camera obscura and the photographic camera.

production, distribution, and consumption of geometric and photographic images. Industrial printing reproduces both geometric and photographic visual products on a large scale by using photomechanical methods. (For further discussion of the technological developments in graphic design, read Philip Meggs, 1983.) A more recent invention, the photocopier, reproduces optical images by electrostatically charging a sheet of paper, depositing a layer of toner, and thermally fusing the charged areas corresponding to the original image. This process has been improved by the introduction of lasers that convert and reproduce information in greater definition and detail. The photocopier enables easy and inexpensive reproduction of images. In the area of motion picture film, the original single-frame photograph becomes more dynamic when projected as thousands of frames that give the illusion of motion.

More recent electronic methods for reproduction, such as video and computer, further extend reproduction capabilities. Video images may seem similar to motion picture film, but many important differences divide them. Motion pictures are based on photographic technology. The motion picture film image is an photochemical analog image. Each image is a photograph that photochemically recorded light levels in discrete, static, individual frames. The image is projected in a series with other images to give the illusion of motion. Broadcast television or recorded video also gives the illusion of motion, but the video image is subdivided into reprojected scan lines, which are stored on magnetic tape. The video camera electronically records and reproduces transmitted and reflected light levels in the optic array, which results in a continuous stream of images. In addition, the output of each medium is different; video is projected on a phosphorescent screen, and photography is presented on film or paper.

The computer is automated technology that can be used to create a wide variety of visual products. The computer can transform mathematical data and calculations into graphs and geometric figures. It also interprets and enhances photographic and electronic visual data from remote sources such as satellites. An individual can also draw and paint with this same technology (see Color Plate 18).

Video and computer technologies are converging as both use digital electronics to store digitally encoded visual information. This technology affects the visual products that can be produced with the computer. Now, digitally coded visual information may be reproduced and transformed in many different ways, instead of simply as a limited number of products like negatives or videotapes. The same digital data may be distributed as video display, magnetic tape, printed, photochemical, and electromechanical media.

Copying, geometric perspective, optical reproduction, mechanical reproduction, and electronic reproduction are all drawings that reproduce ideas or some aspect of the visible environment. All use some aspect of technology. Reproduction technology often has been divided into basic and advanced technologies, with the bias during the modern period toward advanced or "high" technologies. Basic reproduction technology began with primary human instrumental extensions, such as the hand, the pencil, the paint brush, and the hammer. It advanced to other instrumental extensions, such as printing presses, camera lucida, and camera obscura. Advanced technologies, such as photography and photocopying, allow more efficient and plentiful reproduction. For duplication of an image or copying of something seen, these latter technologies have generally replaced older technologies, such as drawing. However, older technologies continue to be used concurrently with more advanced technologies; for example, metric geometries are still required for floorplans and maps.

A *craft* is any basic technology in which production is done by hand. The crafts emphasize reproduction closer to human scale rather than a mass scale of production and have often been considered as humanizing, as with the British Arts and Crafts movement in the nineteenth century, which romanticized hand craft production as preferable to the mechanized production of goods. However, the Arts and Crafts movement served as a symbolic example rather than a viable alternative to the mass production system fostered by the Industrial Revolution. In late twentieth-century mass production, both the scale of production and the organization of labor and technology have dehumanized the process of reproduction. The workers in the craft trades have been transformed into laborers who tend machines and assemble components. Many who continue to practice the crafts using traditional methods do so as leisure activity, although some craftspersons are still self-supporting.

Therefore, basic technologies and fabrication by hand may seem to be no longer needed with advanced technologies. However, advanced technologies cannot be separated from basic technologies. The basic technologies including the crafts are required at the same time as advanced technologies rather than one replacing the other. The production of computer components still requires physical labor comparable to craft skills and extensive divisions of that same labor; some things considered to be made by hand require materials that are mass produced. As a result, no clear distinction exists between what composes basic and advanced technology. Reproduction media have become so sophisticated that they appear basic yet are quite advanced. For example, the simple pencil for drawing is the complex product of many technologies, including forestry and mining. The photographic camera, which appears complex, can be constructed from a coffee can. A pinhole coffee can camera and a 35 mm single-lens reflex autofocus, autozoom camera both can make photographs. The results are not identical, but is one necessarily better or more valuable because of the technology used?

POWER

Advanced technologies in reproduction change the value and nature of the original visual product and affect the number of copies. A visual producer needs to consider how the media used affects the object made in terms of the value of the work, how many times it will be reproduced, and how it will be distributed to the audience.

Here is an example of how reproduction affects the value of a product. Photographs can be precisely reproduced an infinite number of times. Sherrie Levine, a contemporary artist, has made precise photographic copies of the works of various photographers, including Walker Evans (Fig. 4-10) and Edward Weston, both of whom were prominent photographers earlier in this century. She calls these works her own and makes money from them without denying the fact that her photographs are copies. Although photographs can be reproduced in infinite numbers, they can be made more valuable if they are reproduced in limited editions. The photographs of Edward Weston are valuable in part because they were made in limited editions. Levine subverts the idea of the limited edition by easily and directly reproducing Weston's photographs (see Rosalind E. Krauss, 1981).

Reproduction affects the value of the reproduced image, especially innovations in reproduction technology since the European Industrial Revolution. Walter Benjamin, in his essay "The Work of Art in the Age of Mechanical Reproduction," discusses how the power and meaning of the unique artwork has changed when it may be repeatedly reproduced.

Figure 4-10. Sherrie Levine's *Untitled (after Walker Evans: 1),* 8" x 10", photograph, 1981. The artist precisely reproduced this photograph by Walker Evans.

Before artworks could be so easily reproduced, each artwork had an aura derived from its uniqueness, its location in only one place, and its limited audience. One example of an aura is that of the frescoes found in a cathedral where religious rituals take place. The fresco was powerful because it was unique and because of its religious significance. The power derived from artwork with religious significance subsequently shifted to secular visual products. Before printing and photography, this unique image or aura was the most important aspect of an artwork's value. Since the invention of movable type printing in Europe, that power has been progressively diminished with the introduction of methods of mechanical reproduction. Actual first-hand experience of an original visual product becomes unnecessary in order to have some knowledge of it, even though the reproduction is not the full sensory experience of the original work (Fig. 4-11).

Technology changes the effect that artwork and all visual products have on a culture. The power of the visual product becomes located in

Figure 4-11. Fresco from the Villa Madama, Rome. Because this Renaissance fresco is located in a villa, it has had a limited audience. Through mechanical reproduction, you are acquiring some knowledge about it at this moment, without actually seeing the original fresco. School of Raphael, begun 1520, fresco painted by Giulio Romano and framework by Giovanni da Udine.

experiencing the message reproduced by other media, rather than in possessing and experiencing the original object. Greater power comes from distributing this message by reproduction for a mass audience rather than from the possession or experience of the actual object. In the examples used in this text, we discussed many visual products and their significance by using photographic reproductions. Understanding the composition and context of the reproduced objects is an important but different experience than traveling to see each original work.

Early mechanical reproduction such as printing led to the development of media such as photography, motion picture film, and more recently videotape and television. The accessibility and immediacy of visual products made by mechanical means challenge the values associated with artworks such as painting, drawing, and sculpture. As a result of their increased audience, those institutions and individuals who use mechanical means of reproduction gain power and influence. The film industry and the television networks have a cultural and visual power that surpasses the effect of the museum or art gallery.

What does this mean to the artist or designer? The power of the unique visual product has not changed for the individual, who may still travel to see an original work of art and find that experience to be rewarded and exciting. However, unique art objects have been exclusively supported by elite social and economic classes. Others can possess the experience of such precious objects only as part of the mass audience who visits them and perhaps purchase reproductions as souvenirs. Finally, the visual producer can determine what audience will receive the message of the visual product by deciding what media to use.

Modern developments in reproduction technologies have proliferated consumer products and activities in Western countries and produced a crisis of meaning for unique artwork that is easily reproduced. This same crisis of meaning exists for all visual products, even those not considered as art. Reproduction technology today is so efficient that any meaning may be associated with a object or action and assigned a value. In this culture, for example, love has become associated with diverse objects and services such as sending flowers. These associations can be arbitrary, as in the case of love associated with the teddy bear. A real bear may be very threatening.

The arbitrary association of sentimentalized meanings with mass-produced objects results in kitsch. *Kitsch* refers to items or events associated with mass or popular culture. The term is generally considered pejorative. Someone with an elite point of view, whether from education or wealth, may assign the term to anything mass-produced that is seen as lower in class, status, value, and meaning. The meaning associated with kitsch items usually is considered a sentimentalized version of some more profound concept or emotion. For example, the teddy bear represents a simplistic version of love. Because *kitsch* is a pejorative term, its use distorts nostalgic or stereotyped sentiments such as brotherly love, patriotism, the innocence of children, and the wisdom of age and experience.

Kitsch is associated with the visual products of mass culture; the possession of artwork is associated with elite culture. The distinction of art and kitsch is not simply the application of labels or jargon. The distinctions of high and low art are associated with high and low culture and socio-economic classes. The term *kitsch* is applied from an elite point of view to literally anything mass-produced that is seen as lower in class or status. Those people often identified with mass culture do not attach a pejorative label to elite visual products and in fact often aspire to possession of objects such as fine paintings and expensive cars.

Objects or events themselves are not inherently kitsch or art. Human actions and situations comprise the context that defines kitsch and art. Pop artists and surrealists have incorporated kitsch objects into artwork (Fig. 4-12), yet their products are defined as art for two reasons. First, their work is art because it appears in the context of the art museum. Second, their work is not mass-produced, although it may be frequently reproduced. Kitsch and art situations overlap in other instances. Large-scale museum shows are often called *blockbusters* because they attract a mass audience and mass media attention. The division between visual products for an elite and for a mass culture is thus blurred. Much of art history is an attempt to control this crisis by designating new critical categories and terms. Art history defines what objects constitute art—and by exclusion what constitutes kitsch—and sets the standards by which the two are distinguished.

Art and kitsch exist because we have excess capacity to reproduce things and ideas beyond what we immediately need for everyday survival. The differentiation is less a matter of skill than it is one of assigning value that the distinction exists between art and kitsch. The kitsch classification is a way of using power to identify lower-class objects and simultaneously improve the value of or identify upper-class objects. Art and kitsch have greater exchange value than use value. The surplus represented in the production and reproduction of value is one that emphasizes the exchange values of commodities.

Something is valued if it can be used or exchanged for something else. An object can be used directly when it is handled, employed as a tool, eaten, or in some other way directly consumed. A thing also can be used indirectly, as when knowledge is acquired. For example, a book can be directly used to prop open a door and indirectly used to read for information. Objects also have an exchange value. For example, a book has direct exchange value because it may be traded for other things. A book given as a gift acquires an indirect exchange value because it signifies an exchange of affection or implies a future obligation. Art and kitsch have both use and exchange values.

Figure 4-12. Art and kitsch may often be embodied in the same visual product. Robert Rauschenberg, *Skyway*, 1964.

The distinction between art and kitsch objects occurs because an elite culture arbitrarily assigned value and meaning to objects. If you do not understand the distinction between art and kitsch, you may place an undue value on art objects. You may be misled by the belief that art objects are more valuable because they were produced by geniuses whose skills and insights you might not be able to learn. This latter belief would be an example of mystification, which occurs when you do not understand the process of making visual products.

Here are some specific examples to help explain this process of mystification. Currently, many people believe famous artists and designers are geniuses who produce masterpieces miraculously through the mysterious application of creative talent and insights that border on the divine. In this example of mystification, some "famous" visual producers are often accorded mythic and superhuman powers. Some artists and designers produce memorable and outstanding visual products, but they are only a few of the many participants, such as manufacturers, distributors, critics, writers, and audience, who cooperate in the entire process of creating a visual product. In addition, all artists or designers are products of the culture and have been taught by others, learned from others' products, and continually rely on the advice of their peers. The process by which a visual producer makes a product is not mysterious and unknowable, although many contemporary perceptions about art and design emphasize the opposite.

Mystification is not confined to the person who creates visual products. It can also include the products themselves. For example, painting and photocopying are both technologies for reproduction. Both may be used to reproduce precisely some hypothetical image. Nevertheless, the two reproductions have different values and are aimed at different audiences. The painted image implies a limited audience who will examine the single, unique reproduction for both the image and the skill of the painter who manipulated the paint. The photocopied image implies a broad audience looking at multiple copies without considering the skill of the photocopy machine operator or the designers of that technology. Because of the mystification of the artist as genius and because of mass reproduction, the painted image will likely have a greater monetary value associated with it than the photocopied image.

The roles and products of craftspersons may also be mystified. You may believe that a craftsperson has some manual skill, discernment, dexterity, and training that you could never acquire. You may also believe that by being associated with the crafts you may be in touch with an important tradition and humanizing influence in society. The profession of a craftsperson may be very different from what you imagine, however, especially in regard to the number of hours to produce and distribute a piece and whether that same individual actually devoted those hours to it. Recall the discussion about the division of labor.

The use of advanced technology may also result in mystification. The products resulting from such technology are made valuable because the equipment is often expensive and not widely available, the use of the equipment requires special training, and the procedures used in high technology are "unknown" or unrevealed in its products. A level of mystification results when the latest science fiction movie generates imagery with a multimillion-dollar computer. Large-scale projects like films that use many people and reach many people emphasize how mystification accompanies the application of reproduction technologies.

Everything we have been discussing in this section is the result of recent technological innovations, which leads to questions about progress. Concepts of progress are identified with modern thinking about technological innovation. Progress is often represented by the use of reproduction technologies. Frequently it is presented as inevitable and as potentially beneficial. For artists at the end of the nineteenth century, the railway, electricity, and the skyscraper seemed to signal a fast-approaching utopian future based on technological development. However, contemporary artists and designers have questioned the myth of progress after the destruction brought by two world wars and the attempts to use nuclear power for peaceful purposes. Understanding of progress should be based on an awareness of a broad range of technical, social, and cultural factors.

A competent visual producer needs knowledge and skill, especially now as basic technologies become amplified by advancing technologies and the understanding necessary to operate them becomes more complex. Knowledge, access, and competence in the advanced reproduction technologies empower a visual producer. Not only is skill in various media important, but also understanding how the media affects the message of the visual product and what potential audiences are reached with each media. Use of modern reproduction technologies questions the traditions and values of all other media. Many practitioners still work in traditional artistic media such as painting or sculpture, and you may choose to become one of them. If so, you need to be aware of the conflict created by the use of reproduction technologies.

In returning to the story, you go to the college's shop facilities and begin to make the table for your mother. You enlist the aid of some of your friends, one of whom is an accounting major. Another is a poet. They hesitate in participating because they feel they lack the creative power they think you have. After working for a while, they learn some manual skills and even make some suggestions that improve both the fabrication and the look of the finished table. One friend even takes a piece to a local workshop where a component for the table can be machined easily. When the table is finished, another friend comments that your table seems to have design improvements over other tables made in a similar style.

REPRODUCTION ASSIGNMENT 1

Transformations in Reproduction

A drawing is a reproduction of something you experience through visual, verbal, or mathematical information or of something you imagine. A reproduction, however, is not a true duplication; it only partially recreates the original.

Materials

1 sheet bristol paper, 16" x 16"

Ruler

Cutting knife

Several pencils in a range of hardnesses (for example 2H, B, 2B, and 6B)

Procedure

The instructor will provide one poster, a full-color photographic image, 16" x 20", cut into 4" x 4" pieces. Each student selects one piece of the poster, grids the piece into 1-inch squares and correspondingly grids the bristol paper into 4-inch squares.

Draw an enlarged version of the image from the poster fragment onto the bristol paper. Reproduce the poster colors as pencil tones, matching the lightness or darkness as nearly as possible. Use the 2H pencil to reproduce the lightest tones, the B and 2B pencils to reproduce middle tones, and the 6B pencil to reproduce the darkest tones. General tonal differences are most important; add any details if time allows. When the drawing is completed, assemble all the enlarged drawings on a wall to reconstruct the poster image.

Discussion

Discuss the compositions of each individual drawing and the assembled drawings.

Discuss the differences among the drawings. What factors account for the differences—for example, personal choice, personal style, media used?

REPRODUCTION ASSIGNMENT 2

Color Reproduction

Reproducing color is different in every medium. You must follow different procedures and use different primary colors to reproduce a certain color with paint, with a computer, or with markers. Even after you have matched the colors as closely to the original as you can, the computer color, paint color, and marker colors are easily distinguished.

In this exercise, you will study color mixing and primary colors in various media that absorb and reflect the ambient light. Read Appendices A and C before proceeding with this assignment to better understand color perception and color reproduction.

Materials

Pantone markers, one each for process cyan, process magenta, and process yellow

Acrylic paints, painting supplies

1 color photograph, 3″ x 5″

3 acetate sheets, 3″ x 5″

2 sheets of bristol paper, 5″ x 7″

Masking tape

Procedure

Part 1. Bring to class a small color photograph of a few simple items. Affix the three sheets of acetate, one on top of the other, to one sheet of bristol paper with masking tape.

Reproduce the color photograph with cyan, magenta, and yellow as primary colors. Make dots from one color marker on each acetate sheet. Put yellow dots only on the bottom sheet, magenta on the middle, and cyan on the top sheet. Build up dots of color to approximate the colors seen in the photograph. Where the color is light, make very small dots of color spaced far apart. Where the color is dark or intense, place larger dots closer together. Check your progress to monitor color mixing and to keep the images on the three acetate sheets aligned. Overemphasize the yellow dots so that they are visible under the cyan and magenta dots.

As extra credit, add a fourth acetate sheet with black dots for more contrast and clarity of image.

Part 2. On the second sheet of bristol paper, reproduce the same color photograph with acrylic paints. Use ultramarine blue, cadmium red light, and cadmium yellow pale as primary colors.

Discussion

How well did the primary colors for each medium reproduce the colors in the original image? How are colors reproduced in the original photograph? How is the marker reproduction of the photography like color reproduction in industrial printing? How is color mixing in industrial printing like a pointillist painting, such as Georges Seurat's *Sunday Afternoon on the Island of La Grande Jatte* (Color Plate 1), in which the artist mixed colors by a patterned application of small dots of paint?

REPRODUCTION ASSIGNMENT 3

Color Reproduction: Part 2

This exercise is a continuation of the previous project, but here you will study color mixing and primary colors in light-emitting media.

Each medium has a specific and distinct set of color primaries. For light-emitting media, the color primaries are red, green, and blue, commonly abbreviated as RGB.

Read Appendices A and C for information about color perception and reproduction.

Material

1 color photograph, 3" x 5"

1 video camera, monitor, and (optional) video cassette recorder

1 computer graphic workstation with user-controlled RGB color mixing and video camera input (optional)

Procedure

Use the same color photograph you used for the previous assignment.

Using the video camera, reproduce the color photograph on the monitor. Use the color controls on the monitor to change the color balance so that the image is reproduced only in red, then only in blue, and then only in green. Then change the color balance so that the image is reproduced only in red-green, only in red-blue, and finally only in green-blue. If available, use a video cassette recorder to record a few seconds of these different states.

If available, use a computer graphic workstation that allows you to control the red, green, and blue color mixing. Reproduce your photograph again. First use the drawing functions to outline simple shapes from the photograph. Then use the color-mixing functions to reproduce the colors and add them to the computer graphic image. If your computer gives numeric equivalents for the amounts of primary colors used in each mixture, record this information on a separate piece of paper. Save your image on a floppy disk.

Extra Credit

Experiment with color mixing with theater lights and gels projected on various surfaces. This process involves a combination of light-emitting and light-reflecting color mixing.

Discussion

Place the results of this assignment and the previous assignment in a very bright room. Which reproductions seem to have the most saturated colors? Place both in a dark room. Which reproductions now have the most saturated colors? How do ambient light levels affect color perception for light-emitting and light-reflecting media?

Other factors can influence color perception and reproduction in light-emitting media. Discuss standardizing the monitor's color controls and brightness and contrast settings in order to compare colors in different reproductions.

REPRODUCTION ASSIGNMENT 4

Color Shifts in Reproduction

In this exercise, you will study perceptual factors that affect color perception and color reproduction.

Materials

3 sheets of bristol paper, 18" x 24"

Acrylic paints, painting supplies

Colored pencils

Premixed color samples, paint chips, or assorted papers (optional)

Computer graphics workstation with user-controlled color mixing; floppy disks (optional)

Procedure

You can complete this exercise with acrylic paints, colored pencils, pre-mixed color samples, or a computer graphic workstation. If all media are available, divide the class so that various students complete the project with different media.

Make four 1-inch squares all the same color. That color should be low saturation and in the middle tonal range. Surround each square with 3-inch-square samples of various other colors. Experiment to find surrounding colors that cause an apparent shift in your perception of the center color. Try to make two sets of paired colors in which the center colors appear to change as follows:

1. The center squares appear to be two different colors.

2. Each center square resembles the color of the neighboring outer square more than it resembles the other small square it actually matches (Fig. 4-13).

Glue the completed works onto a piece of white bristol paper.

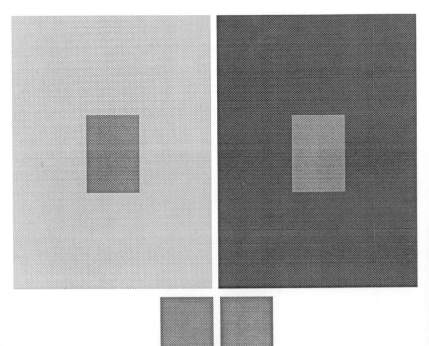

Figure 4-13. The center rectangles are the same tone but seem to resemble the tones of the opposite outer rectangles more than they resemble each other. This example shows how perception of tone can shift. This example is similar to many devised by Josef Albers.

Discussion

What aspects of the physiology of the eye account for apparent shifts in color? Consider the adaptability of the color receptors in the eye and the fatigue factor of the receptors.

Read Josef Albers's *Interaction of Color* (Yale University Press, 1971) for more information about apparent color shifts.

REPRODUCTION ASSIGNMENT 5

Mural/Billboard Project

You can reproduce the same image as a painting, book illustration, mural, or billboard. The medium used influences who sees your visual product and how the visual product is perceived.

A mural and a billboard are similar in scale. However, the mural is often indoors and approached on foot; the billboard is visible from the freeway. The mural may be considered fine art and is generally permanent; the billboard is temporary and usually commercial in subject. The billboard is exposed to a very large and diversified audience. The mural may have a more limited viewing. Because the mural is painted on architecture, it is more monumental and of longer duration, in contrast to the billboard, which is temporarily fixed to a flimsy support. Although a mural may take a variety of shapes, the billboard is usually rectangular. The billboard is seen from highways while viewers are traveling at very high speeds; the mural is more often an image seen at leisure and contemplated by the audience.

However, billboards and murals are similar, and in some instances the distinction between them may become blurred. Both may be vehicles for the same information, are public, and are done in the same scale. Both must be appropriate for the particular surroundings in which they are placed. Some billboard images are painted by hand, although others are printed and still others have moving parts, unusual materials, or lighting as part of the design. Although billboards are generally associated with commercial art (versus fine art), some artists, such as James Rosenquist and Les Levine, were originally billboard painters and have incorporated that imagery into their fine art. In Los Angeles, art projects have been designed for and executed as billboards, and murals frequently line the freeways to be seen by passing motorists.

In this assignment, you will design either a billboard or a mural. You must consider viewer motion of your audience, the distance of your audience from the image, and from what point of view they will see your visual product. You will communicate your idea through small-scale models or other documentation.

Materials

Acrylic paint, painting supplies

Pencil

Paper

Ruler

Camera, film

Procedure

Half the class will complete the mural assignment, and half will do the billboard assignment. The same subject matter should be the theme for both: a prominent topic from the newspaper headlines of the previous week.

As a class, draw up a list of ten possible mural sites on campus and in nearby neighborhoods. Select specific sections of highway as possible sites for billboards.

Make several rough sketches of different ideas for your image. Indicate the surrounding structures and land in your sketches. Keep in mind the potential audience when developing your ideas and under what conditions they will view your visual product. Paint a full-color scale version of the image.

Class Research

The class members should research one of the following topics and present the information to the class:

1. Materials, surface preparation, and painting procedures for mural painting

2. Investigation of local laws or permits that apply to mural painting

3. Possible means to fund a mural or billboard project, such as grants, foundations, and public funds

4. Hiring competent labor and getting insurance

5. Cost for labor, installation, and location rental for billboards

6. Local city ordinances concerning height and locations of billboards

7. Publicity for the project, both during the execution of the project and once completed; investigate local newspapers and art magazines

After students present this information, write detailed steps for the procedures for planning, funding, executing, and publicizing your mural or billboard. Indicate a timetable for how long each task should take to accomplish. As a model, use the algorithm from computer science programming. An algorithm is a sequence of precise statements that describes how to solve a problem in a finite number of steps. It will help you divide the labor necessary for the tasks, list exactly what must be done, and determine the order of execution. This effort is essential for any task performed by a group and helpful for any individual project.

Discussion

What are the difficulties of visualizing a large-scale design from models and diagrams? How would the actual billboard image differ from the model?

Are billboard images less important because they are temporary?

Can this project be planned to allow improvisation while the work is being executed? Who controls the final outcome of the work?

REPRODUCTION ASSIGNMENT 6

Style

Whenever you make a visual product, you are not merely making an isolated object. To some extent, you are also reproducing your own previous work and others' visual products you have seen. In other words, your visual products are done in a combination of your style and also in styles in which others are working. *Style* is the similarity of composition or origin among any grouping of objects. Similarity of composition may be shown through a number of factors, including choice of colors, use of pattern, and proportion of parts within the visual product. Collectively your visual products exhibit your style.

In this assignment you will determine factors of style in other students' work.

Procedure

Bring to class four old, unsigned drawings that the other students have not seen before.

Each student hangs on the wall one drawing that was done in class. Then the class reviews each group of old drawings, trying to match them with one drawing on the wall. Examine the work for identifying traits, favored subject matter, or a persistent style.

Discussion

What drawing habits could be controlled or altered? What long-term interests does each student show? What is the difference between intuition and style?

REPRODUCTION ASSIGNMENT 7

Computer

Whenever you make a visual product, you participate in an act of reproduction that can be extended and multiplied by the use of automation. The most advanced form of automation is the computer, which can make visual products by using commands for numerical values that correspond to electronic circuit functions. Computer programming in what are called high-level languages organizes the commands into many procedures that generate numerical values that may be translated into their geometric equivalents. Highly complex visual objects or the plans for such objects can be generated with advanced technology. In this assignment, you may use an elementary computer program to produce and reproduce complex geometric patterns. In this exercise you will be selecting the number of sides for a closed geometric figure called a *polygon* and will see a series of similar polygons traced within the figure to generate a surface pattern.

Materials

Any computer, whether a large mainframe computer or a smaller microcomputer, may be used to run this assignment. You may have to assign line numbers to each line of the program, which is written in BASIC computer language.

Procedure

Type in the following program:

```
DIM X(21),Y(21)
PI=3.14159

FINDSIDES:
INPUT''NUMBER OF SIDES (20 MAXIMUM)'';N
IF N>20 THEN FINDSIDES
```

```
FOR R=100 TO 0 STEP-4
GOSUB POLYGON
NEXT R

END

POLYGON:
'CALCULATE VERTICES
FOR J=0 TO N
X(J)=120+R*COS(2*PI*J/N)
Y(J)=120+R*SIN(2*PI*J/N)
NEXT J

X(N+1)=X(0):Y(N+1)=Y(0)

'DRAW POLYGON
FOR J=0 TO N
LINE (X(J),Y(J))-(X(J+1),Y(J+1))
NEXT J

RETURN
```

Discussion

After running the program, notice how the pattern of the visual representation changes with different numbers of sides for the polygon because of
the coarseness of the display screen. In very large numbers, these different
polygons may be used to develop visual representations of highly detailed
objects.

POWER

CHAPTER
5

This morning, you are working off-campus in an art gallery as an installer and receptionist. You will be leaving early in the afternoon to go to your position as an unpaid student intern in a nearby design firm. Incidentally, the design firm also uses your gallery to supply paintings and sculpture for some of their design projects.

You have been working in the gallery for several months, and you have been learning a lot about art as a business. You expected that you would be working in a creative and stimulating environment, but you have also become aware of how much the gallery is like any store. The benefits of this job come from associating with prominent artists and observing their interaction with the owner of the gallery. You have also met the collectors who are the gallery's clients and the various art reviewers of the gallery's exhibitions.

While you are at the reception desk, you overhear the gallery owner having a heated discussion with one of the artists represented by the gallery. The artist is angry because the owner has sold very few works over the last few months and has lent the artist's work to both collectors and the owner's friends and associates for display. This was done for extended periods without compensating the artist. The artist argues that the borrowed work cannot be sold because other collectors and buyers cannot see the work. The gallery owner responds that this was done at the gallery's discretion and was meant to create goodwill and a responsive climate for selling the work. The owner also asserts that immediate sales were less important than placing the works in prominent collections and institutions and that this practice was the only way to be chosen for a museum exhibition.

While the discussion continues, one of the collectors arrives and is accompanied by an art reviewer from the local paper. The collector wants to know what the reviewer thinks about a potential acquisition that is currently displayed at the gallery. After studying the painting, the reviewer perceives some problems with the work, stating, "The work doesn't feel right." You wonder about this conclusion because the work has incorporated some classical Greek images you remember seeing in your art history class. The collector decides not to purchase the work but asks the reviewer to come by the house to have lunch. The collector owns other works and wants the reviewer to write an article about the collection for a promotional publication.

You realize it is time to get to your internship at the design firm. You arrive in time to see the delivery of some works by the same artist who was just in the gallery. You wonder whether the works were lent or purchased. On your desk are recently completed design projects that need to be put in folders and filed. You have been promised that in a few more weeks you will be taught how to use the computerized camera and typesetting equipment that are better than the ones the university uses to teach its students. Another employee has called in sick, and you have been given an opportunity to help complete a project. While standing in a common work area, you cut window mats, attach labels, and cover the work with plastic sheets.

As you complete this project, you hear a designer in the next office discuss a project with a client from an interior design firm. You overhear this conversation because the designers' offices are made of temporary dividers that are only 5 feet tall, unlike the large corner office of the firm's owner. That office has a window that looks outside, unlike the interior staff offices whose windows overlook the common work area. The project being discussed involves artwork from the gallery where you work. The client feels that the painting detracted from the project. The designer feels that the painting, because it was made by a prominent artist, enhanced the value of the project.

You become very interested as the discussion continues because the client and designer begin to talk about a sculptor's work that will also be used for the project. You have thought about becoming a sculptor, and the work of this artist has always interested you. The designer remarks that the sculptor's large-scale monumental sculpture was just featured in a museum show in a large city and therefore all the sculptor's work was rapidly increasing in value. The client will buy a sculpture for the project only if the design firm agrees to organize a big publicity campaign about the artist and the installation of the sculpture for this project. The designer agrees because the extra publicity will further increase the value of the work and also because of the potential fee for the designer. In addition, the sculptor has installed a work in a civic plaza that has become controversial because it prevents city workers from quickly reaching their parked cars. The client suggests that this free publicity also will increase the sculpture's value and has already made that sculpture a popular tourist attraction. You remember seeing that work on the local television news program and think that perhaps the designer will save publicity campaign costs with such notoriety. You finish your work and prepare to do some research on why that sculptor is becoming so famous.

THE PERCEPTION OF VALUES

The story contains many examples of power in art and design situations. The power was manifested in the following actions: the art reviewer's negative comments made the collector decide against buying a painting; the gallery owner continued to lend paintings despite the objections of the artist; the designer's semiprivate office represented greater power than the student's but less than the firm's owners have in their private offices; and the sculptor's recent shows and publicity were used to increase the work's value as money and influence.

Power exists as a complex and dynamic set of relations among humans. It can be direct or indirect, concrete or abstract, observable or obscured. It is usually all of these at once, which makes it sometimes difficult to identify. What is important is that it is composed of the directly manifested and indirectly latent relationships among objects and human actions. The relationships among things and people may be evaluated and interpreted as aspects of power.

In its most direct manifestations, power may be the physical, concrete interaction with the world, such as having the path blocked by a sculpture. Power can be direct influence, the "power over someone," or the order impelling someone to do or make something. Direct power also may be the perceptual power of experiencing a visual product for the first time.

An example of the interrelated and indirect nature of power may be the power that the powerless give up, that is, for every instance of someone having power over someone, the subjugated relinquish or give up power. This act of giving up power places the authority for individuals' actions on external agents. These external agents become powerful indirectly through the acquisition and employment of such authority. People slow down when driving past a police car because of such power. Power can be easily institutionalized to create additional influence and values.

More indirect or abstract power can be applied through intermediate media, such as the ability to spend or have money to give orders. The indirect application of power can be seen in the power of wealth, which exists in the perception of one person's relative wealth by others as well as in the capability to use that wealth. Publicity or notoriety often communicates power by using visual products to represent images of wealth or success. Although a book may have a direct power as a doorstop, its indirect power is manifested by its latent knowledge as power. The power of a visual product not only comes in the direct individual perceptual experience but also is amplified when the visual product indirectly moves the viewer to do something else, such as cry or kill, as a result. This power of imagery was shown when a person attempted to assassinate the president after having been influenced by a motion picture that incorporated a similar incident.

From both jobs, as gallery receptionist and as unpaid design intern, you feel a lack of power. All tasks at either location are prescribed by supervisors. You make no decisions about your activities. You cannot even learn to use the computerized camera and typesetting equipment without permission. Power is both action and object; it is simultaneously access to and ownership of technology and objects. Power is manifested directly in the objects but also appears indirectly in the relationships among the visual producers and their clients. You would like to acquire some of this power and influence because you feel powerless to make career moves by yourself. Although the task seems ambiguous and peripheral to the making of visual products, you see the need for power. How do you acquire it?

The jobs with the art gallery and the design firm enable acquisition of power through learning about the interactions among artists, designers, clients, collectors, reviewers, and gallery owners. Education is also a means to gain power. School learning leads to empowerment through knowledge of making visual products in the context of what they mean within culture. Students learn how individuals and institutions confer, use, and exchange power.

A visual producer is empowered by self-expression through craft skill or competence in a medium or process and by communication to an audience. The visual product is an act of communication that expresses both a general message about making visual products and a particular message about an individual's craft skill. An audience member is empowered by fully understanding the messages in visual products. Different persons perceive each visual product differently, yet the range of understanding is defined culturally. The work does not "speak for itself." It is understood only by individually conscious and aware human beings within an environment.

Being powerful requires being competent in making and interpreting visual products within the context of human actions, events, and perceptions. That competence can also be called *literacy*. Literacy is power because it is a cultural competence based not only on linguistic competence but also on complete perceptual competence. A person who is visually literate not only receives and understands visual products but also actively participates in their production. How specifically do you perceive and understand the messages of visual products?

Codes

In general, visual products are messages. Visual products always express and communicate intense personal feelings and a sense of community. Mass communication media heighten this cultural relationship between the personal and the community. Because visual products exist between the personal and the community, the messages of the works are conveyed through a series of codes. *Codes* are conventions that structure the interpretation of visual products. These codes operate in a similar way to the rules of language that help people to read, speak, and write language.

The messages of visual products have multiple meanings that represent the values of their producers and audience. The messages are not always immediately accessible because they are communicated through and structured by codes. For visual producers, this means that they encode the visual product with meaning or value and that the audience for the same visual product decodes that message. Through codes, values are both used and exchanged. For example, the painting encodes the self-expression of the artist. The audience decodes it as many other values, including investment, interior decoration, ownership, and cultural status. These values are changeable, as in the collector's changed perception of the artwork after the reviewer perceived problems with it. This change of mind is an example of a shift in coding and encoding that involves the same object.

Let us look briefly at specific examples of code. Morse code consists of various combinations of long and short sounds that were used to communicate via the telegraph. Combinations of sounds stand for each letter of the alphabet. In addition Morse code has a visual component—dots and dashes that represent the short and long sounds of the code. Morse code arbitrarily assigns meaning to the dots and dashes and to the short and long sounds. The dots and dashes are an arbitrary code with arbitrary referents. A certain combination of sounds does not intrinsically have to stand for any particular letter. What is important is that the code of dots and dashes corresponds to alphabet letters through mutually agreed upon rules of translation. The power of the code exists not in each instance but in the grammatical or logical system that enforces or enables the operation of a code.

As mentioned, codes frequently have visual components. Dress codes are regulations concerning appearance, as some authority decides what people should wear before being allowed to participate in an activity or event. The mutually agreed upon rules for the code do not have to be written down. They are collectively understood. In dress codes, swimwear is not defined as attire for attending church. The rules are never written anywhere, but Sunday best refers to less casual clothing. Even nonchurch-goers understand this code.

Other codes structure understanding of visual products. Under contemporary codes for art, almost anything hung on a wall may be considered art. In Western culture, the frame, the pedestal, the lighting, and the title card are codes that identify an object as art. A person entering a museum knows what not to touch by the implied code that regulates how art objects are presented. If anyone violates that code, the gallery guard will enforce it. In other cultures this code that identifies art does not have the same force or power or even exist at all. As with Morse code, the code's importance is in the system of cultural meanings attached to these arbitrary referents.

When you heard the dispute between the gallery owner and the artist over the display and sale of artwork, whose position did you support? When the gallery owner and artist each perceived the same situation differently, how could the dispute be resolved? For galleries codes of conduct or rules of behavior govern the relationships among galleries, museums, and artists. Between the artist and the gallery owner, these codes place the gallery owner in a position of power. The artist perceives that the gallery controls access to cultural institutions such as museums and collectors. The artist then follows the code of conduct established by the gallery and accepts a percentage of the sales revenues of artwork as opposed to selling the work personally and receiving the total sale price. A visual producer must understand the codes governing a certain situation to acquire competence.

PATTERNS OF VALUE

Coding and decoding must be considered within their general cultural context. Although the collector was making individual decisions about purchasing an artwork, the context for the decision was the contemporary system of values for art as a discipline. An *ideology* is a system of codes that structures the meaning and value of the product and the activity that generates it. An ideology is not a temporary phenomenon but rather a long-term pattern of concepts about a culture that may be influential for decades or even centuries. An ideology represents a systematic pattern of beliefs that enables an individual to have ideas about what a visual product's value is and what it means. Many ideological systems may coexist and conflict within a culture at any moment. As examples, we will describe several current ideologies that deal specifically with visual products, which are called *visual ideologies.*

Formalism

Formalism is a visual ideology that proposes that the meaning and logic of an artwork is contained only within the object itself or the immediate perception of that object. Under formalism, an artwork has a limited cultural context and does not contain social messages as its primary message. Formalists are the group of visual producers who subscribe to this code. They suggest that the composition of the artwork always has the power to determine the meaning of the artwork, apart from context. To the formalist, the subject matter of a work is inconsequential compared to its compositional logic. Therefore, formalists analyze works only in terms of the balance of lights and darks, the handling of the paint, and the balance of shapes and colors within the piece. The formalist would discuss *Still Life with Oysters* (see Color Plate 7) with respect to the placement of figures, the suggestion of mood caused by the handling of pigment, and the organization of colors.

A work has value and meaning in proportion to how much the formalist considers the work as a product of individual genius. Formalism has derived its power through the institutions that support it. The individuals associated with such professional institutions include the various art writers, art educators, and ultimately the artists who come in contact with them. Guilds and academies are early versions of such professional institutions. Formalism remains popular in the twentieth century and is still prescribed by many critics and writers and supported in most art institutions. However, cultural criticism has placed formalism in historical perspective. It has been challenged by other ideologies that have attempted to describe more fully the scope of visual production. (For further discussion of formalism, see Carter Ratcliff, 1974.)

Deconstruction

One ideology that opposes formalism attempts to locate the meaning and value of an artwork in its contextual meaning by dislocating or deconstructing its dominant meaning. That deconstructed dominant meaning is not only the meaning as hypothesized for the period when the painting was produced but also the dominant meanings for all of its subsequent owners and exhibitions to the present day. An analysis of *Still Life with Oysters* could ask what was significant at the time it was painted because it was a manifestation of the growing power and wealth of the Dutch merchant class but could also ask questions about the present value of viewing the painting and about its ownership. This ideology suggests that the meaning of visual products is always contestable. (For further discussion of deconstruction, see Christopher Norris, 1985.)

Other Visual Ideologies

The meaning and value of *Still Life with Oysters* can be interpreted using other ideologies. For example, materialism analyzes the role of visual products as commodities that can be exchanged for currency or other items. *Still Life with Oysters* gains value in relation to the reputation of the artist, the price paid for other works by the same person, the economic and cultural status of the current owner of the work, and the scarcity for works of its kind. These qualities are mutually reinforcing and interdependent. This ideology suggests that the power of the visual product corresponds to economic values. (For further discussion of materialism, see Janet Wolff, 1984.)

Because several visual ideologies exist concurrently, a hierarchy of ideologies emerges, with some dominating and others subservient. The dominant ideology at any one time most strongly characterizes a cultural environment and its systems of value. Although subject to change, the prevailing ideologies assign more specific value and meaning to objects, processes, and ideas. Institutions codify such values through many means, including schools, exhibitions, and communications media such as publicity. In the American art world of the 1950s, formalism was the dominant ideology. The people or groups associated with such institutions who designate such value or control meaning within the dominant ideology are powerful within society.

Currently, gender, race, and class are topics of major ideological alternatives to dominant visual ideologies. (For further discussion on this topic, see Angela Y. Davis, 1983.) For example, feminism is a gender-based ideology that seeks equality for women. One strategy for feminist visual producers is to analyze the relationship between the male-dominated social order and visual products of the past. Feminists seek equitable conditions for the practice of visual production. They analyze artworks in terms of who possessed or owned them, whose point of view is implied in the image, and what social conventions are illustrated. For example, *Still Life with Oysters* represents the images of domestic life and that the world of women is depicted as another male household possession. (For further discussion of feminism, see Griselda Pollock, 1988.)

Thus, when ideological systems are applied to the same works, different values and interpretations of meanings result. Ideologies act as analytical patterns or templates against which not just visual products but all cultural products are measured. These ideologies are not simply patterns used to interpret visual products that already exist, nor are they absolute or fixed in meaning. They are also not accidental but correspond to the historical conditions that influence visual producers as they make new visual products.

PROPORTION

At various times in history, visual products have been evaluated on the basis of theories of beauty, which have been called *aesthetic systems* or *aesthetics*. Aesthetic systems are ideologies that specify idealized codes or propositions for the perception of beauty in visual products or nature. Aesthetics, as a theory of value, is concerned with beauty as seen in proportions and judgments related to beauty, especially moral judgments. These judgments have been institutionalized formally through organizations such as academies and informally through such organizations as craft guilds. For example, the British academy exerted influence on visual production in England beginning in the eighteenth century. Even today, the Academie Française attempts to protect the purity and beauty of the French language from corruption by other languages.

Conventions of female and male beauty from various historic periods provide examples of these proportional aesthetic codes. The ancient Greeks developed canons that determined ideal proportions of male figures in sculpture. Likewise, the female figure has been subject to changing aesthetic proportions. During the Baroque period in Holland, the ideal of feminine beauty was a round-faced, slim-shouldered woman with small breasts and wide hips. In the late twentieth century, thin, large-eyed woman with childlike features were considered highly attractive, as exemplified by anorexic fashion models. During each era, the proportions constituting the ideal human figure changed. The varying proportions were the means by which someone could be judged to be beautiful or ugly. These proportional ideals are often arbitrary and often serve as rationalizations for dominant cultural conventions. However, ideal proportional systems exist, are pervasively applied, and propose what is aesthetically pleasing and what is not.

Advertising uses aesthetics because it suggests that certain products are superior in quality or that personal beauty or status may be enhanced through the use of these products or services. To be effective, an advertisement must create in the viewer a sense of need that can be corrected by some product or service. The audience's diminished sense of personal worth and desire for status are important factors in advertising. (See John Berger, 1973.)

PRODUCTION AND REPRODUCTION

Ideologies do not spring up out of the ground, nor are they maintained by magic. Ideologies must be reproduced, distributed, and consumed through cultural institutions. Such cultural institutions range from the specific professional organizations for visual producers with a specific location, such as a museum, to the more pervasive media industries that communicate visual products and their ideologies by electronic transmission. Such visual products function as information. They can be used or exchanged for something else of value. In cultural history, values continually shift from their original referent in materials to being based on information. This phenomenon recently has been called the *information society*, in which information is based on the acquisition, accumulation, and consumption of data. (For further discussion of the information society, see Daniel Bell, 1976.)

Information is the transformation of data into knowledge. This information is neither book nor object; frequently, it is nothing more than telephone signals or an illuminated computer screen. Just as the information society makes wealth and communication more fluid, it also places value on more ephemeral displays of visual production and the ability to reproduce and proliferate it. Advanced technology can transform the image of a popular monument into digital information to be used for divergent purposes (see Color Plate 13). Concepts such as scarcity have been introduced to motivate individual action in an information society. Scarcity has less to do with objects than it does with desires or wants. Entire industries such as advertising base their activities on the production of desires that do not match needs. Scarcity, necessity, and prestige are constantly being redefined even within this culture; items are assigned high values without any apparent reason. Even in museum giftshops, the value of items from pet rocks to Picasso reproductions are dubious if not contradictory.

ART INSTITUTIONS

Art institutions, such as museums and galleries, maintain visual ideologies and traditions. Artwork takes on added stature, value, and importance when it is displayed in museums. Museums usually have extensive collections, of which they show only a small part. What they choose to show is generally designed to maintain certain ideologies. While the dominant art style produced in America and Europe in the mid-twentieth century was abstract and color based, for example, museums generally displayed Impressionism as the only valid art that was produced in Europe at the end of the nineteenth century. Now, in the postmodern era, Bouguereau, a painter who had previously been considered decorative, sentimental, and decadent, is emerging from the storeroom.

The museum serves as a type of collective memory. The visual products the museum displays reproduce powerful historical imagery. The museum is a collective version of your own memory: Some images from your personal life seem particularly strong and memorable and the visual products in the museum function for society in the same way.

Museums mount special exhibitions that also establish and maintain visual ideologies. Exhibits are used to support the value and status of certain living and dead artists and to certify their importance, which may be partially established already by their sales in galleries. Galleries also are institutions that support and maintain visual ideologies. Galleries generally show a wider variety of contemporary visual products than a museum. Because ideologies represent long-term patterns of thought, however, most of the work shown in both institutions remains within the realm of existent ideologies, despite the appearance of opposition or resistance by individual creative acts.

The visual producer operates within an existing cultural context and makes products that reflect that context. The museum curator, gallery director, and collector are also influenced by that same cultural context. The writers of books and reviewers of visual products present their ideas and critique works based on existing ideologies. A competent reviewer does not simply like or dislike some visual product. Rather, the reviewer questions the meaning of the work as it is defined by current visual ideologies and reproduces that meaning through mass communications media such as a newspaper or magazine.

Educational Institutions

Ideologies are reproduced and distributed through educational institutions. Universities, colleges, and art and design schools teach students current styles of visual production, contemporary ideologies, and current technologies. In addition, your education trains you to fit into the art and design world once you graduate. Your experience in the gallery and the design firm enables you to enter the job market easily after graduation. You may see this as a benefit, but it delimits the notion of art and design production as an autonomous, innovative, creative, or radical activity.

You may be taught in school that visual production is a creative process, and in many ways it is. What you create is contingent on what you have been taught, what materials are available to you, and how you can use your skills to shape the material to make a product that reflects both your self-expression and your social context. However, your training has given you codes of visual production, and your products resemble other visual products. Your work fits into a category that the audience recognizes as art or design work. Your educational institutions provide you with much of your training and information and much information about how you can function in the art and design field. You may feel that you have no room for your own creativity in your visual production and that what you produce has been predetermined by various cultural institutions. Although schools teach you to be "creative and original," you may wonder how this is possible, given institutions that maintain visual ideologies and traditions.

Visual production is more an act of improvisation on a given theme than an act of complete originality. Jazz musicians begin with the structure of a song and, while performing, change and develop it according to their own ideas and the ideas of the other musicians with whom they are playing. In the same way, you also improvise on all the cultural material you have absorbed while you make your visual product. Your visual production can never be totally original, completely spontaneous, or self-generated. The completely original work would make no sense to others as they would be unfamiliar with the elements you use and unable to interpret it. The painting or design you "spontaneously created" bears strong resemblance to other paintings or designs but is primarily an improvisation on them.

Language provides a helpful analogy for this discussion. When you converse with someone, you do not have a script containing everything that will be said. You may start the conversation, but everything else you say depends upon what the other person says and how they say it. To be understood, you both use the same vocabulary and grammatical structure, but each person in the conversation is able to shape the language to express themselves. This is called a *discourse*. Similarly, visual production is improvisation on existing themes. Improvisation is not arbitrary but is individual performance acted in relation to social norms. Improvisation is not invented in a vacuum; it is contingent on what went before and suggests what may follow. It functions like a foreground-background relationship. Your individual performance as you create a visual product is like a momentary foreground against the general cultural background. It is not separate from the background but a distinct part of it. An example of this shifting relationship may be seen in the work of Jackie Winsor, in which the minimalism of the artwork suggests that the viewer consider the larger context for the presentation of visual products, including the role of individual craft, industrial materials, and minimalism as an oppositional response to the formalism of the 1950s (see Color Plate 14).

In the performance of improvisation, freedom or invention must operate in the context of the collective understanding shared by members of the audience. Otherwise, individual self-expression would be incomprehensible to the group. This situation is exactly what you face as you make visual products. Your freedom of expression operates in a context of collective understanding that enables you to communicate your ideas to others.

SYSTEMS OF POWER

Suppose you decide to be a sculptor and wanted to make a living at that occupation. Making sculptures is only part of your task. You may choose to study at a university art department to learn more about your craft, to study contemporary art theory, to receive the criticism of experts, and to begin to acquire a network of associates in your chosen field. During this time, you begin to market your work and perhaps find a collector or two who are interested in your ideas. After graduation, you will need to have your work displayed in a gallery. Having already had some collectors buy your work encourages the gallery to invest time, money, and effort into selling your work. While your sculptures are being exhibited, you want several art critics and reviewers to view and write on the work so that your ideas are explained, your work more widely publicized, and your sculpture validated as important cultural items. After the years have passed and you have had several shows, reviews, and collectors buying your work, you should have a museum show, perhaps in a regional institution but preferably in an art institution in New York, Chicago, or Los

Angeles. After that, a large, hardbound book about your work would be very nice.

This hypothetical career outlines the systems and institutions of power for fine arts, specifically, the university, the gallery, the critic, the collector, the museum, and the publishing industry. These interdependent systems constitute the hierarchies that the artist may encounter as instruments of bureaucracy or careerism. A similar hierarchy exists for any kind of visual product, such as architecture or landscape design. These institutions validate a cultural product; that is, they certify its importance and justify its fame. These institutions define culture. Some visual producers such as Hans Haacke challenge the dominant definitions of culture (see Color Plate 15).

This culture tends to see art and design as separate disciplines. In education, for example, most art classes emphasize expression, particularly self-expression, whereas related classes such as design are "commercial." Art classes discuss the object created in visual production but rarely discuss ways that the artist encodes it with a meaning that the audience decodes and almost never discuss the means by which artwork is circulated. Design classes emphasize communication in that the visual product should reach the widest possible audience.

What has happened is that the act of expression has been falsely separated from the act of communication; expression has been falsely ascribed to artistic activity; and communication has been ascribed to design (see Color Plate 16). However, all visual products, whether classified as art or design, are the inseparable embodiment of both expression and communication within the context of a specific culture. A visual producer such as Barbara Kruger synthesizes both expression and communication in her work (see Color Plate 17).

You can see how this false split between art and design and between expression and communication exists in popular ideas. Practitioners of all areas of visual production experience a general alienation from the rest of the population, and the history of visual production shows increasing divisions among disciplines, especially under industrialization. Historically, many institutions and movements attempted to correct the conception that art and design belong to discrete categories, whether because of technologies used or markets addressed. The British Arts and Crafts movement and the Bauhaus proposed integrated ideologies for the crafts, art, and design. The common ground shared by these movements and institutions is the human basis for visual production. Visual producers may be stereotypically seen either as solitary artists who are misunderstood by all or as designers of advertisements who expediently use any device to capture attention. In actuality, they are rarely one such extreme or the other. Rather, quality design work and artwork are both expression and communication. The effective artist and the effective designer have an idea, an audience, and a means for bringing one to the other. They are often the same individual unencumbered by the disciplinary labels invoked for reasons of power.

We have introduced the concept of power not as an individual act of aggression but as a means to understand and identify interests common to visual producers. We characterize this concept as power because modern art and design have always existed within the context of power relationships, whether dispossessed artists or ministers of culture. We hope that we have made clear that we are not advocating that you as a visual producer aspire to domination or isolation in response. Power exists only among groups of people. For example, artists respond more effectively as groups than as individuals to threats of censorship. We invoke the concept of power in the spirit of envisioning a world with mutual aid and collective action.

POWER ASSIGNMENT 1

Sculpture and Site

Materials

Pencil

Paper

Colored pencils

Camera, film

Procedure

Part 1: Analysis. Divide the class into groups of four. Each group will be assigned a sculpture on campus or in a nearby museum or public area. Analyze the relationship between the sculpture and the site, according to the following points. Each student in the group should complete part of the analysis.

1. *Ground plan:* Take measurements and make an accurate ground plan of the location of the sculpture. Note all open areas, areas of public seating, access paths to sculpture, and any physical or visual barriers to the sculpture.

2. *Sight lines:* Photograph the sculpture from the major paths of approach to the sculpture.

3. *Integrated versus freestanding:* Make sketches or notations for following pertinent points:

   a. Is the sculpture freestanding or on a pedestal?
   b. Is there a distinction between sculpture and surrounding areas?
   c. Is the sculpture similar in style to any surrounding structures?

4. *Lighting:* Note how the sculpture is lit with both natural and artificial light. What is the direction and strength of illumination of natural light?

5. *Audience:* Who sees this work? What is the potential audience, and by what means and speed does the audience approach and see the sculpture (by car, on foot, from above in surrounding buildings)?

   Part 2: Final drawing. Based on the analysis made by the group, each student makes a drawing or set of drawings that alter the sculpture, site, sight lines, and lighting for the sculpture. Take the point of view of one of the following:

1. A city planner

2. A landscape architect

3. An architect

4. A sculptor

Discussion

What is the difference among the points of view of a city planner, landscape architect, architect, and sculptor?

What is the difference between those points of view and the point of view of the public?

POWER ASSIGNMENT 2

Composition and Context: Part 1

Every visual product exhibits interrelated composition and context (Chapter 2). In this assignment, you will study one aspect of the composition of an image, its color.

Materials

Camera

1 roll of color print film, 24 exposures

Procedure

Make 12 photographic exposures of the color blue. Make 12 photographic exposures of the color orange. The objects or scenes you photograph do not matter as long as the resulting image is primarily either orange or blue.

Have the roll of film developed and a proof sheet made from the film.

Discussion

What things were photographed by many class members? Are certain images and items both contextually and compositionally associated with either orange or blue?

Do you commonly associate some qualities or events with certain colors, such as red for passion or green for envy? What is the context that provides colors with these meanings? Do the contextual meanings of colors have compositional reasons?

POWER ASSIGNMENT 3

Composition and Context: Part 2

In the previous assignment, you studied one aspect of the composition of an image, its color. All visual products, however, exhibit interrelated composition and context. In this assignment, you will concentrate on contextual aspects of images, specifically, of kitsch images.

The context determines the meaning and value of an object. For example, a Heinz ketchup bottle has been represented in many ways, as Andy Warhol's *Heinz 57,* a flashlight shaped as a Heinz ketchup bottle, or a bottle of Heinz 57 ketchup. Although the exteriors of these objects are compositionally similar, contextually they are very different. The original function of the ketchup bottle has been transformed by these other applications. In addition, some versions of the ketchup bottle have been contextually defined as art, and others have been defined as kitsch. See Chapter 4 for further discussion on kitsch.

Materials:

Camera

1 roll of color print film, 24 exposures

Procedure

Find and photograph many examples of an image or object whose original function is transformed by its applications. The original image or object can be from fine art (for example, the *Mona Lisa* or Grant Wood's *American Gothic* has been transformed by many different uses and applications), mass culture (for example, the Campbell's soup can transformed by Andy Warhol), architecture (the Empire State building or your favorite monument made into a pencil sharpener), or industrial or home design.

Have the roll of film developed and 3" x 5" prints made of each image.

Discussion

Webster's New Collegiate Dictionary defines *kitsch* as "artistic or literary material of low quality designed to appeal to current popular taste." Consider this definition when you look at the photographs the students made. Are any of the objects kitsch?

Define *camp.* How do you distinguish *kitsch* and *camp?*

A visual product may have varying meaning based on contextual conditions. How does this relate to the concept of encoding and decoding meaning? (See chapter 5.)

POWER ASSIGNMENT 4

Improvisation

Improvisation is individual performance within social brackets. Improvisation is not arbitrary or invented out of the blue but is contingent on what went before and suggests what may follow. The individual performance is like a momentary foreground against the general cultural background. It is not distinct from the background but part of it.

In improvisation, freedom or invention operates in the context of the collective understanding shared by the visual producers and the audience. Otherwise, individual self-expression would be incomprehensible to the group. Improvisation operates in jazz performances and in everyday conversation. In visual production, creativity or originality is actually improvisation.

Materials

Glue stick

Scissors or cutting knife

Acrylic paint, painting supplies

1 sheet illustration board, 24" x 30"

Procedure

Use the results of Power Assignments 2 and 3 as starting points in this assignment. Select and photocopy some photographs or proof sheets from these assignments. Make a collage on the illustration board combining photocopied images with your own drawing and painting. Continue the same themes of the original imagery, but transform it by enlarging and simplifying the images and by your added painting and drawing.

Discussion

How are the class results of this project contextually different from the original photographs upon which they were based?

Discuss how the use of different media and personal interpretation are improvisation.

POWER ASSIGNMENT 5

Communication Design Study

Information can be conveyed in many ways. The various media and methods of communication add contextual information to the message being communicated.

In this assignment, you will study television weather reports to learn how information is changed contextually. Compositionally, the weather reports are all the same, consisting of reports of present conditions, recent past developments, and the forecast. In fact, all reports come from the same source, the National Weather Service. However, each television station encodes other information and messages about the weather and itself while giving the weather forecast. You will develop and use a method to compare how information is communicated verbally and visually and ways to determine other encoded information.

Materials

Video tape recorder

Television

Videocassette tape

Procedure

Work in groups of four for this assignment. Each group is responsible for recording on videotape the weather report from a specific television station at a specific time. All groups will record weather reports from the same day and approximately same time, but from different channels. Review and analyze your weather report, using the following points:

1. *Groundplan:*
   Make as detailed a drawing as possible of the weather report area within the physical space of the television studio; if possible, indicate how that space fits with the news area.

2. *Cameras:*
   Number of cameras used for report: _____

Sequence of shots used and information presented with each shot: _____

Indicate on groundplan the likely camera locations for the broadcast.

3. *Sources and use of images:*

   Amount of time of nonstudio or location footage:

   _____

   Amount of still imagery: _____

   Amount of moving imagery: _____

   Amount of imagery used as text background:

   _____

4. *Graphic information:*
   Record what maps, symbols, and background graphics were used. Use the storyboard format for this part of the assignment.

5. *Kinds of verbal information:*

   Amount of time for reporting weather: _____

   Amount of time for quips, lead-ins, and chatter:

   _____

6. *Other standards:*
   Each group should determine two other quantitative criteria against which your broadcast can be measured. List two nonquantitative criteria that you think are important to analyze the broadcast.

Discussion

Besides forecasting the weather, what other information about the weather, the television station, and the weatherperson was conveyed in the weather report? Do some stations use the weather segment as advertisement, as a public relations tool, as entertainment, or as an educational segment?

The Visual System

The visual system is the eye and brain and their interaction with the environment. The three key factors in perception are the visual system, the available light, and what the person is seeing. In addition, motion is important for perception. This appendix should be read in conjunction with Chapter 1 on perception and with Appendix C on color.

THE STRUCTURE OF THE HUMAN EYE AND ITS INTERACTION WITH LIGHT

Light triggers different sensory responses in nerve cells in the body. For example, the pain of a sunburn is the skin's nervous reaction to overexposure to ultraviolet light. Sight is the nerve sensations of the visual system that are triggered by light. These sensations begins when a certain range of light strikes the retina.

Eyes are roughly spherical. At the front is the *lens,* which focuses light and allows it to pass through the *pupil,* the opening into the eye. The *iris* is the colored part of the eye surrounding the pupil; it expands or contracts to let more or less light into the eye. The light entering the eye strikes the back wall of sphere, which is covered with a membrane called the *retina.* The retina is composed of nerve cells sensitive to light. The *fovea* area in the retina is the location of greatest visual acuity (Fig. A-1).

Your waking environment is full of light. The environmental light by which you see is the available or *ambient light* at that moment. In the daytime, outdoors, ambient light is the sunlight. Light is electromagnetic radiation, which includes radio waves, infrared light, visible light, ultraviolet light, x-rays, and gamma rays. You can see only visible light.

Visible light affects vision both by its quantity and quality. The *quantity* of light is the amount that is present overall. At night, light quantity is

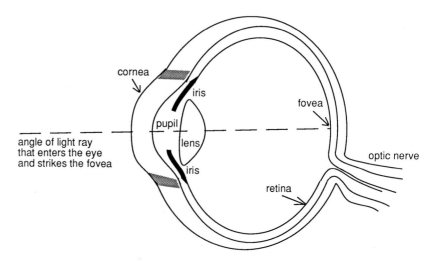

Figure A-1. Cross-section of the human eye.

low, but at noon it is high. The quantity of light must fall within a certain range of vision. If it is too low, you see nothing; if it is too high, you are blinded. Your visual system can respond to a great range of light levels, from a very faint light at night to bright midday sunlight on snow.

The *quality* of visible light is its wavelength composition, to which the visual system responds with the sensation of color. Visible light can produce the sensation of red, orange, yellow, green, blue, indigo, and violet in the visual system. All light components together give the sensation of white light (see Color Plate 3). The ambient light quality changes at different times of day; midday light is different from the light quality of sunset, when red frequencies predominate.

The eye's light-sensitive cells, located on the retina, are called *photoreceptors.* There are two kinds, rods and cones. The *rods* detect varying quantities of light, but no color sensation occurs when the rods are stimulated by light. Rods operate in low light, are spread in more peripheral areas of the retina, and are not associated with sharp vision. The *cones* respond to the quality of visible light. This response is called *color perception.* Cones operate in high light and not in low light, which is why people do not see colors in the dark even though they are still able to distinguish shapes. The cones are concentrated at the center of the retina, the fovea, and represent the area of sharpest vision.

Color vision exists completely within the visual system because color vision is the visual system's biological reaction of light. "Colored" light or "colorful" objects are misconceptions because color is not in the light or the object. Color is quite simply the sensation that results when certain frequencies of light strike certain photosensitive cells. Cones that do not function result in some degree of color blindness. Rods that do not function cause night blindness.

Three kinds of cones enable perception of color. Each kind is stimulated by certain light frequencies. The *R-cones* are sensitive to light from 380 to 700 nanometers (nm) and respond best to 570 nm of light, for red. The *G-cones* also are sensitive to light ranging from 380 to 700 nm of light but peak at 540 nm light, perception of green. The *B-cones* are sensitive to light wavelengths shorter than 540 nm and are most sensitive at 440 nm of light, resulting in the perception of blue.

Color perception is based on pattern. The retina is composed of a pattern of intermingled R-, G-, and B-cones, along with the rods. If two kinds of cones are stimulated at once, other colors are perceived. Red plus blue equals magenta; red plus green equals yellow; green plus blue equals cyan. Maximum stimulation of all three kinds of cones results in the perception of white. Black is perceived when no cones or rods are stimulated (see Appendix C). Most of the colors seen are caused by stimulating all three kinds of cones to some extent.

The visual system adjusts or adapts to different quantities and qualities of light. Balanced perceptions are therefore possible under extremely varying light situations. *Achromatic adaptation* is the ability of the visual system to adjust to different quantities of light. The visual system can achromatically adapt to light ranges of 1 : 1,000,000 in a matter of seconds. Leaving a dark theater to go outside in the daylight temporarily blinds people until they adapt to the new quantity of light.

Chromatic adaptation is the ability of the visual system to adjust to varying qualities of light. A red shirt may look red in daylight, under fluorescent lights, or by candlelight, but the wavelengths of light that reach the eyes are very different in these three situations. Daylight is composed of a specific balance of all visible light. Fluorescent light is composed primarily of light wavelengths that result in the perception of blue and green. Candlelight is composed primarily of light at the red end of the light spectrum. However, the visual system adapts to these environmental shifts in light and to the fact that the light contains more of certain wavelengths. Due to chromatic adaptation, colors in objects seem constant, even though they are always changing as the ambient light changes.

Chromatic adaptation may be triggered by seeing large areas of a single, saturated color. For example, staring at a large patch of saturated color and then looking at a white wall causes a different-colored afterimage (see Color Plate 12). This afterimage occurs because the visual system makes a chromatic adaptation that shifts color perception from the overstimulus of one kind of cones to emphasis on the less-stimulated cones. After a few moments, the afterimage fades, and the visual system adapts chromatically to the white wall.

ORGANIZATION OF THE LIGHT IN YOUR ENVIRONMENT

On a bright day, the environment is full of light reflecting from surfaces, reflected from particles in the atmosphere, and shining from the sun, all bouncing in all directions. Perceptions, however, are organized visual experiences. The first way that light is organized—or patterned—is very basic. When a person looks out straight ahead and not up or down, the light rays above are those from the sun or reflected by the atmosphere. In the daytime, this light is bright and luminous. The light rays below are those reflected by objects or by the earth and are usually a lower light level than daytime sky. This light-above, dark-below condition adds to a person's sense of up and down. This basic distinctive light pattern is immediately apparent over the ocean or over a flat Kansas field; in the middle of a large city with tall buildings and artificial lights, this pattern is not as visible.

Even though ambient light is composed of all rays bouncing in all directions, the light that enters the eyes in the act of seeing is composed only of those rays that shine directly toward the eyes from the light source or that are reflected directly toward the eyes from some surface. In this way light is patterned and made distinct from ambient light. The pattern of light rays that enters the eyes during seeing is the *optic array,* in contrast to the ambient array that is composed of all light rays. The optic array is a structured sampling of available ambient light. The optic array that reaches the eyes is the selective reflection from surfaces and facets of objects that face the eyes at any one instant. Each viewer in every position receives a unique optic array pattern. Read Chapter 1 on perception and James J. Gibson, 1966, for more information on the ambient and optic arrays.

THE PERCEPTION OF OBJECTS

Objects that reflect, emit, or refract light can be seen. These objects, because they reflect, emit, or refract light, also structure ambient light and affect the light that reaches the eyes.

First we will discuss objects that reflect light. When illuminated by the sun or artificial light, these objects absorb some portion of the visible light spectrum and reflect the remainder. That nonabsorbed light, when it reaches the eyes, is what is seen. When the ambient light strikes a red box, the surface of that box absorbs all "nonred" visible light (frequencies corresponding to orange, yellow, green, blue, indigo, and violet) and reflects back the frequency that produces the red sensation in the visual system. In a sense, therefore, we could say that a red object is actually

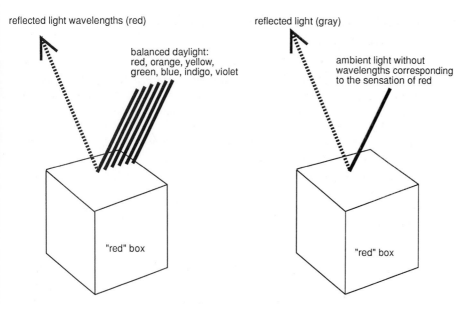

reflected light wavelengths (red)

balanced daylight:
red, orange, yellow,
green, blue, indigo, violet

"red" box

reflected light (gray)

ambient light without
wavelengths corresponding
to the sensation of red

"red" box

Figure A-2. The perception of color depends upon the composition of the ambient light.
"Red" boxes appear gray if illuminated by light that does not contain wavelengths corresponding to the sensation of red.

"not-red," because it absorbs all other colors and "rejects" and reflects
red (Fig. A-2). The perception of reflective colors is dependant upon the
ambient light quality. If the band of the spectrum that produces the optical sensation of red is missing from the ambient light, then red is not seen
at all. If only "green" light is available, the red box appears gray (Fig. A-2).

In addition to color, the box's structure alters the light reaching the
eyes by the way light reflects off its surfaces. From some point on the
box's surface, ambient light will bounce directly to the eyes and reflect a
high quantity of light. At other points, the light glances off the surface
and returns a low light quantity to the eyes. These greater or lesser light
quantities provide the viewer with the object's structural information. In
addition, this process structures and transforms ambient light (Fig. A-3).
A portion of this structured ambient array enters the eyes as the optic
array.

Second, light-emitting objects, such as fire, stars, the sun, artificial
lights, and a television transmission, which are not dependent upon the
ambient light quality for their color, can be seen. However, they must
emit light that is distinguishable in quality and/or quantity from the ambient light to be seen. For example, dim starlight cannot be seen in bright
daylight. Also, in direct sunlight, a television image appears very faded.

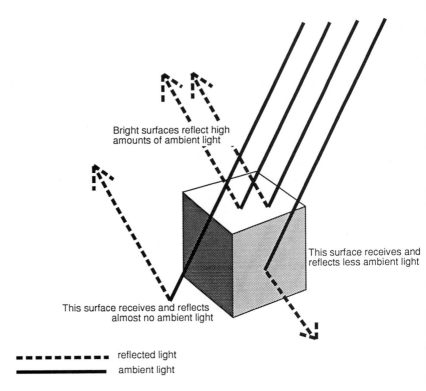

Figure A-3. Ambient light is transformed and structured when it is reflected from surfaces of objects in the environment. Surfaces facing the direction of the light receive and reflect more light than surfaces away from the direction of the light. Bright and dark tonal variations are perceived from surfaces, depending upon whether those surfaces face the light.

At noon, whether a neon sign is off or on may not be readily apparent, but an illuminated neon sign is easily seen in the low night light.

Finally, light can be refracted, that is, deflected or bent, when it passes obliquely from one medium to another of different densities. The bending of light often makes the medium visible. A prism refracts and separates light into bands so that the colors associated with various wavelengths are visible. Among the environmental examples of light refraction, the atmosphere refracts light, causing blue skies, colorful sunsets, and the twinkling of stars. Raindrops suspended in the air refract light that causes rainbows when light hits them at a specific angle. Rippling water bends direct sunlight into bright bands and dark spots on the blue bottom of a swimming pool. Glass of varying thicknesses causes distortions in the scenes beyond it.

MOTION AND HUMAN VISION

The photoreceptors of the eye are designed to detect change, not a constant condition. If neither the eye nor the perceived scene moves at all, fatigue and a curious kind of blindness result. Without motion of any kind, a person would quickly be unable to see. Human physiology has built-in movement to prevent this problem from happening. The eye is subject to frequent head, body, and eyeball movements. In addition, the eye constantly experiences saccadic motion, which is rapid, tiny movements that refresh the retinal image. To further add movement to perception, much of what people observe in everyday life is moving. Without movement, sight is impossible.

Vision is not composed of just a single image. Unlike a photograph, which isolates and frames a scene, vision is continuous and frameless, with sequences of scenes that vary slightly from those that preceded them. Motion is therefore an integral part of vision.

Composition

AREAS OF EMPHASIS

In making a visual product, visual elements must be organized to make them intelligible to the audience or to carry the message that is to be communicated. Each audience member also organizes visual elements to receive the message of the visual product. This organization is the *composition* of the visual product. Composition is not a fixed or static condition. A visual producer organizes visual elements according to past perceptions, experiences, and the culture. The producer and the audience share in the creation of a composition, and it is a mutual act of communication. Do not presume that the everyone sees a visual product the same way. The composition is the result of the interaction between an audience and a visual product.

Two factors are involved in organizing visual elements. The first is the relationship among elements, which is governed by grouping concepts, symmetry concepts, and virtual space. The second factor is the structure and shape of the visual product itself, which affects the organization of the visual elements contained within it and, ultimately, the perception of the visual product.

The composition of a visual product has certain areas that draw more attention, even if the composition appears to be devoid of objects. Usually many visual elements are contained within a composition. These elements are more or less noticeable, depending on their placement within the composition.

The following are the areas of emphasis within a composition, based on the structure of the visual product. Remember that these areas of emphasis are not fixed; they are contingent on the relationships among the visual producer, the product itself, and the audience.

MAJOR AND MINOR AXES

The major and minor axes within any composition's shape are areas of emphasis within that composition. Visual elements placed along the format's major and minor axes are more noticed by the viewer.

An *axis* is an implied straight line, around which shapes may seem to rotate. A figure or shape may be symmetrical around an axis. An axis can also be the straight line implied by direction, motion, growth, or extension. When a person looks downward from an erect posture, the major axis runs through the center of the body, from the top of the head to the space between the feet. This implied line defines the line of rotation, the axis of symmetry, and the line of growth of the body. Stretching the arms outward from the shoulders defines the minor axis of the body. The hips are a lesser minor axis. Bending or stooping creates new axes in the body; in fact, each new change in orientation and position creates new sets of axes.

The major and minor axes are easy to find in the rectangular composition common to many paintings and graphic design products. An implied horizontal line is halfway between the top and bottom edges, and an implied vertical line is halfway between the left and right edges of a rectangular composition. These lines are the major and minor axes, with the longer of the two being the major axis. They form a central cross in the composition. In addition, the diagonals of a rectangular composition are

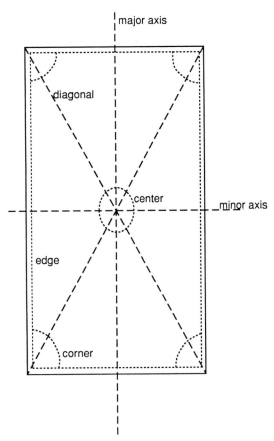

Figure B-1. This diagram shows major and minor axes and areas of emphasis within a rectangular composition.

axes of emphasis (Fig. B-1). A visual product with a nonrectangular composition may have a horizontal and vertical central cross that are the axes; otherwise, the axes parallel the longest edges of the composition (Fig. B-2).

In the case of architecture or sculpture, the major and minor axes may at first seem difficult to find. The perception of buildings and sculptures changes as they are seen from different points of view. Thus, their major and minor axes are different from every different angle from which they are seen (Fig. B-3).

The visual producer structures the vision of the audience by organizing the composition along the axes of the visual product. The gaze of the audience follows these axes. Remember that perception is a continuous series of images because the human eye is constantly scanning. These axes are dynamic entities because they indicate the direction of the viewers' gaze as they indicate the direction of the mass of the product. Therefore, these axes are implicit vectors. A *vector* is an entity that has a direction and is commonly shown as a line with an arrow on one end.

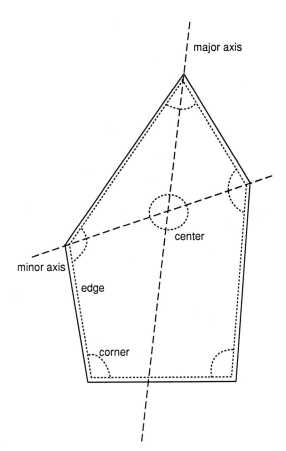

Figure B-2. This diagram shows major and minor axes and areas of emphasis within a nonrectangular composition.

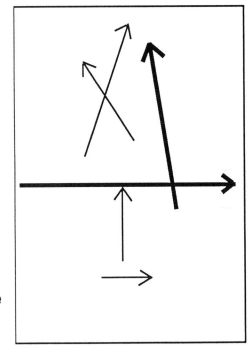

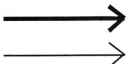 major axis within viritual space

minor axis within virtual space

Figure B-3. These photographs show David Smith's *Cubi XX* from three points of view. The virtual space of each view is different because the virtual space is the perceptual combination of foreground and background. The major and minor axes are different in each view also.

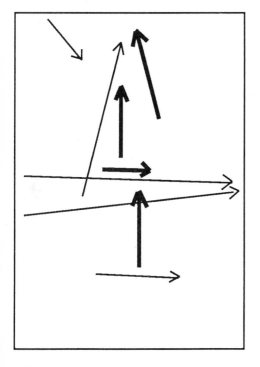

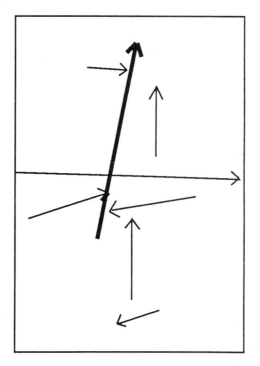

CENTER

The approximate visual center of any visual product is an area of emphasis within the composition. Any visual element placed at the center of a composition is emphasized because of that placement. In most paintings and graphic design, the center is the crossing point of both the major and minor axes and the implied diagonals of the rectangular shape (Fig. B-1).

Nonrectangular compositions also have approximate centers, defined by the intersection of the major and minor axes. In sculpture and architecture, the implied center is different for each possible point of view and is defined by the major and minor axes within that view (Figs. B-2 and B-3).

COMPOSITION BOUNDARIES

The outer edges of a composition are areas of emphasis (Figs. B-1 and B-2). The edges of a visual product are vectors because, along with the major and minor axes, they indicate the directions of the mass of that visual product. When people look at a visual product, their eyes follow not only the major and minor axes but also the edges of a visual product, so that vision is structured by the compositional order.

The corners of any visual product are areas of emphasis within the composition because they represent the meeting of two edges.

Sometimes a visual product is so large that it cannot be seen entirely at any instant. In these cases, the edges of the composition of the total visual product may not structure perception of it. Instead, the visual product is perceived as a group of fields that are defined by the major and minor axes within the visual product. Each of these fields has its own areas of emphasis (Fig. B-4).

THE SHAPE OF THE VISUAL PRODUCT

Different cultures develop typical or standard composition shapes for various visual products. In this culture, paintings are usually rectangular, and buildings are typically based on variations of the cube. In encountering such compositions, an audience tends to ignore them and concentrate on the visual elements within them. The composition in these cases can be said to be *transparent,* in the sense that it is taken for granted or seen as given. It becomes background to the visual elements in the foreground. A composition becomes *opaque* when the audience becomes intentionally aware of its relationship to both composition and elements. Transparency and opacity are present in all visual products. The relative transparency or opacity of a composition indicates how common such compositions are within a culture. For example, boulders or tree trunks as the composition for visual products would be opaque to Western eyes. To Canary Island-

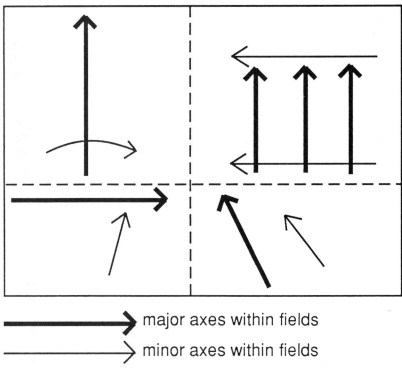

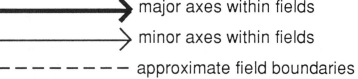

——————————▶ major axes within fields

—————————▷ minor axes within fields

— — — — — — — approximate field boundaries

Figure B-4. Fields contain varying major and minor axes.

ers, who carved faces in large boulders, or to the American Northwest Indians, who carved totem poles, these compositions would be transparent.

An unusual composition for a visual product becomes a point of emphasis in the consideration of that visual product (Fig. B-5). For example, the composition shape of a triangular building or a curved painting becomes foreground, and often that product is identified by its shape. The shape of a rectangular billboard does not draw attention, but a round billboard would be noticed.

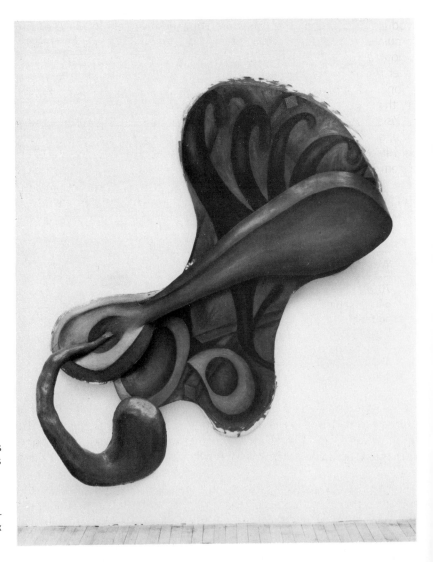

Figure B-5. In this culture, paintings whose compositional shape is rectangular are most common. That shape is relatively transparent for compositions in this culture. Elizabeth Murray's painting does not have a rectangular composition; therefore, the composition is relatively opaque. Murray, *Pompeii*, winter 1987, oil on canvas, 87" x 69.5" x 13".

Color

PERCEPTION

The visual system, available light, and the perceived objects interact to produce color vision. The *cones* are light-sensitive cells in the eye, and stimulation of cones results in color vision (see Appendix A). Color vision is not the same for every individual, due to differing cone sensitivity and other factors such as fatigue. For example, 8.5 percent of the male population and 0.5 percent of the female population are color defective, meaning that their cones do not function "normally."

Visible light ranges across wavelengths from 380 to 700 nanometers (nm), or even over a broader range if sufficient energy is available. Visible light itself is not colored but triggers the sensation of color in the visual system. The varying wavelengths of light determine the *quality* of visible light. By contrast, the *quantity* of visible light is the amount of available light, resulting in the sensation of brightness or darkness. The chart below shows the relationship between wavelengths and color responses in the cones.

Wavelength	Color Sensations	Maximum Cone Sensitivity
700–650 nm	Red	
640–590 nm	Orange	
580–555 nm	Yellow	570 nm: R-cones
540–490 nm	Green	540 nm: G-cones
480–460 nm	Blue	
450–440 nm	Indigo	440 nm: B-cones
430–380 nm	Violet	

The sensation of pure or *saturated* color is experienced if the eyes are exposed to only one wavelength of light. Most color sensations are the result of retinal stimulation by mixed and varying wavelengths of light. These sensations are experienced as duller, less saturated, or *desaturated* colors.

To be seen, an object must change the optic array that reaches the eyes. This change occurs when the object emits its own light or absorbs and reflects ambient light. Color is perceived in objects when they change the quality—or wavelength composition—of the light reaching the eyes.

PATTERN

The colors from the environment can be reproduced with art or design media. To understand color perception and color reproduction, the visual producer needs to know about color mapping systems, whose patternlike qualities help to explain relationships.

Color has to be analyzed and broken down into some basic components to be understood. We will look at two different color identification and mapping systems and study how color is analyzed in them.

The International Commission on Illumination (Commission Internationale d'Eclairage or CIE) developed a system to identify colors with instruments that measure components of light. The *CIE system* determines three numeric values, *X, Y,* and *Z*, which identify colors very much like color identification based on stimulation of the R-, G-, and B-cones. The light from any source or reflected from any surface can be broken down into three numerical values that specifically identify the color. Certain sets of number combinations are also given common names. The chart below lists the CIE numeric equivalent for spectral colors and the dominant wavelength for some common pigments.

Wavelength	X (red)	Y (green)	Z (blue)	Paint Pigments
700: red	11.4	4.1	—	
660: red	164.9	61.0	—	Alizarin Crimson: 628
620: orange	854.4	381.0	0.2	
580: yellow	916.3	870.0	1.7	Cadmium Orange: 586.9
540: green	290.4	954.0	20.3	Zinc White: 569.5
500: green	4.9	323.0	272.0	Emerald Green: 511.9
460: blue	290.8	60.0	1669.2	Cobalt Blue: 474.6
420: indigo	134.4	4.0	645.6	
400: violet	14.3	0.4	67.9	

The *Munsell color system* is based on totally different color components (see Color Plates 9 and 10 and Figs. C-1, C-2, and C-3). In the Munsell color system, colors are organized according to three different qualities: hue, value, and chroma. *Hue* is similar in meaning to the common use of the word *color*. It is the attribute that allows a color to be classified as, for example, red or yellow. *Value* is the perceived or apparent lightness or darkness of a color. Another term for value is *tone*. *Chroma* is the saturation or purity of a color. A high-chroma color is a vivid, pure, or saturated color; a low-chroma color is dull or grayed.

The Munsell color system is arranged roughly as a sphere around a center vertical axis of gray tones, with white at the top and black at the bottom. Like the white to black along the center axis, all colors in the Munsell system are arranged according to value, so that the lightest are at the top of the sphere and the darkest at the bottom. The grays of the

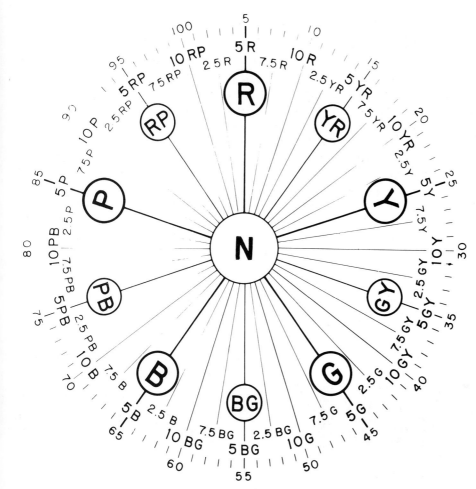

HUE SYMBOLS AND THEIR RELATION TO ONE ANOTHER

Figure C-1. In the Munsell system of color notation, hues are arranged in a circle, with saturated colors at the edges and neutral colors at the center. The ten major hues are the principal hues, which include red (R), yellow (Y), green (G), blue (B), and purple (P); and the intermediate hues, which include yellow-red (YR), green-yellow (GY), blue-green (BG), purple-blue (PB), and red-purple (RP).

central axis and the colors near them are low-chroma or low-saturation colors. Vivid or high-chroma colors are at the outer edges of the sphere. The principal and intermediary hues in the Munsell system are yellow, green-yellow, green, blue-green, blue, purple-blue, purple, red-purple, red, and yellow-red. They are arranged around the outer sphere like the colors in a light spectrum.

Figure C-2. In the Munsell system of color notation, saturated colors are arranged in a ring along the outside of the sphere. Low saturated colors and grays are arranged vertically at the center of the sphere, with light tones at the top and dark tones at the bottom. White and black are located at opposite ends of the vertical axis.

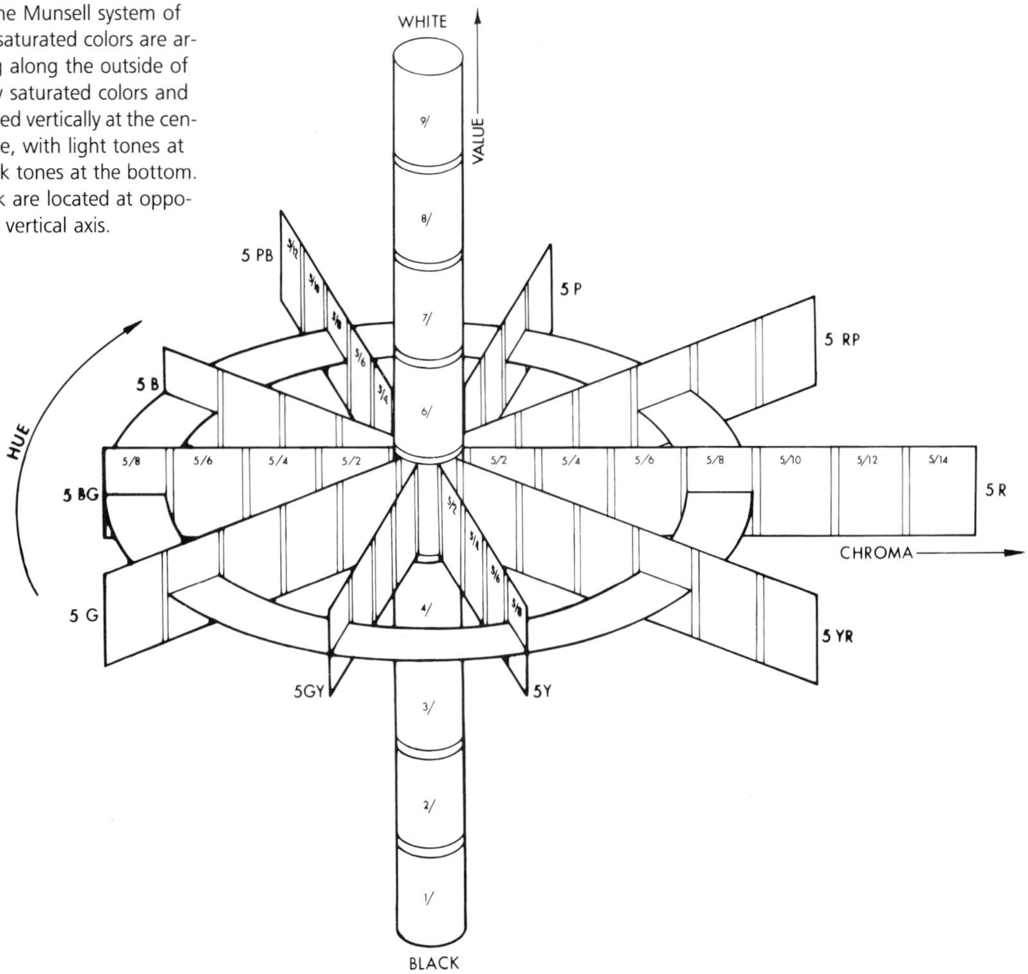

WHITE

VALUE

5 PB   5 P

5 B   5 RP

HUE

5 BG   5 R

CHROMA

5 G   5 YR

5GY   5Y

BLACK

In the Munsell color system, colors close to each other are similar. Similar hues, such as red, red-orange, and orange, are in close proximity around the outer sphere. The varying values of one color, such as light red, red, and dark red, are arranged in vertical columns. The chroma variations of a color, such as vivid red, strong red, red, and grayish red, are arranged along a horizontal axis from the outer edge of the sphere to the center.

Unlike the CIE color identification system, which is based on measurements of light by instrumentation, the Munsell color system is not based on numerical measurements. For the CIE system, the distinctions of color hue, value, and chroma are not important for color classification. The CIE system may seem more objective because it is based on numeric measurements as a method of standardizing color identification. The Munsell system also standardizes color identification. It assigns alphanumeric codes to identify colors, but these codes are not the result of measurement by instrumentation. Also, the National Bureau of Standards has assigned specific color adjectives to be used before hue names to correspond to specific Munsell colors. We used some of these adjectives in the previous paragraph: light, dark, pale, vivid, strong, grayish. When these adjectives are used with hue names, they are not simply vaguely descriptive; they stand for specific colors in the Munsell system.

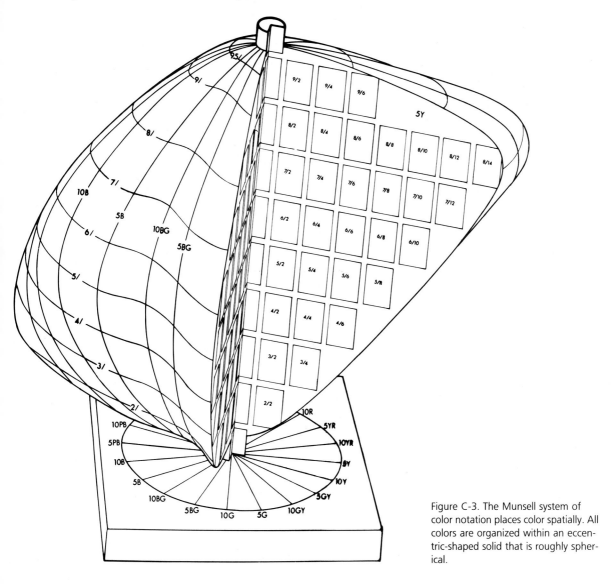

Figure C-3. The Munsell system of color notation places color spatially. All colors are organized within an eccentric-shaped solid that is roughly spherical.

PROPORTION

The Munsell and CIE color classification systems are ways to identify and produce specific colors under controlled conditions. In contrast, color perception cannot be standardized because it is always an act performed by an individual in some particular circumstance, and this experience can never be standardized. Color perception as it is experienced is always relative and proportional. Some of the factors that make color perception a relative, proportional experience are color perception deficiency, chromatic adaptation, and quality of ambient light. In addition, color perception is culturally determined.

Color perception is not the same in every individual. As mentioned above, a significant portion of the population is color-defective, or color-blind to some extent. The color perceptions of even those who have "normal" color vision are affected by very bright light, which bleaches color, and by low light, when colors fade to gray. The ambient light affects color vision. If the ambient light is *fluorescent,* that is, contains an excess of light with wavelengths corresponding to green, then color perception is proportionally more green and less red in everything seen.

However, the highest relativity in color perception is experienced as a result of *chromatic adaptation,* a qualitative adjustment in the visual system that can be explained with an example. Staring at a red dot on a blank page for thirty seconds and then looking quickly to a blank white wall produces an apparent blue-green dot on that wall. The visual system produces that apparent dot because of chromatic adaptation. After staring at red for so long, the visual system makes a qualitative adjustment by discounting the information from the red cones and emphasizing any sensory input from the blue and green cones. The blue-green dot perceived on the white wall is the result of that qualitative adjustment. Then the blue-green dot begins to fade as the visual system chromatically adapts again.

This example of chromatic adaptation is extreme, but it is a phenomenon that occurs to some extent in all color perception. In *Interaction of Color* (1975), the artist Josef Albers described his many experiments in color relativity due to chromatic adaptation. A particular color may appear to change in value, chroma, or hue depending on the colors that surround it (see Color Plate 12; in other texts this apparent change is called *simultaneous contrast*). Large areas of that particular color are less affected by surrounding colors than a small patch of that color (Fig. C-4).

Finally, color perception is relative because it is culturally conditioned. An individual may perceive a color differently because of expectations that are due to cultural conditioning. The assigning of names and attributes to colors is an example of such conditioning or cultural convention. For example, the terms *warm* and *cool* are used in reference to the "color temperature" of various hues. Some books describe yellow, orange, and

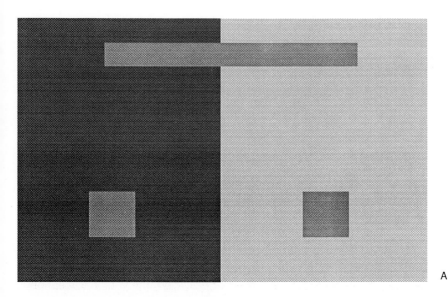

A

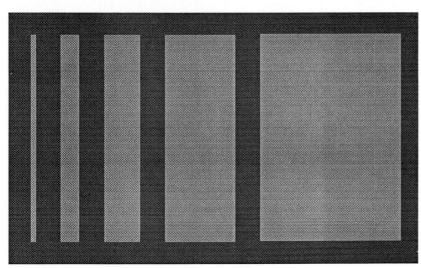

B

Figure C-4. Perception of tone and color is relative. Perception of a particular tone is affected by the tones that surround it. In (A), all of the smaller shapes are the same tone. However, the small squares appear different tonally because of the surrounding lighter and darker tones. In (B), perception of a tone is affected by the size of the area the tone covers. Although all enclosed rectangles are the same tone, they may appear different because of their varying sizes. These examples are chromatic adaptation. Chromatic adaptation operates on the same principles except that it involves color perception instead of simply tonal perception.

red as warm colors and green, blue, and purple as cool colors. Any of these colors in certain contexts could be called either or both warm and cool. No universal agreement exists on the meaning of color in relation to temperature.

As another example of cultural conditioning in color perception, someone in this culture may say that tree trunks are brown, despite perceptual evidence to the contrary. Within different cultures, a desaturated color such as olive may be associated with greens, browns, or yellows. Literary evidence suggests that the ancient Romans did not distinguish between blue and green (Eco, 1985).

PRODUCTION AND REPRODUCTION

Color can be reproduced in a variety of art and design media, both reflection and transmission media. *Reflection media* are those whose apparent colors are the result of the absorption and reflection of ambient light; *transmission media* such as video and television emit light in wavelengths that produce the sensation of colors in the visual system. Reflection and transmission media have different systems of *color primaries.* Primary colors are those that combine to yield the largest number of apparently new colors within a medium.

In painting, the primary colors are red, yellow, and blue. Mixing these primary color pigment particles together creates the perception of other colors. Mixing red and yellow results in the perception of orange. Mixing red and blue results in purple; mixing blue and yellow gives green. Green, orange, and purple may be called secondary colors. (This terminology is not standardized among all color applications. For example, the Munsell color system assigns different colors to the classifications of primary, intermediary, and secondary hues. Charts called *color wheels* are simplifications of the Munsell system. These charts only place primary and secondary colors in an arrangement that often suggests color relationships such as adjacent and opposite or complementary colors. These relationships are also called *color harmonies.* We do not use these terms because of the ambiguity of such words as *harmonies.* Color characteristics and relationships are grossly simplified in color wheels.)

Both primaries and secondaries are high-chroma colors. All other colors are lower-chroma colors, which are the results of color mixtures. Mixing all three primaries results in a color of lower chroma. Some texts identify certain pairs of colors as complementary colors that, when mixed, also result in colors of lower chroma. These color pairs are red and green, blue and orange, and yellow and purple. In fact, mixing pairs of complementary colors is the same as mixing all the primary colors. Green is the mixture of yellow and blue. Mixing red and green is actually mixing red, yellow, and blue, that is, all the primary colors. In painting, juxtaposing discrete paint strokes of primary colors may result in color mixtures. Impressionist and pointillist painting are examples of this kind of color mixture (see Color Plate 2).

In industrial printing, a wide range of color mixtures results from layering separate dot patterns of the primary colors yellow, magenta, cyan, and black. These print primary colors yield all other colors by absorbing and reflecting light, unlike video primaries, which emit light. Each color pattern is a systematic arrangement of dots, and each primary color layer must be placed at a specified pattern angle to provide accurate reproduction (see Color Plate 4). The chart below indicates color mixture and light absorption in industrial color printing.

Primaries	Colors Perceived	Light Reflected
Cyan	Cyan	Green, blue
Magenta	Magenta	Red-orange, blue
Yellow	Yellow	Red-orange, green
Cyan + magenta	Blue	Blue
Yellow + magenta	Red-orange	Red-orange
Yellow + cyan	Green	Green
Black	Black	None (in theory)

The color of a static medium such as painting or industrial printing does not match that of the dynamic medium, video. In video, a wide color range is created from the systematic arrangement of phosphor elements in triads of red, green, and blue repeatedly distributed across a screen stimulated by an electron beam (Fig. C-5). The following chart indicates how color mixtures are created by these triads.

Phosphor Elements		Colors Created
Blue	=	Blue-violet
Green	=	Green
Red	=	Red-orange
Blue + green	=	Cyan
Blue + red	=	Magenta
Green + red	=	Yellow
Blue + red + green	=	White
(No elements)	=	Black

With video color production, red, green, and blue are considered primary colors because they combine to produce all other color mixtures. These transmitted colors are the product of light emissions. As more primaries are added, the mixture's color changes and the color becomes lighter. Transmitted light may be reduced to create darker colors and tones.

Figure C-5. Beams for an electron gun cause the red, green, and blue phosphor elements of the screen to glow, which creates the image on a video screen.

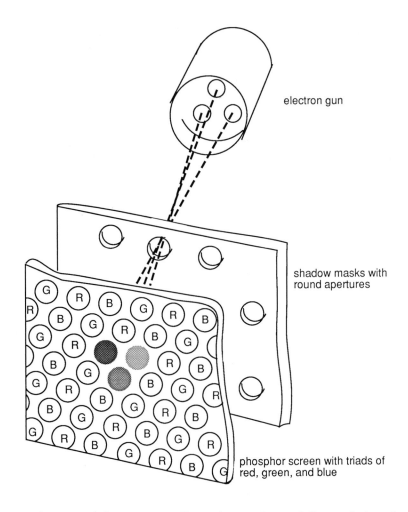

electron gun

shadow masks with round apertures

phosphor screen with triads of red, green, and blue

We have used the terms *quality* and *quantity* to define variations in ambient light. For imagery produced by electronic media such as video or television, the terms *chrominance* and *luminance* are used. These terms refer to standardized quality and quantity of color information reproduced electronically. Chrominance information refers to hue and saturation in the image, and the luminance information is the equivalent of the signal generated by a single color or monochrome video camera. When chrominance and luminance information is broadcast, it is encoded into a single television channel. A television set then decodes that information into pattern combinations of red, green, and blue (RGB) reproduced as an image for consumption. One of the systems for standardizing the television broadcast signal is the National Television Systems Committee (NTSC). It is the electronic definition of pattern for color mixing.

Regardless of medium, whether paint, video, or industrial printing, each system of primaries is related to human color perception. The primary colors for each medium are all perceived by humans using their eyes and brains. The primaries in transmission media correspond directly to the three types of color-perceiving cones: red, blue, and green. In reflection media, the relationship between the primary colors and color perception is more complex. With reflective color primaries, each primary reflects back two light primaries with the third absorbed. For example, yellow reflects back light that stimulates your R- and G-cones. When two reflective primaries are mixed, only one light primary is reflected back, with the remaining two absorbed. For example, mixing yellow with blue results in a perception of green, because it reflects back light that stimulates only G-cones. All reflective primaries used together may reflect back very little light. Thus, with reflection primaries, the addition of more primaries absorbs and reduces available light.

Some texts refer to additive and subtractive color primaries and color mixing by using *additive* to refer to transmission media and *subtractive* to refer to reflection media. The problem with these terms is that additive and subtractive suggest two autonomous color mixing systems, which is not the case. Perceiving all colors, whether reflective or light emitting, requires the same human eye and brain. In addition, some media exhibit the attributes of both light emission and light reflection. With a photographic slide projection, for example, the light is emitted yet a reflective screen is required to view it. An even more extreme example is that of the laser beam, which requires particulate matter in the air to be seen.

One frequent need for color mixing is exact color matching. Color matching must be considered both under fixed and changing light conditions. *Metameric* colors produce the same stimuli, or look the same, under a fixed light condition. Metameric colors produce the same CIE color values under fixed light conditions, but different CIE values when light conditions change. An example of this effect is a repainted section of auto bodywork. The new paint color matches the original color in the shop but no longer matches in the sunlight. *Nonmetameric* colors, also called *isometric colors,* look the same under any light conditions. Metameric color conditions affect all types of reproduction processes such as industrial printing and electronic imagery.

THE POWER OF COLOR

Two additional important areas of color vision are those concerning the ecological uses of color and the cultural context of color. In the ecological approach to perception as discussed by Gibson (1966), color vision improves the ability to distinguish surfaces in significant ways. Discriminating among colors is part of the general ability to discriminate among substances and enhances human survival.

Regarding the cultural context for color, we have already suggested the importance of naming colors as a way of organizing the value or importance of color. In general, color terminology and grouping are culturally and socially determined. Color names and distinctions historically change and differ among human cultures. Ancient Rome and the Maori are examples of different cultures who have developed distinct color systems (Eco, 1985). Some colors have further distinguishing characteristics associated with them, such as white with purity in Western civilizations and white with death in Eastern civilizations. Distinguishing colors and discriminating among color also can relate to the power of one ethnic group over the other on the basis of skin pigmentation or color. In countries such as South Africa, skin color defines the amount of political power a person has. For example, being "colored" or nonwhite gives citizens fewer rights than being white. In America, drinking fountains in some regions were labeled White and Colored to designate and segregate their users.

Linear Perspective and Scaling

COMPARING LINEAR PERSPECTIVE DRAWING AND VISUAL PERCEPTION

Perspective is a technique or process used to represent a space on a flat surface. As such, perspective is a powerful drawing tool and an important one to know how to use. However, linear perspective drawings are only partial representations of visual perception and of space. Understanding the limitations of perspective and how linear perspective drawings are different from visual perceptions is important.

Perspective is a proportional representation because it can show only what can be seen by a static observer looking at a static scene. Also, it can show only what can be seen with monocular vision and is frequently line drawings without color or tonal variation. Linear perspective is different from and an abstraction upon actual perception. The body and the eye are always moving in the act of perception, but a linear perspective drawing implies that the viewer is static. Perspective systems have only one center of vision. However, every time an eye or body moves even slightly, a new center of vision is established, with the eye taking in a different portion of the optic array.

Actual perception has a time dimension to it. It is an accumulation of information from numerous points of view over a period of time, which would be impossible for a fixed viewer with one center of vision to achieve. The comprehension of space requires at least two points of view, achieved through either stereoscopic vision or movement. Linear perspective uses overlapping shapes and receding planes to show space.

Straight edges seem to curve and 90-degree angles do not seem square when seen with the eye's curved retina. In linear perspective they are rendered as straight, whereas in visual perception they appear curved.

Visual perception includes distortions due to distance. For example, the edges of a distant object become blurred, and right angles and squares appear as curves or circles. Other visual changes, for example, the loss of detail, predominance of blue, and effects of heat wave and rain on vision, are due to atmospheric interference. These distortions cannot be adequately depicted with linear perspective.

In addition, peripheral vision cannot be adequately depicted with linear perspective. The scope of human vision is not defined by hard edges but is softened at the periphery. If a drawing covers the whole page, then the distinct edges of the paper define the scope of vision in that drawing. Human vision is not uniformly sharp or focused, but perspective drawings frequently have an equal degree of focus across the page.

Perspective is different from actual perception and exhibits other limitations. Using the complete rules of linear perspective is more suited to drawings created from the imagination or drawings from ground plans and elevations. The rules are very difficult to implement in drawing an actual object or scene. For example, vanishing points are almost impossible to establish and may be a great distance off the page. Additionally, the locations of marks to indicate various distances are difficult to establish, and what is seen with peripheral vision must be eliminated from the drawing. Also, landscapes have few, if any, straight lines in them, and buildings shift, settle, and bend. Linear perspective systems based on straight lines are suited to idealized rendering and can be used only as general guidelines in most drawings from life.

Despite these restrictions, perspective is a valuable tool for visualizing spatial layout and the spatial relationship. This appendix shows some basic features of projective methods of linear perspective.

SCALING

The midpoint of any square or rectangle is located at the intersection of its diagonals (Fig. D-1). Any square or rectangle can be proportionately enlarged by extending one diagonal and generating other proportional rectangles as indicated (Fig. D-1). Several adjoining squares create a grid. Proportional girds may be made by enlarging or reducing the proportions of the basic square (Fig. D-2). These proportional grids may be used to enlarge or reduce pictures by overlaying them onto the pictures (Fig. D-3).

Within any square or rectangle, columns or bands of diminishing width can be created by dividing the rectangle or square in half. The procedure is to find the center, draw a horizontal line through it, find half of that first half, and continue to find halves within each new half (Fig. D-4). This subdivision resembles how bands of space parallel to the horizon line are depicted in diminishing size in linear perspective drawings.

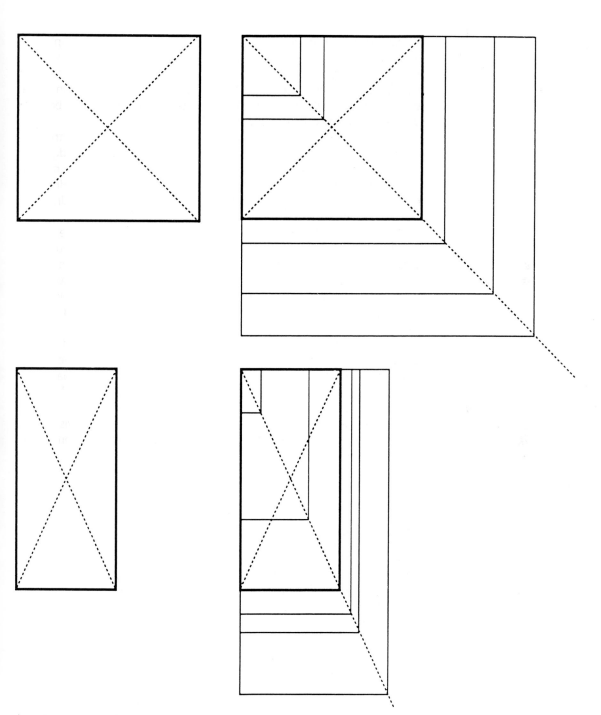

Figure D-1. Proportional shapes. The center of a rectangle or square is at the intersection of the diagonals. Larger and smaller proportional rectangles all share the same diagonal.

Figure D-2. To make a proportional grid, enlarge or reduce a pattern of squares.

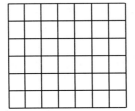

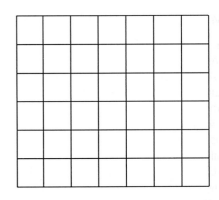

Figure D-3. Any shape can be increased or decreased in size as the scale of the drawing is changed. Place a grid over the original drawing. On another larger or smaller grid, draw the shape again so that the new drawing intersects lines of the grid in the same way as the original drawing intersected the original grid.

Figure D-4. Repeated subdivisions of a square or rectangle.

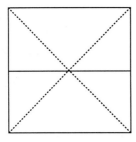

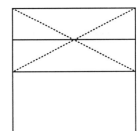

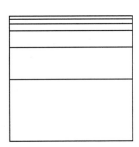

ELEMENTS OF LINEAR PERSPECTIVE DRAWINGS

The page corresponds to a window of vision. Both the page and the window are rectangular in shape, and both cut off the edges of peripheral vision. A linear perspective drawing cannot include what is seen in peripheral vision. The best effect comes from drawing what would be seen through a window with an angle of vision to the outside somewhere between 45 and 90 degrees (Fig. D-5). This effect corresponds to the optic array usually depicted using linear perspective. This limited optic array is also called the *cone of vision* in a linear perspective drawing.

Establishing the *horizon line* is the first step in making a linear perspective drawing. The horizon line is an abstraction of the horizon and a necessary element in linear perspective drawings. However, the horizon is different in many ways from the horizon line. In actual perception, the *horizon* is that edge where the earth "meets" the sky. Because the earth is curved, the horizon also is a curve. It can be seen on very clear days from a plane or from the ocean. The horizon is not a line but the edge of the earth as it curves away. The horizon is the same as eye level. The horizon rises along with a person climbing a hill and sinks as a person lies down on the beach. In drawing, a straight line usually indicates the horizon line. Theoretically, the horizon line extends infinitely, both left and right, off the page. If drawn high on the page, the horizon line indicates a high point of view; a low horizon line indicates a low point of view (Fig. D-6).

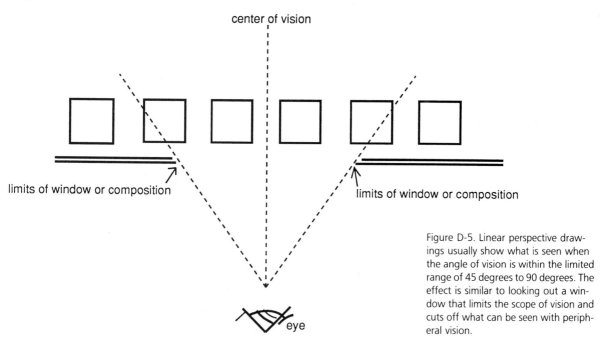

Figure D-5. Linear perspective drawings usually show what is seen when the angle of vision is within the limited range of 45 degrees to 90 degrees. The effect is similar to looking out a window that limits the scope of vision and cuts off what can be seen with peripheral vision.

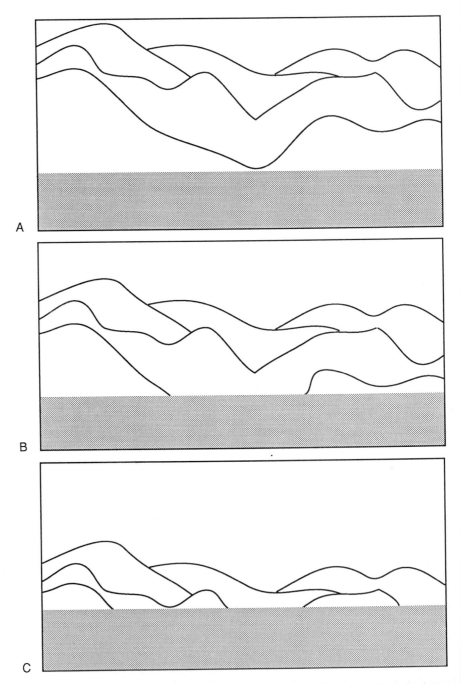

Figure D-6. Eye level corresponds to the horizon. These three diagrams indicate visual perception of mountains beyond the horizon: (A) indicates a high eye level; (C) indicates a low eye level; (B) indicates an eye level between (A) and (C).

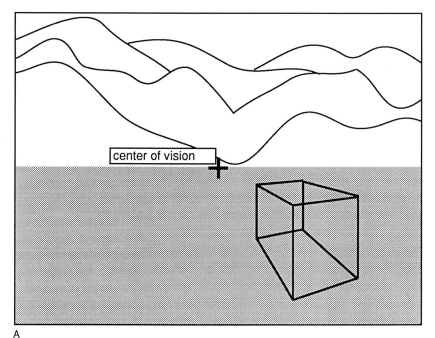

A

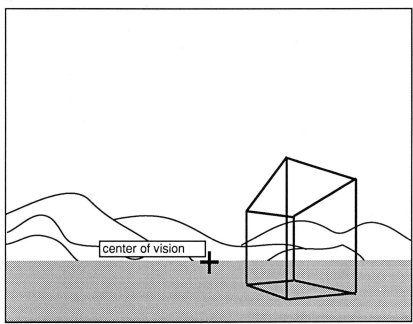

B

Figure D-7. These diagrams indicate high (A) and low (B) eye levels with boxes placed relative to the horizon line and center of vision.

The *center of vision* in a linear perspective drawing is the point of the horizon line where the horizon line intersects a hypothetical viewer's sight line, looking out straight ahead. Items in the actual optic array are placed in the linear perspective drawing according to how they correspond to the center of vision. Items to the right of the center of vision would be placed on the right side of the page; things to the left would be placed on the left side of the page. Similarly, items located above eye level would be placed above the horizon line in the perspective drawing; items below eye level would be placed below the horizon line (Fig. D-7).

The concept of a center of vision is an abstraction of foveal and peripheral perception. *Foveal perception* is the area of sharpest vision, in contrast to *peripheral vision,* which is blurred and indistinct. The foveal-peripheral relationship also is a specific foreground-background relationship. In perspective drawings, the center of vision is a point that corresponds the center of foveal vision.

Vanishing points represent the points to which the edges of some planes recede in linear perspective drawings. They can be located anywhere on the horizon line. Planes that are not horizontally parallel and vertically perpendicular to the horizon line recede to a vanishing point. Various linear perspective systems use different configurations of vanishing points.

TYPES OF PERSPECTIVE SYSTEMS

The simplest type of perspective system is the *one-point perspective schema.* One-point perspective is used to draw an object that has at least one plane parallel to the plane of the page. The vertical and horizontal lines are parallel or perpendicular to the edges of a rectangular piece of paper. All planes perpendicular to the facing plane recede to the vanishing point (Fig. D-8).

The next type of perspective system is the *two-point perspective schema.* Two-point perspective is used to draw an object with no planes parallel to the plane of the page but with an edge closest to the person drawing. That edge is drawn on the paper and properly located in reference to the horizon line and the center of vision. Planes to the left of the edge recede to a vanishing point on the left. Planes to the right recede to a vanishing point on the right. The more that is seen of a receding plane, the further away from the center of vision is the vanishing point. The less seen of a plane, the closer the vanishing point is to the center of vision (Fig. D-9).

A further development is the *three-point perspective schema.* Use three-point perspective to draw an object in which only one point is closest. Locate that point on the paper in reference to the horizon line and center of vision. All planes recede and are distorted by the effects of all three vanishing points (Fig. D-10).

Four-point perspective schema approaches the effect that results from photographing a scene or object with an extreme wide angle or "fish-eye" lens. It may be used for unusual effects when drawing from the imagination but is not used to draw from ground plans or elevations. An example of this kind of perspective can be seen in the mirror in the background of Jan van Eyck's *Giovanni Arnolfini and His Bride* (1434) in the National Gallery, London.

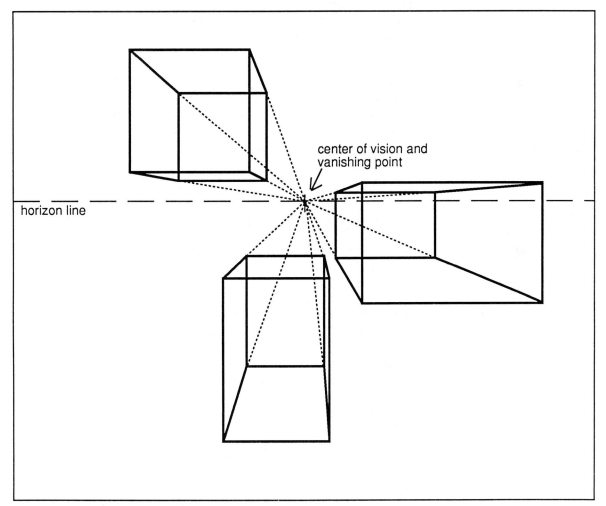

Figure D-8. In one-point perspective drawings, one plane of each shape is closest to you the viewer. Locate that plane first in relation to the horizon line and center of vision. The edges of all planes perpendicular to the closest, frontal plane recede to the vanishing point.

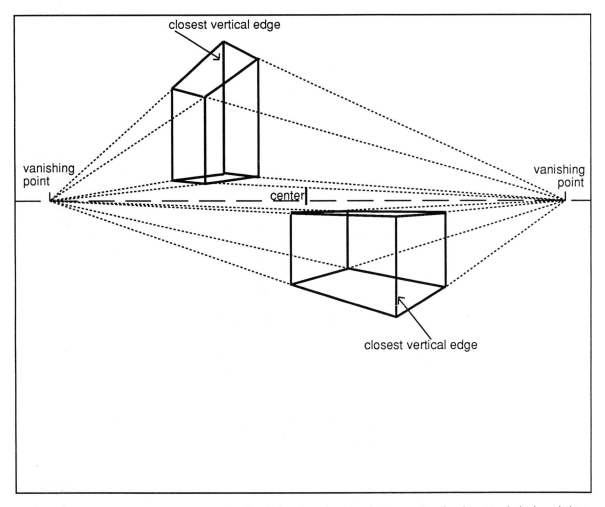

closest vertical edge

vanishing point

center

vanishing point

closest vertical edge

Figure D-9. To draw a shape in two-point perspective, the closest vertical edge relative to the center of vision and the horizon line must be located. The edges of all planes converge at one of the two vanishing points.

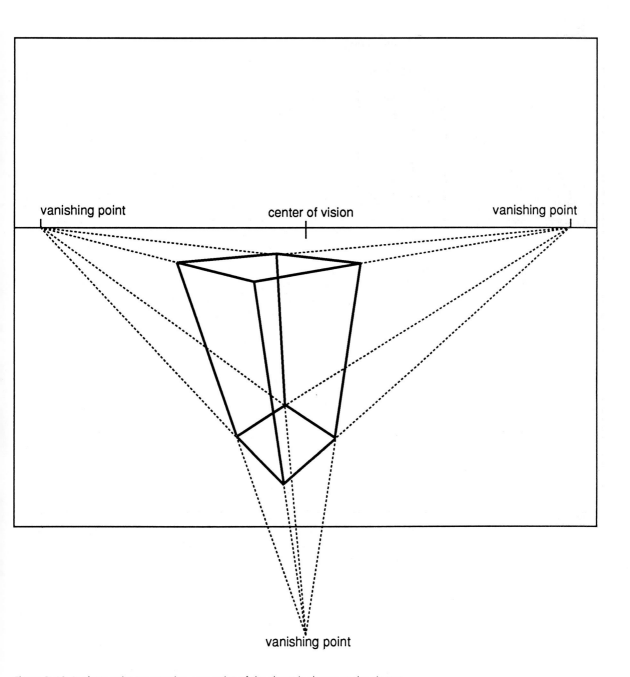

vanishing point   center of vision   vanishing point

vanishing point

Figure D-10. In three-point perspective, one point of the shape is closest to the viewer. Locate that point first relative to the horizon line and center of vision. The edes of all planes converge toward one of three vanishing points.

Glossary

Abstract: Not concrete; the conceptual experience of things or events; a concept or appearance apart from any particular instance or object. A visual produce may be an abstract experience if it refers to events or objects that are not present.

Achromatic adaptation: The ability of the visual system to adjust to different quantities of light; the visual systems can achromatically adapt to light levels of 1 : 1,000,000.

Ambient light: The total available light at any moment.

Anthropometry: The study and comparison of human body measurements, using knowledge of human size, reach, and strength to produce better architectural spaces, urban design, and product design.

Architectural design: The planning and construction of physical structures such as bridges, buildings, and their interior spaces.

Atmospheric perspective: The depictions of spatial relationships that reproduce the blurring, loss of detail, and blueish cast of distant objects.

Aura: A radiant glow that is used by art theorists as a metaphor for the ritual value of an individual artwork based on its uniqueness, its location in only one place, and its limited audience; the concept of an aura has been undermined by mechanical reproduction.

Aural sensory input: Information from the environment received through the sense of hearing.

Axiometric projection: Paraline drawing.

Axis: An implied straight line, around which shapes may seem to rotate.

Axonometric projection: Paraline drawing.

B-cones: One of the three kinds of cones responsible for color perception; the B-cones are sensitive to light wavelengths shorter than 540 nanometers but are most sensitive at 440 nanometers of light, resulting in the perception of blue.

Binocular vision: Also called *fusion;* the use of both eyes at the same time, which results in depth perception in vision.

British Arts and Crafts movement: A nineteenth-century social and cultural movement that influenced twentieth-century art, architecture, and design; it revived the awareness of the crafts in moral opposition to the factory production of the Industrial Revolution.

Camera lucida: An early example of optic reproduction in which prisms or mirrors are used to reflect an optic array from the environment as an image onto a flat surface, so that its outline may be traced.

Camera obscura: Early examples of optic reproduction in which an optic array from the environment is focused through a lens and projected onto a flat surface in a dark chamber.

Chroma: Intensity of hue; the saturation or purity of a color, as measured by its freedom of mixture with white. A high-chroma color is a vivid, pure, or saturated color; a low-chroma color appears dulled.

Chromatic adaptation: The ability of the visual system to adjust to varying qualities of ambient light and to perceive a certain color as the same under these varying conditions. Chromatic adaptation is one factor that makes color perception a relative experience.

Chrominance: The way in which hue and saturation are broadcast in a television image. Chrominance information standardizes color quality for images produced by electronic media such as video or television.

Code: Codes are rules that structure interpretation of visual products; *code* refers to the system of rules that governs the assignment of referents to the message.

Commodity: An article of commercial exchange such as information or objects. Visual products are commodities.

Comparison: One of the grouping concepts in which elements are grouped according to similar aspects, including size, shape, color or tone, location, and direction/orientation.

Competence: An aspect of power; the ability to perform the act of visual production.

Composition: Combined with context, composition is the organization of visual elements, including these three primary conditions: (1) materials constituting the visual product; (2) physical and mental human labor transforming these materials into visual elements, meaningful symbols, and visual information; and (3) the audience that organizes visual elements in space and time.

Concrete: Not abstract; the immediate perceptual experience of actual things or events. A concrete experience is often a direct experience of the environment with all the senses.

Cones: Light-sensitive cells in the eye that result in color vision when stimulated by varying wavelengths of visible light. Cones respond to the quality of visible light. Cones operate in high light and are concentrated at the fovea, the area of most acute vision.

Consumption: The use of visual products according to needs or the satisfaction of wants.

Context: Combined with composition, context includes these three conditions: (1) the economics of visual products, such as prices of artwork and supplies; (2) the communicative network providing the meaning for visual products; and (3) the institutional framework of visual production, including schools, galleries, and design firms.

Contiguity: A grouping concept that groups elements that touch.

Convention: Rule of behavior or action governed by usage or custom. Also a grouping concept that groups elements according to habit, convention, or the accumulated experience of the visual producer or audience.

Corner: The junction of two differently slanted surfaces.

Cultural producers: All the human participants in the process who use and give cultural meaning to visual products, including audience and visual producers.

Desaturated colors: Colors that exhibit low chroma and are perceived as dull as neutral.

Descriptive geometry: A method of drawing that reproduces the geometric interrelations of parts within a whole object.

Dimetric paraline drawing: A version of a paraline drawing in which an edge is shown as closest to the viewer, with all planes receding at a 15- or 45-degree angle.

Distribution: The circulation of visual products. Marketing and displaying visual products are examples of the distribution of commodities.

Division of labor: Proportional production, in which the entire task of production is divided among many individuals. Artist, gallery owner, critic, and collector represent a division of labor in cultural production.

Documentation: In visual production, documentation includes written and visual descriptions, such as drawings, plans, photographs, or diagrams, that communicate and idea or a proposed visual product. It may also be a record of a visual product that may no longer exist.

Edge: The transition from one area or surface to another in the environment, which results in discontinuities in the optic array.

Edge-in-depth: A discontinuity in the optic array that results from one surface behind and partly hidden by a closer surface. Edge and edge-in-depth may be indistinguishable from a single point of view.

Empowerment: Enabling or gaining competence; the reclaiming of power for those who have been systematically or institutionally denied power.

Ergonomics: The application of biology and engineering data to problems relating humans and machines.

Field: A subdivision of the perceived optic array determined by point of view and the center of an individual's attention.

Fluorescent light: Light emitted from a glass tube with an excess of wavelengths resulting in the perception of green.

Foreground-background relationship: A continually shifting relationship that structures the optic array; it is the result of paying more attention to some elements within optic arrays, which then become the foreground, and less to other elements, which then constitute the background; also center-periphery relationships in perception.

Form: Shapes that are structured or systematized; in some visual ideologies, form is identified primarily with concepts of beauty.

Fovea: The area in the retina that is the location of greatest visual acuity.

Fractals: Recently developed mathematical processes that generate geometric shapes that can simulate natural patterns and that model the growth and complexity of nature.

Frames: The boundaries of visual products, defined by the outside edges of canvases, photographs, or screens.

Fresco: The technique of painting with water-soluble color into wet plaster; the resulting painting is fixed to an architectural surface and is not movable.

G-cones: One of three kinds of cones responsible for color perception. The G-cones are sensitive to light ranging from 380 to 700 nm of light, but peak at 540 nm with the perception of green.

Glide: A symmetry transformation in which an element is repeated along an axis. In a one-directional glide, elements are reproduced in a line. A two-directional glide results in a planar pattern. A three-directional glide yields a network, where elements are repeated in length, width, and depth.

Grouping: The structuring of random items and events of the visual environment into usable information. Grouping concepts include comparison, contiguity, proximity, simplicity, motion, and convention.

Halftone: A method of representing tones and colors with dots that are produced by photographing an object through a fine screen.

Haptic sensory input: Information from the environment received through the sense of touch.

Horizon line: In drawing, a straight line that is a visual convention that stands for the horizon; theoretically, the horizon line extends infinitely, both left and right, off the page.

Hue: The attribute that allows a color to be classified, for example, as red or yellow or blue; similar in meaning to the common use of the word *color.*

Human engineering: The study of the personal and cultural spatial needs of humans and their interaction with surrounding space; also called *body metrics.*

Industrial printing: The mechanical reproduction of printed images and text in large numbers.

Information design: The planning, production, distribution, and consumption of messages. Most contemporary information design emphasizes visible and audible messages using advanced technologies. Television and cinema are examples of information design.

Information society: A current cultural phenomenon in which values shift from their original referent in materials to being based on information, which is the acquisition, accumulation, and consumption of large quantities of data.

Iris: The colored part of the eye surrounding the pupil; it expands or contracts to let more or less light into the eye.

Isometric paraline drawings: A version of a paraline drawing in which all axes except the vertical are rotated 30 degrees from horizontal, and frontal and receding lines maintain original proportions.

Iteration: Repetitive reproduction that results in the evolution of style.

Kinesthetic sensory input: Sensory experience derived through the bodily movements and tensions in muscles, tendons, and joints.

Kitsch: Pejorative term referring to events or mass-produced objects associated with mass culture and arbitrarily associated with sentimentalized values.

Lens: Focuses light and allows it to pass through the pupil, the opening into the eye.

Line: The continuous extension of points between any set of two points.

Linear perspective drawings: Diagrams that indicate the spatial relationships among objects and the observer and reproduce a single monocular point of view.

Literacy: An aspect of power; the ability to understand or receive visual products and actively participate in their production. Visual literacy requires perceptual and cultural competence.

Luminance: In a color broadcast image, the brightness of the image that is similar to the signal generated by a single color or monochrome video camera. Luminance information standardizes monochrome aspects of images produced by electronic media such as video or television.

Luminous objects: Objects that can be perceived because they emit light.

Mass communication media: Means of communication that reach large numbers of people, for example, television, newspaper, or radio.

Mass culture: The culture of large social groups, established by mass communication media.

Meaning: What is signified, indicated or understood through the symbolic qualities of visual products.

Media: The plural of *medium;* most visual products are communicated not through one single medium but through a combination of media. Paintings are often communicated by photographic reproductions and verbal descriptions.

Mediated: Transmitting and altering perceptual experience by some intervening mechanism, instrument, or medium.

Mediation: The transformations of perceptual experience by media that alter, distort, expand, or reduce direct experience.

Medium: The material or technical means that emits information.

Metameric colors: Colors that produce the same stimuli, or look the same, under a fixed light condition but may appear different under varying light conditions.

Metric drawing: Restricted perspective drawing that reproduces the spatial relationship in a single plane of an object or structure.

Mirror: A symmetry transformation in which an element or elements are repeated and reversed across an axis.

Motif: A recurring thematic element in a visual product.

Motion: A grouping concept in which movement in the same direction is a basis for grouping. The different speeds of various moving elements may be a basis for grouping. These concepts may be found in visual products such as motion picture film, video, performance art, and kinetic sculpture.

Munsell color system: A spatial method of organizing colors according to hue, value, and chroma.

Neutral: Desaturated or dull colors; colors having little or no decided hue.

Nonmetameric colors: Colors that look the same under all light conditions; also called *isometric colors*.

Object: Something physical or mental of which the subject is consciously aware. In addition, perception of object occurs in patterns in which few elements occur within the frame.

Object design: The production, distribution, and consumption of a wide range of items, such as artwork, crafts, photographs, graphic design, industrial objects, personal use objects, and design objects.

Oblique paraline drawings: A version of a paraline drawing in which frontal planes are shown with horizontal and vertical lines, and receding planes are drawn with all edges parallel at a 30- or 45-degree angle from the frontal plane.

Opacity: Not transparent; a quality of some visual element that is unusual or difficult to understand and potentially a foreground element to which the audience pays attention.

Optic array: The rays of light that enter the eyes as distinct from all rays of light in the ambient array.

Optic sensory input: Information from the environment received through the sense of sight.

Order: The structure of the elements perceived in a visual product. A linguistic analogy would be that of syntax or word order.

Paraline projection: A projection of objects and space showing frontal planes with vertical and horizontal lines parallel to the viewer and the page; receding planes are shown as diagonals that are parallel to each other.

Pattern: An arrangement or structuring of random visual elements or sensory perceptions.

Penumbra: The partially illuminated fringe of a shadow.

Perception: Sensory input; the information acquired through the use of sight, touch, hearing, tasting, smelling, and kinesthetic sensations.

Peripheral vision: The area of blurred vision lying outside the direct line of sight.

Periphery: Surrounding or outer areas, in contrast to the center.

Personal space: The sense of space around the body necessary for comfort in social situations. Personal space is different in different cultures.

Perspective: The geometric depiction of spatial relationships on a flat surface; the resulting drawing is a proportional representation of space that implies a static observer, static scene, and monocular vision; it is frequently without color or tonal variation.

Photoreceptors: The eye's light-sensitive cells located on the retina.

Pigment: Powdered coloring matter that is mixed in a liquid to make paint.

Point: The basic unit of pattern that is repeated and organized structurally; the basis for creating complex spatial patterns.

Pop art: An art style, especially in painting and sculpture, that uses the techniques and imagery from mass communication media, such as comic strips.

Power: The ability to do, act, produce, understand, and influence; also, the ability to control others. Power exists in the complex and dynamic relations among humans.

Practice: The conventional or habitual use and exchange of visual products. Visual producers also engage in critical practice. Critical practices are the interpreting and evaluating of the making of visual products.

Primary colors: Those colors that combine to produce the largest number of new colors; each art and design medium may have its own set of primaries.

Production: The making of visual products. It ranges from the fabrication of individual objects and the conception of ideas to the mass production of commodities.

Projective geometry: A method of drawing that reproduces the spatial interrelations of parts within a whole object. The spatial configurations in the projective method are similar to the x, y, and z axes in the coordinate system, with all lines in depth shown parallel to the z axis at a 45-degree angle from the horizontal and vertical axes.

Projective linear perspective: A method of depicting spatial relationships on a flat surface, in which vertical and horizontal planes are depicted as lines parallel to the viewer and the page; receding planes are shown as converging diagonal lines.

Proportion: The scalar, relational, and dimensional aspect of perception and visual production; also the relation of compositional parts within the visual product and the relation of that product to its audience.

Proximity: A grouping concept in which near elements are grouped.

Pupil: The opening of the eye.

Quality of visible light: Wavelength composition of visible light, to which the visual system responds with the sensation of color.

Quantity of visible light: The amount of visible light present.

R-cones: One of three kinds of cones responsible for color perception. The R-cones are sensitive to light from 380 to 700 nanometers but best respond to 570 nm of light, which results in the sensation of red.

Referent: A sign or symbol that refers to something else, or the thing that a symbol stands for.

Reflection media: Media that rely on light reflected from surfaces to be seen, for example, painting and photographic prints.

Reflective objects: Objects that depend upon ambient light to be seen.

Refraction: The bending of a light ray as it passes obliquely from one medium to another of different densities. A prism refracts and separates light into bands so that the viewer can see the colors associated with various wavelengths.

Reproduction: Iterative production. The process or system of production that proportionally ranges from the eye to mass media technology as re-productive devices.

Retina: The membrane covering the back inner wall of the eyeball; it is covered with photoreceptors.

Rods: Light-sensitive cells that are sensitive to varying quantities of light but that produce no color sensation. Rods operate in low light and are spread in more peripheral areas of the retina.

Rotation: A symmetry transformation in which an element is repeated around a center or axis. Boat or airplane propellors are examples of rotational symmetry.

Saccadic motion: Rapid, involuntary, tiny jumping movements made by the eye that refresh the retinal image.

Saturated color: Undiluted color. The sensation of pure or saturated color occurs only when the eyes are exposed to one wavelength of light.

Scale: The proportional relationship; the relative size of things compared to the perceiving subject. In visual products such as painting, photography, and video, scale is the size of visual elements relative to the size of the frame that surrounds them.

Shape: A closed area whose boundary is established by a continuous edge.

Shape grammars: The study of shapes and their systematic organization, which compares shapes for similarity and prescribes rules for their transformation. Although shape grammar primarily involves geometric shapes, it has its sources in morphology and typology, which study the evolution of biological structures and types.

Simplicity: A grouping concept in which elements are grouped to produce regular, simple, relatively symmetric, and closed relationships. Unconnected parts will be seen as connected when the connection results in fewer structural features or in a completed shape. This also is called *closure,* which is a variation on simplicity.

Slant: An oblique or inclined surface. Visually, a continuously modified surface can indicate slant.

Social division of labor: Physical or mental work that is divided among several persons in order to produce, distribute, or consume a product. Social and technical divisions of labor are interdependent.

Status: An abstract value of relative prestige or position. Status is represented in a hierarchy by higher social standing, participation in elite cultural activities, and the consumption of privileged objects.

Style: The similarity of composition or origin among a group of objects; specific similar characteristics among a set of visual products.

Subject: The one who perceives, as opposed to the object of perception.

Surface texture: The arrangement of the constituents of any material as it affects the appearance or feel of the exterior of that material.

Symmetry: Correspondence of parts in position or in reference to an axis. Symmetry guides the construction and perception of regular patterns in which elements are divided and/or repeated systematically, mathematically, or geometrically. Symmetry is also a grouping concept.

Technical division of labor: All natural and technological resources other than direct human labor that are used to produce, distribute, and consume a product. Social and technical divisions of labor are interdependent.

Technology: The means to provide for human needs; the methods and processes for handling the totality of human sustenance.

Tone: The eye's response to different quantities of light, with more perceived light referred to as *bright* and less perceived light referred to as *dark;* also called *value*.

Transmission media: Media that projects light in order to be seen, such as television and computer display terminals.

Transparency: The quality of some visual element being familiar or common and therefore becoming a background element to which the audience does not pay attention. A transparent element is considered as given or taken for granted.

Urban design: The planning and organization of architectural design in a large-scale urban environment. Urban design is the design component of urban planning that emphasizes the organization of structures and services in an urban environment.

Value: Contextually, the relative worth, utility, or significance of visual products. Compositionally, the perceived or apparent lightness or darkness of a color; also called *tone*.

Vanishing point: In perception, a point where parallel edges receding from the viewer seem to come together. In a linear perspective drawing, a point on the horizon line toward which diagonal lines indicating receding planes converge.

Vector: An entity with both magnitude and direction, which is commonly shown as a line with an arrow on one end.

Virtual space: The visual completion of an object, including its spatial patterns. An object's spatial pattern consists of its surroundings, the perceived context, and the object itself.

Visible light: Electromagnetic radiation between the wavelengths 380 to 700 nanometers, to which the human visual system responds with the sensation of color or tone.

Visual conventions: Commonly accepted symbols, processes, and styles that occur in and are understood only within the context of a specific culture.

Visual literacy: An aspect of power; specifically, the perceptual competence required to produce and understand visual products.

Visual producer: One who participates in the production, distribution, and consumption of art and design products. Visual producers constitute a subgroup of the larger group of cultural producers.

Visual products: The output of visual producers.

Visual system: The eye and brain as a cognitive system and how it interacts with the environment.

References

Adams, James L., *Conceptual Blockbusting: A Pleasurable Guide to Better Problem Solving,* San Francisco: San Francisco Book Co., 1976.

Albers, Josef, *Interaction of Color,* New Haven, CT: Yale University Press, 1975.

Arnheim, Rudolf, *Art and Visual Perception: A Psychology of the Creative Eye,* rev. ed., Berkeley: University of California Press, 1974.

Arnheim, Rudolf, *Visual Thinking,* Berkeley: University of California Press, 1980.

Becker, Howard S., *Art Worlds,* Berkeley: University of California Press, 1982.

Bell, Daniel, *The Coming of Post-Industrial Society: A Venture in Social Forecasting,* New York: Basic Books, 1976.

Benjamin, Walter, *Illuminations* (ed. Hannah Arendt, trans. Harry Zohn), New York: Schocken Books, 1969.

Berger, Arthur Asa, *Seeing Is Believing,* Mountain View, CA: Mayfield Publishing Company, 1989.

Berger, John, *Ways of Seeing,* New York: Viking Press, 1973.

Burgin, Victor, *The End of Art Theory: Criticism and Postmodernity,* Atlantic Highlands, NJ: Humanities International Press, 1986.

Caplan, Ralph, *By Design: Why There Are No Locks on the Bathroom Doors in the Hotel Louis XIV, and Other Object Lessons,* New York: St. Martin's Press, 1982.

Cornsweet, Tom N., *Visual Perception,* New York: Academic Press, 1970.

Croney, John, *Anthropometry for Designers,* rev. ed., New York: Van Nostrand Reinhold, 1981.

Crow, Wendell, *Communication Graphics,* Englewood Cliffs, NJ: Prentice-Hall, 1986.

Curtis, William J. R., *Modern Architecture since 1900,* Englewood Cliffs, NJ: Prentice-Hall 1982.

Davis, Angela Y., *Gender, Race and Class,* New York: Random House, 1983.

Dickie, George, and Sclafani, Richard, eds., *Aesthetics: A Critical Anthology,* New York: St. Martin's, 1977.

Dondis, Donis, *Primer of Visual Literacy,* Cambridge, MA: MIT Press, 1973.

Eco, Umberto, "How Culture Conditions the Colours We See." In *On Signs,* Marshall Blonsky, ed., Baltimore: Johns Hopkins University Press, 1985.

Foster, Stephen C., *Critics of Abstract Expressionism,* Ann Arbor, MI: UMI Research Press, 1980.

Gassen, Arnold, *Handbook for Contemporary Photography,* Athens, OH: Handbook, 1970.

Gibson, James Jerome, *The Ecological Approach to Visual Perception,* Boston: Houghton Mifflin, 1979.

Gibson, James Jerome, *The Senses Considered as Perceptual Systems,* Boston: Houghton Mifflin, 1966.

Gombrich, E. H., *Art and Illusion: A Study into the Psychology of Pictorial Presentation,* 2d ed., Princeton, NJ: Princeton University Press, 1969.

Greenberg, Clement, *Art & Culture: Critical Essays,* Boston: Beacon Press, 1961.

Greenberg, Donald, et al., *The Computer Image: Applications of Computer Graphics,* Reading, MA: Addison-Wesley Publishing Co., 1982.

Gregory, R. L., *Eye and Brain,* 3d ed., London: Weidenfeld and Nicolson, 1979.

Guilbaut, Serge, *How New York Stole the Idea of Modern Art: Abstract Expressionism Freedom and the Cold War* (trans. Arthur Goldhammer) Chicago: University of Chicago Press, 1983.

Hagen, Margaret, *Varieties of Realism: Geometries of Representational Art,* Cambridge and New York: Cambridge University Press, 1986.

Handhart, John, ed., *Video Culture: A Critical Investigation,* Rochester, NY: Visual Studies Workshop Press, 1986.

Heskett, John, *Industrial Design,* New York: Oxford University Press, 1980.

Hoke, John Ray, Jr., *Ramsey/Sleeper Architectural Graphics Standards,* 8th ed., New York: John Wiley and Sons, 1988.

Kelly, James J., *The Sculptural Idea,* Minneapolis: Burgess Publishing Co, 1981.

Kerlow, Issac Victor, and Rosebush, Judson, *Computer Graphics for Designers and Artists,* New York: Van Nostrand Reinhold, 1986.

Koberg, Don, *The All New Universal Traveler: A Soft-System Guide to Creativity, Problem Solving, and the Process of Reaching Goals,* Los Altos, CA: William Kaufmann, 1981.

Korties, B. J., *Graphic Software for Microcomputers,* Duxbury, MA.: Kern Publications, 1981.

Krauss, Rosalind E., "The Originality of the Avant-Garde" *October* 18: 46–66. (Fall 1981).

Kuspit, Donald B., *Clement Greenberg, Art Critic,* Madison: University of Wisconsin Press, 1979.

Lawson, Bryan, *How Designers Think,* London: The Architectural Press, LTD, 1980.

Lucie-Smith, Edward, *A History of Industrial Design,* New York: Van Nostrand Reinhold, 1983.

Lucie-Smith, Edward, *Story of Craft: The Craftsman's Role in Society,* Oxford, England: Phaidon, 1981.

Lynton, Norbert, *The Story of Modern Art,* Ithaca, NY: Cornell University Press, 1980.

Mandelbrot, Benoit B., *The Fractal Geometry of Nature,* New York: W. H. Freeman, 1983.

Mayers, Ralph, *The Artist's Handbook of Materials and Techniques,* rev ed. expanded, New York: Viking Press, 1981.

Meggs, Philip B., *A History of Graphic Design,* New York: Van Nostrand Reinhold, 1983.

Minnaert, M., *The Nature of Light and Color in the Open Air* (trans. H. M. Kremer-Priest), New York: Dover Publications, 1954.

Mitchell, William J., *Computer-Aided Architectural Design,* New York: Van Nostrand Reinhold, 1977.

Monaco, James, *How to Read a Film: The Art, Technology, Language, History and Theory of Film and Media,* rev. ed., New York: Oxford University Press, 1981.

Nelson, Glenn C., *Ceramics: A Potter's Handbook,* 3d. ed., New York: Holt, Rinehart & Winston, 1971.

Nicolaides, Kimon, *The Natural Way to Draw: A Working Plan for Art Study,* Boston: Houghton Mifflin, 1941.

Norris, Christopher, *Deconstruction: Theory and Practice,* New York: Routledge, Chapman and Hall, 1985.

Papanek, Victor J., *Design for the Real World: Human Ecology and Social Change,* 2d ed., New York: Van Nostrand Reinhold, 1984.

Pollock, Griselda, *Vision and Difference: Femininity, Feminism and the Histories of Art,* New York: Routledge, Chapman and Hall, 1988.

Ratcliff, Carter, "Art Criticism (Part V): On Clement Greenberg," *Art International,* 18: 53–58. (December 15, 1974).

Rees, A. L., and Borzello, F., eds., *The New Art History,* New York: Humanities Press International, 1988.

Richardson, John Adkins, *Art the Way It Is,* 2d ed., Englewood Cliffs, NJ: Prentice-Hall, 1980.

Richardson, John Adkins, *Modern Art and Scientific Thought,* Urbana: University of Illinois Press, 1971.

Saff, Donald, and Sacilotto, Deli, *Printmaking: History and Process,* New York: Holt, Rinehart & Winston, 1978.

Seldes, Lee, *The Legacy of Mark Rothko: An Expose of the Greatest Art Scandal of Our Century,* New York: Penguin Books, 1974.

Sidelinger, Steven J., *Color Manual,* Englewood Cliffs, NJ: Prentice-Hall, 1985.

Steadman, Philip, *Architectural Morphology: An Introduction to the Geometry of Building Plans,* London: Pion, 1983.

Steadman, Philip, *Evolution of Designs: Biological Analogy in Architecture and the Applied Arts,* Cambridge and New York: Cambridge University Press, 1979.

Stiny, George Nicholas, *Pictorial and Formal Aspects of Shapes and Shape Grammars,* Ph. D. dissertation, University of California, Los Angeles, 1975.

Swirnoff, Lois, *Dimensional Color,* Basel, Switzerland, and Boston: Birkhäuser Boston, 1989.

Weisberg, Robert, *Creativity: Genius and Other Myths,* New York: W. H. Freeman, 1986.

Whitney, Patrick, *Design in the Information Environment,* New York: Alfred A. Knopf, 1985.

Wolff, Janet, *The Social Production of Art,* New York: New York University Press, 1984.

Reproduction Credits

Figure B-3: David Smith, *Cubi XX,* 1964, University of California, Los Angeles.

Figures B-4, 3-8, 2-23: Royce Hall, University of California, Los Angeles.

Figure B-5: Elizabeth Murray, *Pompeii,* winter 1987, oil on canvas, 87" x 69.5" x 13", Gersh Collection, Los Angeles. Photo: Geoffrey Clements. Photo courtesy Paula Cooper Gallery, New York.

Figure C-1: "Hue Symbols and Their Relation to One Another," Courtesy: Munsell Color, Macbeth, Division of Kollmorgen Corporation, 2441 N. Calvert St., Baltimore, Maryland 21218.

Figure C-2: "Munsell, Value and Chroma, Scales in Color Space," Courtesy: Munsell Color, Macbeth, Division of Kollmorgen Corporation, 2441 N. Calvert St., Baltimore, Maryland 21218.

Figure C-3: "Munsell Color Solid Cutaway, to show Constant Hue 5Y," Courtesy: Munsell Color, Macbeth, Division of Kollmorgen Corporation, 2441 N. Calvert St., Baltimore, Maryland 21218.

Figure 3-1: Multipurpose Building, Commonwealth Avenue Elementary School, Siegel Sklarek Diamond, A.I.A. Architects.

Figure 3-4: Early Childhood Education Center, University of California, Irvine, Client: Regents of University of California. Siegel Sklarek Diamond, A.I.A. Architects. Floorplans, elevations, model, and landscape plan.

Figure 3-6: Eadweard J. Muybridge, *Horse and Rider at a Gallop,* from *The Attitudes of Animals in Locomotion, 1878–79.* Salt print, 7.5" x 8.875", courtesy, J. Paul Getty Museum, 17985 Pacific Coast Highway, Malibu CA 90265-5799.

Figure 4-1: Four-color magazine ad by Southwestern Bell featuring a trucker using a SWBT pay phone. Ad produced for Southwestern Bell for Darcy Masius Benton and Bowles-St. Louis.

Figure 4-4a: East Elevation, Multipurpose Building, Commonwealth Avenue Elementary School, Siegel Sklarek Diamond, A.I.A. Architects.

Figure 4-4b: *Egypt: The Pool in the Garden,* fragment of a wall painting from an unlocated Theban Tomb. Facsimile painting by Nina M. Davies. Date of original, New Kingdom Dynasty 18, reigns of Tuthmosis IV or Amun-hotep III, late 15th to mid-14th centuries B.C.; dimensions of original fragment: 72 x 62 cm. The original fragment is now in the British Museum, London. Courtesy of The Oriental Institue, of The University of Chicago, Chicago, Illinois, 60637. Photograph P. 33323/N. 21478.

Figure 4-6: Sanjo-Den youchi no emaki *(Scroll with Depictions of the Night Attack on the Sanjo Palace)* from the Heiji monogatari emaki *(Illustrated Scroll of the Events of the Heiji Period),* detail, Japan, Kamakura period, second half of the 13th century. Handscroll: Ink and color on paper; 41.3 x 669.7 cm., Fenellosa-Weld Collection. Courtesy, Museum of Fine Arts, Boston.

Figure 4-8: Sanredam, Pieter-Jans, *The Choir and North Ambulatory of S. Bavo in Haarlem,* November 1634,'' pen and brown ink and watercolor, 39.1 x 37.6 cm., J. Paul Getty Museum, 17985 Pacific Coast Highway, Malibu CA 90265-5799.

Figure 4-10: Sherrie Levine, *Untitled (After Walker Evans: 1),* 8" x 10", photograph, 1981 (Photo courtesy Mary Boone Gallery, 417 West Broadway, New York City, New York).

Figure 4-12: Robert Rauschenberg, *Skyway,* 1964, oil on canvas, mounted on panel, Dallas Museum of Art purchase, The Roberta Coke Camp Fund, The 500, Inc., Mr. and Mrs. Mark Shepherd, Jr. and the General Acquisitions Fund.

Color Plate 1: Georges Seurat, *Sunday Afternoon on the Island of La Grande Jatte,* 1884–86, oil on canvas, 207.6 x 308.0 cm, Helen Birch Bartlett Memorial Collection, 1926. 224. © 1889 The Art Institute of Chicago. All Rights Reserved.

Color Plate 7: Davidsz de Heem, ''Still Life with Oysters,'' 1653, 14.25" x 20.875", oil on panel, collection: Los Angeles County Museum of Art.

Color Plate 9: Munsell Color Tree. Courtesy: Munsell Color, Macbeth, Division of Kollmorgen Corporation, 2441 N. Calvert St., Baltimore, Maryland 21218.

Color Plate 10: 5R Glossy Chart, Munsell System of Color Notation. Courtesy: Munsell Color, Macbeth, Division of Kollmorgen Corporation, 2441 N. Calvert St., Baltimore, Maryland 21218.

Color Plate 14: Jackie Winsor: *Interior Sphere Piece,* 1985, mirrored glass, paint, 31" x 31" x 31". Photo courtesy Paula Cooper Gallery, New York.

Color Plate 15: Hans Haacke, *Metromobiltan,* 1985, 140" x 240" x 60", Fiberglas construction, 3 banners, photomural, The John Weber Gallery, New York.

Color Plate 16: Jenny Holzer: *Under a Rock,* 1986, installation, granite benches and LED signs, Barbara Gladstone Gallery, New York; and detail, *Untitled with Selections from UNDER A ROCK* (People Go to the River. . . .), misty granite, 17.25 x 48 x 21" (Photo courtesy Barbara Gladstone Gallery, New York).

Color Plate 17: Barbara Kruger, *Untitled (Your gaze hits the side of my face),* 55" x 41", photograph, 1981 (Photo courtesy Mary Boone Gallery, 417 West Broadway, New York City, New York)

Index